16.89/JON

Family
Systems
Therapy

UNIVERSITY OF EVANSVILLE
HARLAXTON COLLEGE LIBRARY
HARLAXTON MANOR
GRANTHAM. LINCS,

WILEY SERIES IN FAMILY PSYCHOLOGY

Series Editor

NEIL FRUDE

University of Wales College of Cardiff

Childhood Illness: The Psychosomatic Approach
Children Talking with Their Bodies
Bryan Lask and Abe Fosson

Family Systems Therapy
Developments in the Milan–Systemic Therapies
Elsa Jones

ELSA JONES

Family Systems Therapy

Developments in the Milan–Systemic Therapies

UNIVERSITY OF EVANSVILLE
HARLAXTON COLLEGE LIBRARY
HARLAXTON MANOR
GRANTHAM, LINCS.

JOHN WILEY & SONS
Chichester · New York · Brisbane · Toronto · Singapore

Copyright © 1993 by John Wiley & Sons Ltd,
Baffins Lane, Chichester,
West Sussex PO19 1UD, England
National 01243 779777
International (+44) 1243 779777

Reprinted January 1994, November 1995

All rights reserved.

No part of this book may be reproduced by any means,
or transmitted, or translated into a machine language
without the written permission of the publisher.

Other Wiley Editorial Offices

John Wiley & Sons, Inc., 605 Third Avenue,
New York, NY 10158-0012, USA

Jacaranda Wiley Ltd, 33 Park Road, Milton,
Queensland 4064, Australia

John Wiley & Sons (Canada) Ltd, 22 Worcester Road,
Rexdale, Ontario M9W 1L1, Canada

John Wiley & Sons (SEA) Pte Ltd, 37 Jalan Pemimpin #05-04,
Block B, Union Industrial Building, Singapore 2057

Library of Congress Cataloging-in-Publication Data

Jones, Elsa.
Family systems therapy : developments in the Milan–systemic
therapies / Elsa Jones.
p. cm. — (Wiley series in family psychology)
Includes bibliographical references and index.
ISBN 0-471-93825-4 (paper)
1. Family psychotherapy. I. Title. II. Series.
RC488.5.J63 1993
616.89'156—dc20   92–30568
                                                         CIP

British Library Cataloguing in Publication Data

A catalogue record for this book is available from the British Library

ISBN 0-471-93825-4 (paper)

Typeset in 10/12pt Palatino from author's disks by Photo·graphics, Honiton, Devon
Printed and bound in Great Britain by
Biddles Ltd, Guildford and King's Lynn

CONTENTS

FOREWORD

The systemic revolution in family therapy thinking and practice, that began with the work of Mara Selvini Palazzoli and her colleagues in Milan, Italy, in the early 1970s, continues to boil along. After two decades the wave of new ideas and technical innovation they began has not yet crested. Selvini herself, and her erstwhile collaborators Luigi Boscolo and Gianfranco Cecchin, while they have gone in separate directions and no longer work together as a team, bring to their new work the same qualities of intellectual rigor and honesty that began the seminal process. They continue to do research, to explore new possibilities, to face the inconsistencies in their thinking. And they continue to absorb new ideas and to relate without flinching to such currently significant topics as feminism and violence in families.

While Selvini has tended to stay at home in Milan, Cecchin and Boscolo are formidable travelers and teachers. In their journeys over the years they have stimulated and interacted with an important group of colleagues internationally, learned from them and assimilated aspects of their critiques and innovations. On this list we place, among others, Penn and Hoffman, Goolishian and Andersen, Tomm, Campbell and Draper, and Keeney. Elsa Jones is among the outstanding teachers and conceptualizers who have become fellow travelers on this stimulating journey. Her long experience with the strategic model is the basis for this summary volume.

Her work adds to the growing literature on the systemic therapies and will certainly make an important place for itself, being both comprehensive and lucid. Elsa Jones is a highly intelligent, no-nonsense sort of person. She is a clear thinker, an experienced therapist, and has the invaluable ability to write simply about complex subjects. She is also a passionate and involved woman who tackles difficult questions and does not fudge the contradictions she may see in the interest of a spurious consensus. The chapters are filled with clinical wisdom; the case histories are spare and effective, rounded enough in their description to give us a sense of the essential points the author wishes to make, and yet not overwhelming with unnecessary detail.

Jones suggests a number of reasons why therapy may have blossomed in the 20th century: the need, for example, for 'paid intimates' in a fragmented urban life; that the expectation of the good life includes, for the first time in human history, states of psychological well-being. New clinical technologies, family therapy, or new theories of human development, may serve the adaptive interests of the marketplace or create a marketplace of their own. It has been observed that psychoanalysis and its associated value system of autonomy and self actualization served the need for upper-middle-class mobility following the Second World War. Systemic, Milan style, therapy promises to give us tools for powerful interventions while severely constraining our ambitions for social engineering or large-scale social change. In these trying times it may create a livable space for therapists with this paradoxical 'change/no-change' configuration. For families, it emphasizes the necessity and possibility that the therapist is a facilitator, gifted and inventive perhaps, but only a facilitator nevertheless, and thus returns power to the family.

My comments, in this foreword, cannot hope to do much more than indicate a few of the intriguing elements of this mode of conceptualizing and working. I have always been impressed, for example, with the deliberate fashion in which the Milan group conveys meta-messages to the families, by carefully choreographing the presentation of the therapeutic team and the therapeutic situation. Family therapists have made use of such formalized presentations of themselves to clients from the very beginning, and the field is distinguished by being thoughtful and self-conscious about these presentations. Family therapists have been aware that the very act of convening a family is rich in messages that induct famly members into a certain view of themselves, of the nature of the problem, the direction of favorable change, and even how this might come about.

By their formal design of the interview structure and by adhering to this structure without deviation, the Milan group and their students have crafted a set of powerful therapeutic tools in and of themselves. This extends, as Jones notes, to the very formalities of language choice which are designed to remind the therapists and the families that something else is at play here. Not, so-and-so *feels* this or that but so-and-so *shows* this or that.

One must go back to the early days of Freudian psychoanalysis to find a therapeutic technology as paradigm-driven as is systemic family therapy. To an extraordinary degree the Milan group strove for epistemological purity with particular attention in the beginning to the work of Gregory Bateson and that attitude continues to characterize their work. Currently the overwhelming interest among systemic therapists in second-order cybernetics is, I think, the most important example of this. In teaching and in clinical work with families, and in consultation to institutions, the consequences of this paradigm are persistently explored: What if we are, as in the drawing by Escher, the hand that draws the hand, that draws the hand, that draws the hand . . . and on into an infinite loop?

What does it mean to co-create? How does this view inform our therapeutic work? It is a dizzying and unsettling way to look at things—at least, at first. And one can understand medical fundamentalists clinging to the raft of 'objective reality' in the storm-tossed seas of relativism. Social construc-tionism seems to introduce equally difficult problems at the other end of the ideological spectrum: abuse of power, as the prime instance, challenges this relativism, or appears to. We 'know' that men oppress women, therapists oppress patients, adults sexually abuse children. How is this 'knowing', these convictions, to be distinguished from other fervently-held realities? A related problem in the therapeutic arena concerns how one distinguishes the glibly facile (dare I say manipulative?) reframing or positive connotation or paradoxi-cal prescription? As therapists, and as teachers of therapists, we make those distinctions based on such vague, but persistent, criteria as an assessment of the *integrity* of the person and the *authenticity* of the intervention. We expect therapists to be ethical, coherent, authentic, *and they are*! The reference for these judgements always lies outside the system being analyzed, and is informed by the *purposes* (called 'intentionality' by some) of the judge.

It is true enough that 'the map is not the territory,' and also true that the map *is* the territory. We have ideas about ideas, and in that sense, maps about maps. One of my favorite Picasso stories concerns the occasion when he painted the portrait of a wealthy man's wife, charging, of course, a very high fee for this. The portrait, not surprisingly, had one eye and three noses. The patron bridled at paying the fee, saying, 'That's not my wife.' 'Oh?' said the artist. 'Yes,' continued the patron, pulling out a photograph from his wallet, 'Here is my wife.' Picasso looked at it for a moment and said, 'She's so small.' The question of purpose comes in here again. One can compare two valid maps, perhaps the collector's purpose was to flatter his wife and own a Picasso; the artist's purpose, perhaps, was to earn a high fee and have some fun.

Purpose, as I am using the term, connotes a synthesis of aspects of the context. These are the aspects that lead the participants to join in the creation of a new system, the therapeutic system, for our purposes. Purpose decides which language system will be used, for example, *biomedical* or *psychosocial*. Purpose invokes the comparison processes by which judgement will be made as to the goodness of a result.

An interesting bias among therapists favors change over stability. While this is understandable it is, at times, wrong minded. Jones, for example, observes, 'If we were to look back in 10 or 20 years' time, would we see our systemic therapies . . . invested in the prevention of change, rather than the open exploration of flexibilities?' But change is not the only goal. Much of what healers are called on to do is to stabilize systems that are in some kind of deviation amplifying, runaway, mode. A couple flailing at each other in pain and frustration may need calming down before they can begin to listen to any other kind of intervention. I have found often that assuming the attitude that 'things are desperate but not serious' can be quite useful at times of escalation crisis. Most experienced therapists convey this notion without explicitly saying it.

Jones considers why there is a dwindling team literature—perhaps some clues to that lie in the economic realm. What does it mean that we develop a theory of therapy and an intervention technology that depends upon a *seemingly* uneconomic arrangement? Consider the basic elements of the Milan team approach, with its working rules of a pre-session, the interview itself (including an in-session consultation), the assignment of a task, and a post-session discussion by a two-to-five person therapy team. Add to this the observation of the team that the client group may make in the reflecting team format. This appears to be a dinosaur of the therapeutic format, doomed to extinction under the impact of economic necessities. Do we train people to do something they are never going to be able to do thereafter—except when they train others? Is it all a bit reminiscent of psychoanalysis, that ultimately, on its four-or-five hour a week schedule would be carried on with no one other than cinema stars and analytic students in training, where indeed the term 'interminable' seems to apply?

Third-party payers and government funders may not be willing to underwrite such formats. Yet, there may be considerable justification for working as a team with particularly difficult problems and these methods may help design new methods of work. To mention some early, and still under-appreciated work along these lines, Peter Laqueur[1], the inventor of multiple family therapy, usually worked in a format where five or six families, with two or three therapists and a couple of video technicians, arranged themselves in space so as to both express and reflect on (the reflecting team in its first incarnation) interaction processes in each other's families. Most of Laqueur's work took place in state hospitals with poor psychotic patients and their families. I mention it here simply to indicate that some of the underlying theory

---

[1] Laqueur, H.P. (1976). Multiple Family Therapy. In *Family Therapy Theory and practice*, P.-J. Guerin, Jr. (ed.), New York, Gardner Press.

and technology may in the future be adapted in a socially responsible and economically feasible way. The cost of a team is still only a fraction of the true social costs of inadequately treated social breakdown.

The other economic basis for this mode of working it that it is in fact *an efficient use of resources*. If these constraints are made explicit, which they rarely are, the format may justify itself on clinical cost/benefit grounds. While we have a hunch that this is so, we do not know this for sure (knowing for sure that we do not know anything for sure), and future research must make a serious effort to demonstrate this. If there is any doubt about the validity of this on a case basis, one should carefully read the description, in Chapter 2, of the work with the psychotically depressed mother.

The essence of the argument would be that the total social cost and the total social burden are substantially reduced, even though the service provided *appears* to be more expensive because it uses more people. If future dysfunction is prevented, if symptomatology is reduced for other than the index patient, if protracted and non-productive modes of therapy are avoided, the cost/benefit ratio tilts substantially in the direction of team approaches of the sort described here. But this cannot be taken on faith, or simply asserted. The methodological problems of demonstrating this kind of cost-effectiveness are severe, and, it should be noted, one buys into another reality structure if one talks about improving dysfunction or reducing symptomatic behavior. But, in my view, this is the multiverse in which indeed we do well, and we are authorized and supported in our work according to a set of principles with which we certainly would not fully concur, although as citizens and tax-payers they might interest us.

The misuse of power in families and in the therapeutic situation have been of increasing concern in recent years in the world at large and in the family therapy literature. Jones is on sure ground here. She is familiar with the literature and has grappled long and hard with some of the apparent contradictions—exploring the connections between abuse of power and such concepts as Maturana's notion that instructive interaction cannot take place. One cannot control the direction of a system's response. The other major concern is with complementarity, that sets of behaviors reciprocally reinforce each other. Of course, this is exactly what happens in abusive power situations. The beating is structurally coupled to compliance; the submissive child stimulates the adult's sexual advance.

At the moment of any criminal act, the perpetrator has no more choice than does her victim. Constraints converge until the *act* takes place at which point we can only say with the poet,

Could have,
Would have.

The social contract rests on assuming that the murderer could have *not* committed her crime, a condition that pertains during all the time that she might have been dreaming of it, but had not yet fired the shot. But it is an assumption that makes no sense at all *after* the fact. Chaos theory and meteorology all tell us that the hurricane can hit the coast at an infinity of possible points—a statement that includes the *time position* as well as the space position of the observer/observed system. Once the time line moves on, that is after the fact, there is only one place the hurricane could have hit: where it did hit. Although, on a fractal coast line that space point continues to be indefinite as well. Perhaps her aim was poor and the charge is only 'Assault, with intent to kill'.

The chapter on power will reward readers well. It is a full exploration of these connections, and a clarification as well. Problems, as Jones is well aware, remain, in that as therapists, particularly with difficult and complex cases, we are required to switch conceptual frames, for example, from being social control agents to promoting change in family organization. Such transition points are inevitable; as a male feminist therapist, I will change lenses and descriptive languages at a different point in the therapy than would a traditional female therapist.

Jones is, of course, fully aware of all this, pointing out the significance of social constructionism in regard to its introducing issues of ethics and meaning into the systemic therapies.

Family therapists propose to get paid for their work, and therefore something of value must be exchanged. What is that? Since therapists are not running an escort service, or a phone sex business, they provide something other than companionship or the co-construction of erotic stories. One can minimize power, sanitize it, share it; one can acknowledge its complexities and vagaries, for example, that there are ways that clients hold therapists in thrall. The exchanges are multilayered. But, something of value must be exchanged. What is that?

We might close by noting that the therapist is constantly shedding power to gain power. If one is an expert on human behavior, problems in living, mental illness or—even more benignly—an expert in patterns of communication, or the characteristics of living systems, one has power and is privileged to charge for one's time. To be an expert is hardly a criminal offense, but it does imply a status difference. And the privilege to charge for one's time is quite a privilege.

DONALD A. BLOCH
New York, September 1992

SERIES PREFACE

When I started to teach Family Psychology, over 20 years ago, there was a distinct shortage of material. Then, as now, the prevailing view was that Psychology was an empirical science and that lecture content should be firmly grounded on research findings. Case studies were permissible, but only as illustrations of population-based evidence. In Britain, at least, interventions which were not based on behavioural approaches were generally regarded as totally ineffective and the theories upon which they were based were dismissed as 'merely speculative' at best and as 'fanciful ramblings' at worst.

My earliest attempts to fill my lectures with psychological research studies on the family were hardly successful. My consultation of social psychology textbooks (which would, I imagined, provide me with a lead into the relevant literature) yielded very little. It was a rare index that contained a 'Family' entry. If it did appear then the reference was usually to a single page. By contrast whole chapters were devoted to 'Eye Contact' and 'Risky Shift'. I searched for a book entitled *The Psychology of The Family*. My quest was not entirely in vain, for such a book had appeared at the turn of the century under the authorship of Wilhelm Wundt, one of the founding fathers of experimental psychology. It proved a learned tome, but was in essence a work of 19th-century anthropology. How different psychology might have been (and how much easier my task of lecture preparation) if this study by Wundt had proved as seminal as those conducted in his famous laboratory.

In the end I did manage to cobble together some sort of course. Partly, I drew on developmental psychology. There were lots of mother and child studies (fathers had not yet appeared on the scene, and siblings were only 'rivals' who disturbed the individual's development). I also drew upon sociological studies, focusing heavily on any parts that I could pass off as psychology. Psychiatry proved a rather rich seam;

there were many studies of family life and depression, family life and schizophrenia, family life and eating disorders, etc.

I am not sure, in retrospect, whether students who took the course in those early days felt that they were being given a raw deal. I became aware very early on that I was giving a course on *Hamlet* without mentioning the prince. Where were the studies of interactions within whole families? Where was the empirical exploration of relationships between intimates? (volumes were devoted to studies of how strangers interacted when they met for the first time).

The answer was that, at that time, there were few such studies, at least within 'mainstream' psychology. I failed to plunder the rich offerings of psychoanalysis (in five years' University training I had had one lecture on psychoanalysis, and this not sympathetic), and despite two years' clinical training I had not heard the term 'Family Therapy'.

Since those early days a lot has changed. There is now a viable 'Family Psychology', with journals, divisions of professional associations, societies, and all of the other institutions and ephemera that mark the acceptance of a new sub-discipline. The pressure for change has come partly from within psychology, with a growing realization that 'relationships' are entities that are separable from individuals and worthy of study, and the realization that intimate relationships are a key factor in the individual's development, adjustment and well-being. Books on 'social support' have grown a lot thicker in recent years. Emotional expression within the family is now recognized as an important prognostic factor in schizophrenic relapse. Family violence has been studied as a specific form of human aggression. There are many more examples of links forged between traditional psychological topics and aspects of family life. And not all of the interest has been 'applied'. Increasingly attention is paid to theories of family interaction and family groups.

Some of the pressure for change has come from the growth of inter-disciplinary work, more evident in applied settings than in academic collaborations. Psychologists (especially those who work in clinical settings) have increasingly worked side by side with those from other professions whose training has emphasized the centrality of family life and has provided them with a language that can be used to understand families. Increasingly, psychologists have been influenced in their thinking, and in their ways of dealing with problems, by social workers and psychiatrists. And one approach which has been especially powerful in influencing modes of thinking about the family is that of Family Therapy.

This continues to be the fastest growing 'school' of psychotherapy. Predominantly North American in origin, this approach is now increasingly influential in Europe (including Eastern Europe). As Elsa Jones shows in this book, Family Therapy is more than a therapeutic approach, and certainly more than a set of techniques. Family Therapists are thinkers as well as doers, and their writings over the past decades have provided a rich language and a truly encyclopaedic range of concepts with which to understand family life. 'Family Therapy' (despite the upper case initial letters) is not a single approach but a very diverse collection of insights, theories, descriptions and prescriptions for working with 'systems'. It is not *just* an approach to therapy (it offers many an insight into healthy systems too) and it is not just about 'families' (the principles apply, with a little revision, to many different kinds of social group). These days much 'Family Therapy' is not about therapy and not about families. And yet it continues to be a source of much of the best theorizing, and much of the best empirical research, on family life and family dysfunction.

Had I been aware of Family Therapy in that dim and distant past, and had the sense to recognize how much it offered, the prince might have played centre stage. But since that time the approach has become even more sophisticated (through much more diverse) and can offer even more to those who wish to grapple with the complexities of family life. Elsa Jones' book provides a thoughtful yet exciting insight into Family Therapy. It is a 'meaty snapshot' (Family Therapists appreciate the power of metaphors—even mixed ones) of 'work in progress'.

NEIL FRUDE
Cardiff, November 1992

PREFACE

A BRIEF HISTORY OF FAMILY THERAPY

Family therapy, like many another invention, has developed
from many strands, so that it is hard to pin down the exact
place and time when it was first used. According to Luepnitz
(1992)[1] and Braverman (1986) many of the ideas that have
influenced family therapists in the twentieth century were
already present in the work of nineteenth-century social and
community workers and were then rediscovered in the
thirties, forties and fifties of this century, primarily by
American researchers and therapists.

These theorists and practitioners studied the influence of
interactional contexts on the lives and symptoms of individuals, and by the nineteen-sixties were writing about the
application of these new insights in therapy (Ackerman, 1958,
1966, Bateson, 1978a, Bell, 1967, Bowen, 1966, Boszormenyi-
Nagy & Framo, 1965, Jackson, 1968, Minuchin et al., 1967,
Satir, 1964, Wynne, 1961, and others). The work of many of
these early practitioners emerged from psychoanalysis, which
has perhaps had a more significant influence on family therapy
than is always acknowledged. In addition contributions from
elsewhere (e.g. Bowlby, 1949, Laing and Esterson, 1964,
Skynner, 1969, 1976, and Stierlin, 1977) in Europe, and the
ideas of cyberneticians (Wiener, 1948), mathematicians (Von
Neumann & Morgenstern, 1944, Whitehead & Russell, 1910),

---

[1] The fact that family therapy is seen as belonging particularly to the
twentieth century represents, according to Luepnitz, the sort of 'creation
myth' in which certain versions of history are given a privileged status
above other, subjugated versions. Another example of such a creation myth
would emerge if one were to study the healing practices of non-Western
societies (e.g. Bührman, 1984) where families and other community networks
have traditionally been involved in the resolution of individual difficulties
and distress.

chemists (Prigogine, 1976) and systems theorists (Von Bertal-anffy, 1968) all added to the richness of the tapestry called family therapy.

The work of the people most often seen as the early family therapy innovators soon became clustered around certain characteristic approaches, which all found a common basis in the view that interactional patterns between people (particularly in families) contributed significantly to the difficulties individuals experienced, and that these difficulties could be untangled more efficiently if the whole family were to participate in therapy. Each of these early family therapists influenced others and developed a following, which in some cases began to be regarded as 'schools'. The two schools which, early on, became most prominent were those of Structural family therapy, associated in particular with the work of Minuchin and his associates such as Aponte, Auerswald, Barcai, Montalvo, Walters and others (Minuchin, 1974, Minuchin et al., 1967, 1978), and of Strategic family therapy. The latter has been associated most specifically with the work of the Mental Research Institute in Palo Alto (Beavin, Fisch, Jackson, Watzlawick, Weakland, and others, e.g. Watzlawick et al., 1967, 1974) as well as with Haley (1964, 1976), Haley & Hoffman (1968) and Madanes (1981). Some of the most influential pioneers such as Erickson, Satir or Whitaker (cf. for example Erickson & Rossi, 1976, Satir, 1964, or Whitaker, 1975) have resisted classification by being, as Bloch puts it, 'magnificent exemplars, they teach by being' (Bloch, 1981, p. xiv).

This brief Cook's tour does not attempt to give a full exposition of the complexity of the varieties and mutual influencing of family therapy as it developed (e.g. the contributions of Bowen (1966, 1978), or the germinal work done by numerous family therapists in disseminating the theory and skills of this new approach, such as Bloch (1973) and his colleagues at the Ackerman Institute in New York, or Skynner (1969, 1976) in London). The intention, rather, is to place family therapy in its widest sense on a map in order to give a background to the particular approach, namely Milan-systemic therapy, which will be discussed in this book.

As will be described in more detail in Chapter 1, Milan-systemic therapy grew out of these established earlier models of family therapy, which have themselves continued to change and to influence and be influenced by one another. The theory and practice of the original four members of the Milan group (Luigi Boscolo, Gianfranco Cecchin, Giuliana Prata and Mara Selvini Palazzoli) was particularly stimulated, in its early period, by the work of Watzlawick and his colleagues, and also by the continuing exploration of the ideas put forward by Gregory Bateson. The original Milan group separated during the late seventies and early eighties (cf. Jones, 1988, Pirotta, 1984). Selvini and Prata pursued their interests in the search for predictable methods and classifications of families with 'psychotic' members (Selvini, 1986, Selvini et al., 1989) and their work is often now regarded as having returned to a closeness to their origins in strategic and structural ways of working (Simon, 1987). Boscolo and Cecchin have, via their training of family therapists world-wide, been participants in the evolution of a variety of styles of therapy originally based on their work. The approach discussed in this book is identified with the model of the original Milan group, and with the developments associated most specifically with the evolving styles of Luigi Boscolo and Gianfranco Cecchin and their followers and associates.

THE STRUCTURE OF THE BOOK

Chapter 1 sets out the ideas which underlie the practice of systems-based therapy in general, the working method in the classic Milan-systemic model, and the recent developments that are associated with the work of Milan-influenced systemic therapists in particular. These ideas are fleshed out in the later chapters which deal with applications of the model

The word 'theory' will be used throughout the book to describe the intellectual underpinnings of this method of therapy. Nevertheless, it is important to acknowledge that, from the point of view of the 'hard' sciences (Popper, 1972) family therapy, like many other psychotherapies, cannot lay claim to a theory in the sense in which it is generally understood in the scientific community.

Chapter 2 describes working with teams and one-way screens, which has been intimately associated with the Milan-systemic approach. All the clinical work described in the book, even where the focus may be on family patterns or family-therapist interaction, must be read in the context of the therapist/author having worked throughout with consultation from peer team members.

The theoretical ideas and practice issues developed in the first two chapters form the basis for the detailed descriptions of work with clients given in the next four chapters. Thus the ideas explored in Chapters 1 and 2 are illustrated via their application in clinical work, and at the same time the descriptions of therapy gain depth from their placement against the theoretical background.

Chapter 3 discusses work with families, with the focus on a detailed examination of a first session.

Chapter 4 discusses work with families at different life stages.

Chapter 5 discusses work with couples.

Chapter 6 discusses systemic ways of working with individuals.

Although the chapters have been divided into these traditional categories (families, couples, and individuals), this division is perhaps less important than might at first appear, since Milan-systemic practitioners claim that the method has general application. Nevertheless, considerations which are of particular interest in work with different client configurations can be focused on by using this structure.

No attempt has been made to discuss all 'categories' of clients for whom this approach might seem relevant, since again it is assumed that there is a generalizability to the approach, and in addition the categorization or diagnosis of clients does not fit comfortably with systemic ideas. Examples of therapeutic work have been chosen, therefore, more with an eye to variation and difference, and to the illustration of particular aspects of theory or technique.

All the clients discussed in this book have given written permission for material deriving from the work with them to be used for purposes of teaching and publication. Nevertheless every effort has been made to disguise their identities from outsiders by altering names, ages, and many other details of their circumstances. All the examples (with the exception, self-evidently, of those in the chapter on training) derive from work in which the author was the therapist.

Chapter 7 deals with questions about the use and abuse of power, a topic which has in recent years become of increasing interest, theoretically and pragmatically, for therapists of all persuasions. Particular applications of Milan-systemic therapy have been seen by critics as inadequate in their responsiveness to ideas about power and inequity, and this chapter deals with the significance of this issue for theory and practice.

Chapters 8 and 9 discuss applications of systemic thinking to groups other than families, namely consultation to professionals and working groups (Chapter 8) and the training of family therapists (Chapter 9).

The Postscript is intended to draw together some of the many strands of thinking developed in the book, and to offer scope for some wider speculations about the context and meaning of family therapy in this latter part of the twentieth century.

THE CONTEXT OF THE BOOK

Slogans currently in favour in the field covered by this book include 'everything said is said by someone' (Maturana & Varela, 1988), and 'the observer is part of the observing system' (derived from Von Foerster's ideas about observed and observing systems (1981)). These ideas are discussed in Chapter 1, but are relevant here in that they indicate that we cannot speak of a truly objective description, but rather of a description constructed by an observer with a particular perspective, history, and investment in the meaning of the description; an observer, moreover, who is inescapably part of that which is being observed, and who influences observations in the act of making them.

It must therefore be acknowledged that this description of 'developments in the Milan-systemic therapies' is my description, my version of history, herstory and meaning, and my responsibility. The ideas I put forward are shared with many other therapists who would place themselves within the same part of the family therapy territory as the one I occupy, and my ideas continue to be significantly shaped by input from others, as will be evident from the references provided. Nevertheless the emphases I choose, and the picture that emerges from my presentation, cannot but be subjective.

I have used the female pronoun for the therapist throughout the book, and female or male pronouns for clients, as relevant.

Much of the case material used in the book derives from work done at the Family Institute, Cardiff, where I worked from 1984 to 1992, but many other influences and working contexts are also represented. In the early nineteen-seventies I was introduced to the ideas of Gregory Bateson and Don Jackson of the Palo Alto group by my colleague David Norris in Johannesburg, following family therapy training visits from Don Bloch and his colleagues from the Ackerman Institute. In the late seventies and early eighties, as a Sheldon Fellow at the Tavistock Clinic, I encountered Gianfranco Cecchin and Luigi Boscolo of the Milan group, which was to prove a turning point in my own development. I am particularly indebted to Gill Gorell Barnes (trainer) and John De Carteret (fellow-trainee) for our shared early struggles with these new and revolutionary ideas.

Work in a variety of psychiatric settings, as well as at the Institute of Family Therapy (London), provided the experience which, together with the explorations of the Cardiff team, have shaped my current opinions. When speaking of the Cardiff team it is necessary to acknowledge that this team is not a fixed entity, but is more like Bateson's grandfather's axe, which has over the years changed all its components several times, but to which a fixed identity nevertheless continues to be attributed. Thus in addition to having worked with teams in other settings, I have been a member of the Cardiff team while it changed its components several times.

Most of the team examples in the book are taken from work with a team that included Philippa Seligman and Bebe Speed.

TERMINOLOGY

I have used traditional terms and structures in this book, even though I share the interests of many colleagues (e.g. Wynne et al., 1986, Goldner, 1991a) in engaging in a critique of the accepted meanings of the terms we use, and in searching for structures and words that might better describe what we do. In the end my justification for staying with (still) comfortable terminology has to be the desire for ease of communication. However, it would function as a useful context marker to signal at the start of this book that the terms used should be thought of critically in order to elicit what undesired meaning they may convey, and what meanings may be obscured by their use. These issues are also taken up in Chapter 7, where the concept of 'deconstruction' is discussed, and in Chapter 9, where the problem with words like 'therapy', 'client', 'consultation', etc. are examined. We are all inevitably organized by the culture within which we live (Goldner, 1992a), and therefore by its received meanings and habits. Although we cannot escape this, we can engage in a 'subversive discourse' in relation to its terms and structures. I will, in this section, discuss some terms used in the title of this book: 'Family Systems Therapy: Developments in the Milan–Systemic Therapies'.

Family is a word which continues to be used by all of us as if it has a unitary meaning, despite the fact that we are well aware—or should be aware, as mental health professionals— that significantly large numbers of people do not live in traditionally structured families at all (e.g. Kiely & Richardson, 1991). The usual connotation of 'family' is of an intact, two-parent, heterosexual couple, with not too many and not too few children, where the woman is the homemaker and the man is the breadwinner. This image is hard to sustain when we acknowledge that, world-wide, women work much longer hours for less pay than men (Myers, 1985), or that in Western post-industrial countries many families consist of single parents with children, remarried or 'reconstituted' families, childless couples, gay and lesbian couples with or without children, or single people. Persisting with the idea of 'family', rather than 'families' makes it likely that all these ('deviant') configurations will regard themselves, or be regarded by others, as not forming 'proper' families.

Systems and Systemic are terms which have been claimed by most family therapy models (cf Chapter 1 for a fuller discussion), and which have been the source of rancour between proponents of different 'schools' (cf Lask & Speed, 1992). One of the sillier manifestations of ownership of this word and its meaning is the phrase, redolent of orthodoxy and exclusivity, 'but that's not/you're not systemic!' It is evident that we use the phrase 'systems' or 'systemic' more in relation to how we wish to position ourselves *vis-à-vis* other family therapists, than in relation to our customers or consumers or clients or patients, many of whom would not understand, or necessarily agree with, the specific use that family therapists have made of the word 'system'.

Therapy is a term (as discussed in Chapter 8) which can carry connotations of illness and cure, which do not fit with current systemic views on the autonomy of systems or the role of the 'therapist'. However, it also carries associations of healing and wholeness, which may seem more desirable to therapists and their clients.

Developments suggest an image of progress, growth and change for the better. Some dictionary definitions (Chambers, 1988) for the word 'develop' are: 'to bring to a more advanced or more highly organized state ... to cause to grow or advance ... to evolve'. The assumption that recent changes in the field of family therapy represent progress may be misleading or risky. That is, we may claim that our ideas are changing, but change may be seen as progressive, retrograde, or trivial; the meaning (good, bad) will be attributed to it by an observer. Assumptions current in dominant world cultures have held that development must necessarily represent an onwards and upwards movement, and that this will be good. This view has continued to be held by many even when the consequences of unbridled growth are now manifestly threatening the survival of the earth. Thus a critical stance towards this word will enable one to bear in mind that (a) the changes and developments perceived by systemic therapists like myself may not be nearly as significant as we think they are when we talk of a 'new epistemology', 'second-order cybernetics', or 'paradigm shifts' (cf Chapter 1 and Postscript for discussion of these terms) and (b) that we do not yet know what the consequences of these new developments may be, for ourselves or for our clients.

Milan–Systemic is used to signify the work of the original Milan team ('classic Milan'), the work of Mara Selvini Palazzoli and her associates, of Giuliana Prata and her associates, or of Luigi Boscolo and Gianfranco Cecchin and their ex-trainees and associates. The work discussed in this book aligns itself with the latter group.

My hope is that this brief discussion will function as a relevant introduction to this book, where ideas and actions will be described with commitment and enthusiasm, but where these same ideas and actions will also be made available for open-minded scrutiny.

> Let me then conclude with a warning that we social scientists would do well to hold back our eagerness to control that world which we so imperfectly understand. . . . Rather, our studies could be inspired by a more ancient, but today less honoured, motive: a curiosity about the world of which we are a part. The rewards of such work are not power but beauty. (Bateson, 1978a, p. 240)

ELSA JONES
Cardiff, July 1992

ACKNOWLEDGEMENTS

My heartfelt thanks go to the following:

My colleagues, past and present, in many settings, and in particular Philippa Seligman, Bebe Speed and Brian Cade of the Cardiff Family Institute team that I joined in 1984. Our collaboration, mutual support, exploration, and disagreements have helped to shape my ideas.

My feminist friends and colleagues, particularly Virginia Goldner, whose courage and clarity have helped to give a voice to previously silenced discourses.

Luigi Boscolo and Gianfranco Cecchin without whose work this book would obviously not have been written at all. Their continuing responsiveness to feedback sets the tone for the flexibility and evolution of the model associated with them.

Clients, trainees and workshop attenders, whose creativity has contributed to my understanding, who have required me to test the appropriateness of my ideas in practice, and from whom I hope never to stop learning.

Barnardos, the parent organization of the Cardiff Family Institute, who generously supported the writing of this book with time, money, and the sympathetic ear of Dave Smith, Assistant Divisional Director, Wales and the South West Division.

The series editor, Neil Frude, whose unflappability, experience and steady guidance were invaluable.

And last, but most emphatically not least, my friend and colleague Bebe Speed, whose generous and rigorous reading of the work in progress contributed significantly to whatever clarity it may possess.

CHAPTER 1   Family systems therapy

Family therapy, based on the idea of families as systems of humans in interaction with one another, is relatively new. From the nineteen-forties onwards, a variety of therapists and theoreticians have elaborated the ideas which, in continuously developing forms, influence the current practice of systems-based therapies.[1] The origins of family therapy could be said to come from two impulses: the first is that of therapists (e.g. Bell, 1967, Boszormenyi-Nagy & Framo, 1965) who found that their clinical practice, whether with children or with adults carrying serious diagnoses such as schizophrenia, was unsatisfactory, and who therefore started to involve family members in therapy; the second impulse arises from the work of theorists, especially those researchers and therapists involved with the ideas of Gregory Bateson (e.g. Bateson et al., 1956, Haley, 1964, 1976, Haley and Hoffman, 1968, Jackson, 1968).

This search for more useful explanations of the difficulties encountered by human beings led to the adoption of systems thinking and cybernetic explanations for the theory and practice of family therapy. The building blocks of this approach ('systems', 'cybernetics', etc.) will be discussed below, as will the evolution of concepts, some of which have remained central to systemic theory, and some of which have undergone considerable revision.

While this chapter will inevitably deal with complex theoretical formulations, it may be useful to keep some pragmatic focus

---

[1] This version of the origins of family therapy is, as Luepnitz (1992) points out, a 'creation myth, according to which the field was conceived by brave white male psychiatrists' and which ignores or subjugates the 'writings and methods of (the) 19th century social workers and community activists' (pp. 3, 4)

in mind. When an individual complains of personal distress, or when others, whether family or professionals, regard that individual as distressed, the usual Western psychological response has been to deal with that person alone. However, once the meaning, maintenance and resolution of individuals' distressed feelings or actions are seen as being connected to their ongoing relationships with others, it begins to make sense to involve those others in the therapeutic process. This has implications not only for how many people will be invited to meet together for the purpose of therapy; once the therapist thinks of behaviour and its meaning as being influenced by interaction and context, it becomes necessary to evolve theories which take account of phenomena other than those within the internal personal or biological world of the individual.

WHAT IS A SYSTEM?

Based on the work of Von Bertalanffy family therapists adopted the idea of a family as an open system, that is '. . . a system in exchange of matter with its environment, presenting import and export, building-up and breaking-down of its material components' (Von Bertalanffy, 1968, p. 149). A system can then be described as a group of elements in interaction with one another over time, such that their recursive patterns of interaction form a stable context for individual and mutual functioning; to the degree that the system is open, interaction with elements outside itself will exert mutual influence.

Thus Mr and Mrs Brown, and little Johnny and Mary, are seen as 'elements' which mutually influence one another while living together, growing and changing with the passage of time. Change will occur inevitably, e.g. as part of biological and life-stage changes, which will in turn alter relationships, for example when the children start school, or become adolescent; nevertheless, the style of relationships, ways of seeing each other, and 'rules' for interaction will be relatively stable. The family is seen not as a closed unit, but as one which interacts also with other individuals, groups and contexts, such as, for example, extended family, friends, and colleagues, as well as with larger systems such as the community, and with outside events, such as war or economic crisis.

The elements within systems—individual human beings, when we are considering families—are regarded from the perspective of their interactions with other elements, that is 'the attributes by which they are identified herein are their communicative behaviours (as opposed to, say, intrapsychic attributes). The objects of interactional systems are best described not as individuals but as persons-communicating-with-other-persons'. (Watzlawick et al., 1967, p. 120). This is not to say that their intrapsychic condition is not of interest, or that the utility of an intrapsychic perspective is denied, but that the focus, in a systems perspective, is on the relations between units. When considering a system it is important always to remember that any system could also be described as a sub-system of a larger system, and could itself be divided into subsystems. A statement by Arthur Koestler (1964) has been much quoted in discussions of the relation between systems and their environments:

> A living organism or social body is not an aggregation of elementary parts or elementary processes; it is an integrated hierarchy of semi-autonomous sub-wholes, consisting of sub-sub-wholes, and so on. Thus the functional units on every level of the hierarchy are double-faced as it were: they act as whole when facing downwards, as parts when facing upwards. (p. 287)

From this it follows that a system does not necessarily have a fixed status; essentially the designation of a system is a distinction drawn by an observer. To put this in practical terms, family therapists choose to work with families, which they designate as systems. Therapists in different cultures might disagree with each other as to the exact delimitation of the family—e.g. are the grandparents part of the family system or outsiders regarded as intruders by the therapist? It is important for therapists to remember—and it is too often forgotten—that although families are biological relational units, with different configurations and memberships in different cultures, the attribution of system characteristics and properties to them is something done by an observer.

The Characteristics of Open Systems

In regarding the family as an open system, an assumption is made that the family (as distinct from its individual members) shows certain system characteristics. These can be summarized briefly as follows:

Wholeness, that is the interrelation and interdependence in the behaviours of family members;

Wholeness includes *non-summativity*, that is the property of being more than the sum of its parts, which is particularly relevant to the consideration of ideas such as supra-individual interactional patterning;

Feedback, that is the assumption that a system will respond to input from its members or from the environment with the amplification or inhibition of pattern, in such a way as to ensure its own continuance;

Equifinality, which means that the same consequences or endpoints may be reached from different starting points or triggers, since the organization or process of the system is more significant than its initial condition or any identifiable 'cause'.

If we apply these system characteristics to the hypothetical Mrs and Mr Brown and their children, we could say that system wholeness would underlie their sense that being part of this family is different from, and more than, being part of a crowd in a shopping mall, and that their individual identities are part and parcel of the family identity. Johnny and Mary would be influenced during their growing up by family patterns which would seem to have a force greater than that of statements or actions by individuals. Their worldly aspirations, their beliefs about relationships or gender roles, their pictures of themselves will have been influenced not only by specific interactions with family and community members, but also by the rules and myths about family functioning transmitted via the thing called 'the family'.

In this early view of system functioning the emphasis was largely on the maintenance of stability ('homeostasis' or 'morphostasis'), so that attention would have been focused on, for example, the ways in which Mr and Mrs Brown would have responded to Mary's early signals of independence, in such a way as to keep her within the family. This would interact with the idea of equifinality: when the parents' increase in vigilance and nurturing (i.e. by signalling to Mary that she was a child who continued to require parenting) was responded to by Mary's increasingly assertive demands for recognition of her autonomy, the system observer would not necessarily conclude that this endpoint had been reached intentionally, or that it had a single identifiable cause. Rather, the responses and adjustments to input and feedback would be seen as having built up to the endpoint of adolescent 'rebellion' and parental 'overcontrol'.

Cybernetics and Family Systems

A number of ideas crucial to the development of family systems thinking were elaborated by Bateson (1978a). Following the original definition (Wiener, 1948) of cybernetics as the study of self-regulating systems, with particular reference to machines, concepts were extrapolated which have continued to influence our ways of explaining interaction in human systems. This includes the concepts of information, circularity, feedback, punctuation, redundancy, and map and territory. These concepts will be mentioned briefly, in order to map the evolution of systems thinking as applied to therapy. For fuller discussions the reader is referred to the originals, in particular to Bateson (1978a, 1980) and to Watzlawick et al. (1967).

According to Bateson human systems are more adequately described in terms of *information/communication*, rather than in terms of energy. His example, often quoted, is useful:

In general in communicational systems, we deal with sequences which resemble stimulus-and-response rather than cause-and-effect. When one billiard ball strikes another, there is an energy transfer such that the motion of the second ball is energized by the impact of the first. In communicational systems, on the other hand, the energy of the response is usually provided by the respondent. If I kick a dog, his immediately sequential behaviour is energized by his metabolism, not by my kick (1978a, p. 379)

In addition, the dog's response will be influenced by his view of the relationship with the kicker and other relational experiences, i.e. he might bite or run away.

The ideas of *feedback*, and *recursiveness* or *circularity* have been crucial in enabling systems therapists to conceive of human interactions in ways which move beyond simple determinism. Human systems are regarded as showing *circular interaction*, i.e. action a might lead to action b, which might lead to action c, which might in turn give rise to action a. Thus individuals are seen as both responding to feedback and eliciting it in relation to those significant others with whom they interact; that is, they interact recursively. *Feedback* can be characterized as positive (eliciting more of the antecedent behaviour) or negative (eliciting less of such behaviour). The idea of feedback in circular interaction then offers an explanation of how human systems remain stable or change.

In observing the interactions of families, therapists would attempt to distinguish those repeating patterns which are not describable merely as pragmatic responses to the current interaction, but are seen to be characterized by *habit* (Bateson, 1978a) or *redundancy*; that is they are laid down at levels of meaning which are habitual, may not be available immediately to awareness, and are repetitive. Observation of such patterning then can be used by observers to achieve a better understanding of repeated interactions which may seem neither logical nor satisfactory to the participants. (It will be noted later in this chapter that the objectivity here attributed to the observer's perspective was to be called into question as systemic theory evolved.)

In the carrying out of such observation the observer *punctuates* (i.e. selects, organizes, privileges, highlights) the sequences of interaction observed; this is similar to the punctuation carried out by an observer who distinguishes a certain group of people as a system. Thus an observer may punctuate lineally, that is place the frame of observation 'such that the sequence does not come back to the starting point' (Bateson, 1978a, p. 242) (e.g. his anger towards his wife is caused by his mother's neglect); or an observer may punctuate circularly or recursively (his angry action towards his wife is a response, from his point of view, to her withdrawal from him—and this may or may not be influenced by his perception of the similarities between his wife and his mother—whereas her withdrawal is her response to his anger, which in turn elicits his response and so on). It is obvious that a circular view of patterning does not presuppose an initial cause (or at any rate does not see it as essential to the understanding of the current pattern), is capable of considering the views of the participants without being obliged to attribute blame to either, and can be expanded to consider feedback responses to context, history, meaning systems and so on, as well as to current behaviours.

A further important concept, derived by Bateson from Korzybski (1941) is the idea that *the map is not the territory it represents*. That is, that messages do not consist of, and are not identical with, the objects they denote; our representations of reality are not to be confused with the realities themselves. This concept will be further discussed below in considering the influence of constructivist ideas on the development of systems therapy.

THE MILAN METHOD

Following the work of the family therapy pioneers, 'schools' of family therapy soon evolved. In addition to those approaches associated with the names of Nathan Ackerman (1958, 1966), Murray Bowen (1966, 1978), Virginia Satir (1964) and others, the mainstream of family therapy practice centred around the models of structural family therapy, identified particularly with the work of Salvador Minuchin (1974), Minuchin et al. (1967, 1978), and strategic therapy, identified in particular with the work of Jay Haley (1964, 1976) and Madanes (1981), and of the Mental Research Institute in Palo Alto (e.g. Watzlawick et al., 1967, 1974). These major models will not be discussed here; the further development of systemic thinking and practice will be explored by considering the significant turning point which occurred in the late nineteen-seventies when the contributions of the Milan group began to influence the international family therapy field.

The arrival, in quick succession, of a number of publications (Selvini et al., 1977, 1978, 1980a, 1980b, 1980c, etc.) made a considerable impact on the family therapy community, so that by the early nineteen-eighties Milan-oriented therapy teams were to be found in many countries.[2] This approach as described in the above publications is, nowadays, referred to as the 'classic' Milan approach, and has been fully described both in the Milan team's own writings (Selvini et al., 1977, 1978, 1980a, 1980b, 1980c, etc.) and in those of others, e.g. Cronen & Pearce (1985), Hoffman (1981), Speed (1985), and Tomm (1984a, 1984b). Since the separation of the four original co-workers in the late seventies and early eighties their ways of working have diverged, and the work of Luigi Boscolo and Gianfranco Cecchin, in particular, has become recursively looped with the changes and explorations pursued by themselves and their erstwhile students, influencing and being influenced by one another. These developments will be discussed in the latter part of this chapter; the core ideas and applications from the classic Milan period will be summarized first.

The earliest work of the Milan group, described in their book *Paradox and Counterparadox* (Selvini et al., 1978) expounded

---

[2] This way of working has generally been referred to as 'Systemic'; this usage will be followed here, while acknowledging that it may be invidious, since all the mainstream family therapy approaches are to some degree or other based on systems ideas. What has perhaps distinguished the Milan group, originally and after their division into several groups in the eighties, is their interest in the larger three-generational and professional systems with which client families are involved.

the ideas they had developed from working with families with a schizophrenic member, designated by them as 'families in schizophrenic transaction'. They characterized their early work as research, and worked in particular with families with schizophrenic or anorexic members, who had often been referred by other professionals who considered the families to have been unresponsive to their own approaches. The provenance of these clients is not insignificant: a close study of all the pioneering family therapy orientations will reveal a more than trivial relationship between their preferred methods and the kinds of families and referral contexts in relation to which the early ideas were developed.

Taking as a basis the idea that the family was 'a self-regulating system which controls itself according to rules formed over a period of time through a process of trial and error' (Selvini et al., 1978, p. 3), they applied ideas derived from the Palo Alto group (Watzlawick et al., 1967) and, later, increasingly from direct study of Bateson's work (e.g. 1958, 1978a, 1980), to develop their own characteristic style of explanation and application. Using the idea that all behaviour could be regarded as communication, they interested themselves in the 'rule-maintaining' characteristics of communications and behaviours, and assumed that 'the way to eliminate the symptom is to change the rules' (Selvini et al., 1978, p. 4). Thus, rather than focusing on micro-elements of interaction, as other family therapists had done, they searched for what came to be called the 'nodal point' in a system, that is, the point where 'the maximum number of functions essential to its existence converge' (Selvini et al., 1978, p. 4), on the assumption that change here would lead to changes throughout the system. They described the families with which they worked as 'pathological' and rigid systems, and assumed that such systems would experience the possibility of change as threatening. They therefore sought for ways of working that would be powerful enough to overcome such rigid 'family games'.

Consideration of the way in which paradoxical or double binding communications played a part in the history of these families (Bateson et al., 1956, Sluzki & Ransom, 1976), led to the development of the therapeutic counterparadox in order to 'undo' the family's paradoxical situation. The use of paradox in therapeutic messages has to some extent been criticized— partly due, perhaps, to its wholesale application by therapists who liked the idea but had not fully taken on board the rigorous theoretical analysis underlying the technique, nor the idea that, as 'counterparadox', it was meant to occur in response to pre-existing paradoxical communication binds in the client families. Nevertheless, it is worth while looking at some of the building blocks behind the technique, as the Milan group's observations about multigenerational family patterning have continued to contribute to their and other therapists' creativity.

As Bateson and his colleagues (1956) conceived of paradoxical communication, it required several components: messages communicated between two or more persons at one logical level or in one mode (e.g. verbal or non-verbal) which were contradicted at another, in a relationship context such that the participants felt unable either to comment (or 'meta-communicate', i.e. communicate about the communication) or to leave the field of the relationship. Added to this is the idea of such communications being repeated over time (Cronen et al., 1982). The content of the messages is likely to refer to what Bateson calls negative injunctions, that is their basic meaning threatens punishment or the loss of love and relationship, so that the recipients find themselves in a situation of 'damned if they do and damned if they don't'. These are not single or discrete units of communication which can be isolated by the observer—Bateson later commented on the futility of such attempts by saying one might as well count the number of bats in a Rorschach inkblot—but can be regarded as characteristic of a style of communication between family members.

By applying these and other Batesonian ideas—e.g. that of symmetrical and complementary patterns of interaction,[3] of

---

[3] Bateson (1978a) describes symmetrical interaction as that in which the behaviour of A elicits a similar kind of behaviour from B, which in turn elicits more of the same behaviour from A. For example, if A gives B a lavish gift on B's birthday, B might feel obliged to respond with an equally

the possibility of different communicational 'languages', namely the digital (largely verbal) and the analogic (largely non-verbal)—the Milan group developed a way of describing the interactions of family members, over several generations, as engaged in a struggle for the definition of relationship (cf *Some core ideas*' below for further discussion of this concept).

While the early contributions of the Milan group applied particularly to their work with the families studied in their original project (Selvini et al., 1978), i.e. those with schizophrenic or anorexic members, many of their ideas and methods proved to be of general value in the family therapy field. Some of these will be mentioned briefly.

Working Method

One-way mirrors had long been used for training purposes in family therapy (Montalvo, 1973): this meant that a supervisor on one side of a one-way mirror could directly observe and intervene in the work of a trainee therapist interviewing a family on the other side of the mirror or screen. The group behind the screen would be invisible to the family and therapist; the family would be aware of and in agreement with the presence of the observers (cf Chapter 2 for a more extended discussion of teamwork and the use of the one-way screen). The Milan group started to use this technology for peer consultation, since the different perspectives of the therapists and of the team behind the screen allowed them to put together a double description (Bateson, 1978a) of family interaction. Initially they used a co-therapy pair (usually a man and a woman) in the room with the family and another

---

lavish (or even more lavish) gift on A's birthday, and so on.

Complementary interaction consists of an action by A which elicits a different but mutually fitting behaviour from B, which in turn stimulates more of A's mutually fitting behaviour, and so on. For example, nurturing behaviour from A might be responded to by dependent behaviour from B, which elicits more nurturing from A, etc. Either of these two patterns— symmetry or complementarity—can become pernicious and go into 'run-away', if they are not regulated by systemic restraints.

pair behind the screen; this was fairly quickly abandoned in favour of one therapist working with the family while the rest of the team observed.

Thus one therapist works with the clients, another therapist or team are behind a one-way screen and may call the therapist out of the room in order to share ideas and elaborations of hypotheses. The session is classically divided into five sections: pre-session, for discussion of referral information or a summary of the previous session, and for the elaboration of hypotheses; the bulk of the interview between therapist and clients; the in-session consultation, where therapist and team share and elaborate ideas; the final part of the session, where the therapist returns to the family in order to explore these ideas further, or give them a task or ritual to perform between sessions; and the post-session discussion between therapist and team.

Sessions were typically spaced at longer intervals than were then considered usual; in the classic period these were likely to be one month apart. The rationale was that enough time was required to allow the system to respond to the impact of the therapeutic intervention, so that in the next session, the evidence of this 're-calibration' would be available for observation. As time went on, this fixed interval lapsed, and Milan-oriented therapists are inclined to decide the intervals between sessions on the basis of the available feedback, and frequently in consultation with clients. In general, therapy was limited to ten sessions; thus this approach (few sessions at long intervals) has been called long brief therapy.

Some Core Ideas

The struggle for definition of relationship

The Milan group's efforts to understand the intense, multi-generational patterns of mutual disconfirmation which they observed, particularly between the parents in these families, led them to formulate the idea that each person in such a partnership finds himself or herself wanting to be confirmed, and to control the relationship and its definition, but afraid to make the attempt to do so overtly for fear of final disqualification if the effort were to fail. The Milan team postulated that such intense patterns of behaviour were the result of similar interactions gradually building in intensity over several generations, and invoked Bateson's ideas about the way in which positive feedback loops in interaction could go into 'runaway', as well as ideas, derived from General Systems Theory, about the way in which systems could use autocorrective mechanisms in order to retain their homeostasis (stability). They saw each member of the couple then resort to 'the only solution: the avoidance of any definition of the relationship' (Selvini et al., 1978, p. 24), whereas the identified patient's behaviour was seen to act as the corrective (negative feedback/homeostatic) input which restrained the family from change. An example would be where an adult 'psychotic' child behaves in such a way that the family's evolutionary progress through various developmental stages becomes frozen in time, by virtue of the adult child remaining the responsibility of their parents. Such processes then underlay the paradoxical styles of communication in the family.

The Milan group's view of these patterns of mutual *dis*qualification extended to encompass their view of the family's relationship with therapy; thus the family's behaviour towards therapists and therapeutic interventions was seen as attempts to disqualify the therapy, and therapists and family also therefore risked becoming locked in a struggle for definition of relationship. It is this line of thinking, and the unfortunate metaphor of the 'family game'—which derived originally from Von Neumann's game theory (Bateson, 1978a, and Von Neumann & Morgenstern, 1944), rather than from the popular meaning of the word—which led to the use of much adversarial metaphor and thinking in the group's approach, and which has since been repudiated by them (e.g. Selvini & Selvini, 1991).

Showing and being

In order to free themselves from what they described as the 'tyranny of linguistic conditioning' (Selvini et al., 1978, p. 51) the Milan group changed their language so as to remind themselves constantly that appearance and reality were not necessarily synonymous. That is, instead of saying that someone is sad, or aggressive, or dependent, etc. they would use the expression 'to show' : X *shows* (in the context of therapy) a sad expression (cf also Bateson, 1978a, 1980). This then enabled them to begin to be freer to ask what the relational meaning of such a communication might be, and to remain focused on interactions *between* family members, rather than becoming preoccupied with the behaviour of individuals.

Hypothesizing

Hypothesizing consists of the elaboration, by therapist and team, of speculations, guesses, assumptions and explanations about the family situation, on the basis of information about the family available at that stage of the therapy, as well as on the basis of normative assumptions and the therapist's experience with other families. Like null hypotheses in research, the refutation of a hypothesis by subsequent inquiry is not considered a failure, but is seen as furthering understanding.

The intention of hypothesis-making is to guide the therapist's discussion with the clients; hypotheses are not required to be true, but rather to be useful, so as to provide the therapist with a starting point. This guides the therapist's activity, keeps it from becoming random, while at the same time introducing potential new meaning into the family pattern. As hypothesizing became common practice it was realized that practitioners would do well to guard against the danger of 'falling in love' with hypotheses or even 'marrying' them (i.e. regarding them as true and unalterable); the cure for this is to construct more than one hypothesis at the same time. Hypotheses are required to be systemic, that is to address the whole relational system.

The Boscolo/Cecchin Milan team nowadays tend to group their hypotheses into three clusters: hypotheses about alliances, about individual and family premises and myths, and about communication in the family and within other linked systems (Boscolo et al., 1987)

Circularity

Circularity refers to the way in which the therapist conducts the interview, by responding to feedback from the family, and by seeking information about relationships and about difference—that is difference between people, relationships, events, etc. and over time. This concern with circularity in the interview mirrors the theoretical convictions about circularity in systemic interaction, and is associated with Bateson's dictum that we cannot think in terms of knowledge about things but only about relationships between things, people, etc. From this search for information about difference a number of techniques arose that guide the questioning style of Milan-oriented therapists, such as triadic questions (e.g. asking person 1 about their perception of an aspect of the relationship between persons 2 and 3), questions about specific interactive behaviour, ranking questions (e.g. asking for a ranking of who, at a particular point in the family's history, was closest to a particular person, who next, and so on (cf Selvini et al., 1980b). The many therapists who claim influence from the Milan group have elaborated the applications of these types of questions (cf for example, Penn, 1982, 1985, and Tomm, 1987a, 1987b, 1988).

Neutrality

Since this concept has caused more furore in the general therapeutic community than perhaps any other emanating from this group, it is perhaps as well to start off by quoting their original definition. 'By neutrality of the therapist we mean a specific pragmatic effect that his [*sic*] other total behaviour during the session exerts on the family (*and not his intrapsychic disposition*)'(my italics) (Selvini et al., 1980b, p. 4). They go on to explain that they would expect clients, after a session, to have many views about the therapist, but not to see the therapist as having sided with one or other member or having formed a judgement about them. The family may repeatedly experience the therapist as allied with one or other member of the family as that person's views are being elicited, but since this is a constantly shifting process the therapist should be seen as allied with everyone and no one. In the Milan group's view the therapist should in fact occupy a 'meta-level' in relation to the family, that is the therapeutic point of view should be different from that of the family and its individual members if it is to be of any use.

The stance of neutrality came in for repeated criticism, being seen as demonstrating coldness and aloofness on the part of the therapist, a lack of opinions and values, and even a failure to take responsibility when this could be seen as necessary. Cecchin responded to these critiques (1987) by redefining neutrality as 'curiosity'. He proposed that an attitude of curiosity would enable a therapist to remain alert to the multitude of possible explanations and patterns relevant to the family and the family–therapist relationship; such a stance would be one that 'celebrates the complexity of interaction and invites a polyphonic orientation to the description and explanation of interaction' (Cecchin, 1987, p. 406). Thus instead of searching for a true and final description of family problems, a curious therapist would be able to continue to question, for example, how a family's descriptions fit together, and how they fit with the therapist's descriptions; this is seen as an approach that is aesthetic, non-judgemental, non-directive and respectful.

Positive connotation

Positively connoting the problem-maintaining behaviours of all members of the system, and in particular that of the symptomatic member, is designed to give therapists access to a systemic grasp of the meaning that not changing has, at a certain moment, for the system. The therapists thus free themselves from blaming one or more members of the system for their inability to change, or their hurtful or strange behaviours. The therapist comments to the family on the positive role played in the maintenance of the system by their behaviours. For example, a child behaving psychotically may be described as attempting to keep alive the memory and presence of a dead grandparent, with the intention of obliging the parents to cooperate, thus averting the threatened break-up of their marriage, or with the intention of assuaging the parents' grief; obviously such descriptions would depend on the particular family histories and patterns. There are several levels and intentions to such a positive connotation.

Positive connotation is not merely a technique, but requires that the therapist and team should strive to obtain the sort of understanding of the system that will make sense of behaviours which otherwise would seem to be insane or malicious. The therapist seeks for a formulation that will allow a child's psychotic symptoms, a parent's contradictory concern and indifference, the family's ambivalence towards change, to be seen as meaningful contributions to the survival of the system, and at the same time allow them to be described in such a way that their meaning can be altered. Positively connoting all such acts as serving the maintenance of system coherence is seen as a way of both gaining entrance to the system's world of meaning, by respecting it and acknowledging its internal logic, and of preparing the way for change or challenging the status quo.

Positive connotation is classically followed by a therapeutic suggestion to maintain symptomatic behaviour or to slow down the rate of change. The therapist describes to a family their dilemma, and the way in which their behaviours heretofore—and that of the 'identified patient' in particular—can be seen as maintaining the system, and at the same time prescribes the behaviours complained of, if only for the time being. The addition of a time-clause into such a positive connotation and paradoxical prescription is perhaps one of the most crucial elements: it is as if the therapist is saying

> We think we can understand why you are all behaving in this way, and that your behaviour is motivated by good intentions and the desire for survival—you need to be careful not to change too fast *until* you and we can be sure that the unknown

consequences of change will not be worse than the situation you face now.

Positive connotation is not the same as reframing, which is a technique generally used in many family therapy approaches, and is defined (Watzlawick et al., 1974) as changing 'the conceptual and/or emotional setting or viewpoint in relation to which a situation is experienced and to place it in another frame which fits the "facts" . . . equally well or even better, and thereby changes its entire meaning' (Watzlawick et al., 1974, p. 95). While there are similarities, it has to be borne in mind that a reframing can be positive or negative, and does not necessarily attempt to encompass all of the relationships within a system over time.

Positive connotation was often experienced by therapists and by clients as problematic. It could imply that the disturbed or disturbing behaviours of family members were functional, or good, or that the family needed such a symptom. Positive connotation, and the prescription of no change, could therefore seem sarcastic or indifferent. Thus Boscolo and Cecchin (Boscolo et al., 1987) now think more about the 'logical connotation' of system functioning, that is, the therapist tries to understand how a unique system works, what constrains it from change, and even whether it ought to change.

Rituals

The work of the Milan team is particularly associated with the devising of elegant rituals designed to bring about major change in the complex functioning of families. These ritual actions or series of actions, prescribed in minute detail by the therapist and team, are to be performed by all or most family members, sometimes on several occasions. They are designed to address aspects of family relationships seen as significant by the therapists, but at the level of action rather than primarily at the level of words. When language is involved, this is often prescribed as part of the ritual. Because the ritual therefore involves family members in a powerful experience at the analogic or non-verbal level it is seen as highly conducive to change. (Indeed, it is presumably because of this profound capacity to influence and change human behaviour that ritual has always played such an important part in all societies.) Rituals have to be tailor-made for families, and need to grow out of the specific therapist-family experience.

The 'odd and even days' prescription (Selvini et al., 1980c) could be regarded as a sub-category of rituals, which has proved of great value to therapists, in the use it makes of the element of time. Thus aspects of an apparently insoluble—and often paradoxical—dilemma are separated out by prescribing different parts of the pattern at different times. For example parents, who are locked in a mutually disqualifying parenting pattern, may be asked to take turns to parent, e.g. mother on odd days, father on even days. Such a separation would be likely to have the effect of freeing a child from having to obey mutually contradictory injunctions.

DEVELOPMENTS IN THE SYSTEMIC THERAPIES

It can be difficult and confusing to attempt to give a name to the recent developments associated with the Milan approach. As Lynn Hoffman points out (1988), when she was in the process of finishing her seminal textbook *Foundations of Family Therapy* (1981) the field had already started to shift in a way that she likened to a paradigm shift. This constant process of evolution and self-questioning is perhaps what most characterizes this therapeutic approach. Since the idea of responsiveness to feedback, recursiveness, or co-evolution is built into its very foundations, this is not surprising.

Following the break-up of the original Milan team (cf Jones, 1988, Pirotta, 1984), those systemic approaches influenced particularly by the work of Luigi Boscolo and Gianfranco Cecchin have variously been called Post-Milan, or Second-order (Hoffman, 1985), Second-order-cybernetic or Observing-system systemic therapy (Von Foerster, 1981, 1990). The latter terms will be discussed below. I have difficulty in accepting a definition of something which rests only on the idea of it coming after something else. As Margaret Atwood (1990) says '. . .post this, post that. Everything is post these days, as if we're all just a footnote to something earlier that was real enough to have a name of its own'. What the term 'Post-Milan' attempts to convey is the work that is associated with Luigi Boscolo, Gianfranco Cecchin, and their ex-trainees and associates in many different parts of the world, all of whom have continued to influence each other, as well as to struggle together to incorporate the ideas of therapists not directly associated with their approach, and of some scientists and philosophers outside the field of family therapy. Some of these contributions will be discussed below. This discussion will not be exhaustive, but will attempt to explicate some key concepts which have been adopted by family therapists, and to consider their practical implications.

Second-Order Cybernetics or Observing Systems

From the beginning of the development of systems thinking, cybernetics—'the science of communication and control in man and machine' (Wiener, 1948)—has been fundamental to the way that family therapists tried to understand the circularity of organization in family pattern, stability and change, that is, the phenomenon of recursiveness within systems. What has now been called First-order Cybernetics is concerned, first, with questions relating to the way in which systems maintain their organization (e.g. processes such as morphostasis or stability, negative feedback or restraint, and rule systems), and second, with the way in which systems change their organization (e.g. processes such as morphogenesis or change, positive feedback or amplification, escalation or schismogenesis (Bateson, 1958), and adaptation). This approach is characterized by an assumption that the observer stands outside the thing observed, and is therefore *objective*. This makes it possible to intervene from the position of a detached observer, who remains unaffected by the interaction, and who is in a position to make objective observations and judgements; in the case of human systems this would entail judgements of pathology, dysfunction, normative goals, and an interventive stance in relation to what needs to be changed in the observed system.

Second-order cybernetics (or the cybernetics of cybernetics) concerns itself with recursive connections between systems, and the complexity of layers of cybernetic processes. From a second order perspective the observer is seen as part of that which is being observed, and also as crucially implicated in *constructing* that which is being observed. Readers acquainted with some of the more generally available conclusions from quantum physics (e.g. Capra, 1975) will recognize that this shift of perspective on the part of family therapists is only an adaptation to a general and highly significant change in the way that our world, and our place within it, is being construed by scientists and philosophers from many different disciplines. In contrast to the first-order ideas mentioned above, the focus in second-order cybernetics is on concepts such as recursiveness, reflexivity, and the autonomy of systems (Sluzkí, 1985, Von Foerster, 1981, 1990).

Von Foerster (1990), one of the architects of this approach, illustrates it by considering how advances in neurophysiology and neuropsychiatry made it possible to begin to

> write a theory of the brain. . . . What is new is the profound insight that it needs a brain to write a theory of the brain. From this follows that a theory of the brain, that has any aspirations for completeness, has to account for the writing of this theory. And even more fascinating, the *writer* of this theory has to account for her- or himself. Translated into the domain of cybernetics: the cybernetician, by entering his own domain, has to account for his own activity; cybernetics becomes cybernetics of cybernetics, or second-order cybernetics. . . . This perception represents a fundamental change not only in the way we conduct science, but also how we conceive of teaching, of learning, of the therapeutic process, of organizational management, and so on and so forth; and— I would say—of how we perceive relationship in our daily life. (Von Foerster, 1990, p. 5)

This new perception has also influenced the way in which research is structured, so that part of the perennial split between researchers and clinicians is beginning to be resolved, as researcher-clinicians develop research methods which embody second-order-cybernetic thinking. This means that researchers take account of the view that research is not an inert activity which allows for objective observation, without changing that which is being observed. Thus studies are designed to allow for the impact of research activity (whether negative or potentially therapeutic) on those persons being studied, and to enable responses to the research to be fed back into the research process, demonstrating systemic recursiveness (cf for example Doherty, 1986, Fruggeri & McNamee, 1991, Kaye, 1990, McNamee, 1987, Roper-Hall, 1991 and Steier, 1991).

To return to the idea, discussed above in relation to Bateson, that the map is not the territory: Von Foerster (1990), like other of his colleagues, now takes a stance which could be taken to proclaim that the map *is* the territory. What this means is that the map is all we can know of the territory, and therefore constitutes our reality, regardless of what other 'realities' may be deemed to exist, or indeed not to exist. There would be degrees of difference in where, on a 'reality continuum', systemic family therapists and the theorists they follow would align themselves (Dell, 1985). Some would argue that reality consists only of the constructions and distinctions brought forth by observers; others would remain closer to the world-view expressed by Bateson, which suggests that reality, or territory, does exist, but that our knowing of it is profoundly affected by the limitations of our senses, as well as by our active role in constructing that which we observe. However, these are distinctions within a broadly constructivist position (cf the discussion below under *Language and meaning*), which has contributed significantly to the way in which family therapists currently view the nature of their work.

These ideas are not all new, and rest on a philosophical heritage (e.g. Wittgenstein, Kant) as well as earlier psychological approaches hitherto largely ignored by family therapists (e.g. Kelly, 1955). Of crucial importance is how therapists understand the status of the knowledge they claim to hold (about themselves, the world, and others). Von Glasersfeld

(1984, 1987, 1988) posits that all we can know as we bump up against whatever is out there is based on our knowledge of viability (i.e. whether we survive or not); that is, we can argue that there is a fit between our actions and other events, persons and so on, but this does not constitute a knowledge of the nature of those others. Surviving in the world suggests only that our behaviour is adequate or viable. Thus a therapist interacting with family members can, when therapy has been concluded to mutual satisfaction, decide that her actions (words, behaviours, meaning-attributions) found a fit with those of family members; since arguably many other actions would have done likewise she has no basis for claiming the 'truth' of her unique explanation of the family or of her perception of them. From this, then, comes the idea that therapist and family (or other meaningful system) together co-construct or co-evolve new ways of describing the family system, such that it will no longer be seen or experienced as problematic. It is clear that these ideas are interconnected with 'post-modernist' ideas in many fields other than that of therapy, where the consequences of regarding all 'narratives' or versions of 'reality' as equally valid are being explored.

The Organization of the Living

The Chilean biologist Humberto Maturana and his colleague Francisco Varela have made a considerable and controversial impact on the family therapy world. Rather than cybernetic (self-regulating) systems the concern here is with autopoietic (self-generating) systems (Maturana & Varela 1972, 1988). Maturana's ideas are based on his work in the field of biology, and have been criticized both for being irrelevant to the field of psychotherapy, and for being unoriginal, solipsistic and flawed (cf for example, Birch, 1991, Keeney, 1988, Kenny, 1988). Nevertheless, many of these ideas, whether relevant and original or not, have found their way into family therapy discourse (Varela, 1989), and those that have directly influenced practice will be discussed.

Maturana places *objectivity in parentheses* (one might, more usually, say: in quotation marks) because 'an observer has no operational basis to make any statement or claim about objects, entities or relations as if they existed independently of what he or she does' (1988, p. 30). By drawing distinctions the observer 'brings forth' that which she or he then claims to know, to see, or to experience. This is a constructivist position, in that everything said is said by an observer, and there is no possibility of referring to objective truth or reality in order to choose between descriptions. Indeed, Maturana sees reference to objective reality as a sort of bully-boy tactic, designed to club the other person with the weight of one's own subjective argument.

Since objectivity in parentheses makes it impossible to decide on the real truth or the final explanation where different views come into contact with one another, Maturana therefore puts forward the idea of multiple realities, the 'multiverse' (Mendez et al., 1988). This idea has proved fruitful in family therapy, as it has freed therapists from the search for investigation and diagnosis in relation to clients, and—more importantly—has underscored the necessity to approach all versions of reality proffered by clients *and by the therapist* as equally valid.

All living systems (composite unities) are *structure-determined*; that is, 'nothing external to a structure-determined system can specify the structural changes that it undergoes as a consequence of an interaction' (Maturana, 1988, p. 36). What this means for therapists is that in interaction individuals will react in coherence with their own internal structures; it is these that specify all of the possibilities of action, interaction, change, etc., that are possible for that individual to undergo. If we think back to Bateson's dog, discussed earlier in this chapter, it is the dog's structure that specifies how it will react, not Bateson's kick. In Maturana's terms, then, the kick is seen as a *perturbation*, which may or may not *trigger* a response, but the kick cannot specify what that response may be. Taking the discussion out of the metaphoric realm of biology and recasting it in the metaphoric language of relationships raises some obvious questions as to its applicability (cf Chapter 7 for further discussion). Nevertheless, it has been useful for family therapists to consider the idea that the interaction of element A with element B may act as a perturbation which may trigger a response, but the nature of that response, if any, will be (wholly, according to Maturana) specified and determined by the structure of the perturbed unit. In family therapy folklore this has been codified in John Wayne's words: 'A man's gotta do what a man's gotta do.'

It follows from the idea of structure determinism that *instructive interaction is impossible*. That is, A cannot unilaterally determine what B will do. The lesson family therapists have taken from this is that it is incumbent on them to behave in ways, to the best of their ability and skill, that make it more likely than not that their actions will function as sufficient perturbation, in the context of good-enough fit, to trigger a reorganization of the individuals and the family group they are seeing. What form that reorganization takes will have more to do with the family members' history, meaning systems, relationships and relationship rules and myths, perception of the relationship with the therapist and so on, than with the specific content of the therapist's action or message. This does not necessarily mean that therapists have to give up what Maturana calls their 'passion for change', or their intentionality or activity in relation to clients; it merely means that they have to accept that they cannot fully predict or determine their clients' responses.

While Maturana's ideas and those of constructivism generally have influenced the practice of family therapy, they have also been criticized from a variety of perspectives (e.g. Hoffman, 1990, Keeney, 1988, Minuchin, 1991, Speed, 1991a), particularly in their more radical application. The concern here is that too sweeping a transposition has been made from the world of biology or machines to that of human beings and their complex relational networks, and also that, in acknowledging the inevitable subjectivity of knowledge, radical constructivist stances, when adopted by therapists, allow for an amoral, 'anything-goes' kind of approach to therapy, which denies the therapist's responsibility for her actions, and ignores the (experienced) reality of injustice or violence, and the context in which individual 'autopoietic units' live.

Language and Meaning

A number of family therapists have found metaphors for the ways that client families and therapists interact which owed less to the world of science and more to that of language, literature and social contexts. Anderson and Goolishian have been exploring human systems from the point of view of communication, that is of human systems as 'language-generating and, simultaneously, meaning-generating systems' (Anderson & Goolishian, 1988, p. 372). (Incidentally, wherever family therapists turn for new ideas, and however we react against old ideas, all our answers, so far, can be seen to be rooted in the highlighting of some aspect or other of Gregory Bateson's work. Perhaps family therapy will only achieve a 'paradigm shift' once a real alternative to Bateson is discovered!)

Anderson and Goolishian (1988), Hoffman (1990), and others have put forward the idea of therapy as conversation, which becomes organized around a 'problem', whose meaning, like all other meaning, is socially constructed, so that change (the 'dis-solving' of the system coalesced around the problem) is seen as the 'evolution of new meaning through dialogue'. In line with the concept of observing systems, they see the therapist as a participant-observer and a participant-manager of the therapeutic conversation. Thus the therapist's role is seen as facilitating the kind of conversation likely to lead to the dis-solving of the problem and therefore of the therapeutic system that formed in relation to the problem, and the development of new 'narratives', which are not organized around a problem. The therapist's role is non-directive, and it is assumed that there is a 'kind of systemic wisdom that delicately balances natural systems' (Atkinson & Heath, 1990a, p. 145) so that it is not necessary for therapists to engage in active, interventive strategies. Psychotherapists familiar with the work of Carl Rogers may see some similarity in the clinical application, if not all of the theoretical formulation, of these ways of working.

In their search for a constructivist position that will also make sense within the observable world of human relationships, family therapists have turned to social constructionism (which is often confused with constructivism, but clearly different, as the following discussion will show). A definition from Shweder and Miller (1985) will help to clarify this. They discuss three general kinds of theories of category formation:

> (a) realist theories, which argue that 'people categorize the world the way they do because that's the way the world is'; (b) innatist theories, which argue that 'people categorize the world the way they do because that's the way people are'; and (c) social construction theories, which argue that 'people categorize the world the way they do because they have participated in social practices, institutions, and other forms of symbolic action (e.g. language) that presuppose or in some way make salient those categorizations' (Shweder & Miller, 1985, p. 41)

Thus type (a) would correspond to a first-order stance, type (b) to a constructivist stance, and type (c) would begin to offer a way for critics of constructivism to integrate their acceptance of the idea of the constructed nature of knowledge with their desire to include perceptions about the influence of context, power, consensus and lived experience in it.

A social constructionist position (Gergen, 1985, Gergen & Davis, 1985) makes it possible to include the history of social structures, and the role of language in shaping what is experienced as real, within the meaning systems of individuals and families. Thus it becomes possible to re-integrate ideas which, from a rigidly constructivist position, could not be made to fit into systemic theory. Foucault's (1980) exploration of the history of ideas, and the way in which dominant discourse can determine what it is appropriate to discuss (and think), has enabled family therapists, and particularly its feminist critics, to take a meta-stance to their own theory (a sort of cybernetics of cybernetics of cybernetics!). In particular, Foucault's ideas have made it possible to consider the role of power relations within society without attributing the intention to exercise power to those individuals seen to be participating in a dominant discourse. Since such power operates independent of the intentions of individuals, under-standing requires instead an analysis of the position from which such power is exercised. In particular his wide-ranging questioning of how certain ideas become privileged in certain eras is a powerful corrective against the temptation to begin to believe that a final answer has been found. This then also requires of family therapists, like others in the 'mental health field', to ask themselves how their own preferred ideas fit into the dominant social discourse, what its relation is to power, and what other potential discourses have been subjugated by virtue of the success of the views currently held to be valid. As Cecchin and his colleagues suggest (in press) the 'adoption of a position of irreverence is to be slightly subversive against *any* reified "truth"'—and this includes the 'truth' of current family therapy theory too.

PRACTICAL IMPLICATIONS

The focus for systemic therapists currently is less on technique, and more on the attitude of the therapist, which is likely to be self-conscious, multi-positional, alert to openings (Boscolo et al., 1987), realistic about the possibility of bringing about change, and 'disrespectful' (Cecchin et al., in press). These attitudes are likely to be demonstrated by the therapist's awareness of, and curiosity about, her own participation in the observed system, and her willingness to keep an open mind about explanations, different perspectives, and potential outcomes, without becoming non-positional. Alertness to 'openings' involves looking for indications, within the conversation of family members, of flexibility towards the consideration of alternatives or the introduction of variation by the therapist. The therapist seeks for the logical connotation of system behaviour, that is, for an understanding of how things come to be the way they are, without necessarily straining to frame this as 'good' or 'positive'. While not assuming that she can change or direct others, the therapist may nevertheless offer views, or suggestions for change, as part of the ongoing exploration in which all members of the therapeutic system are engaged, and will attempt to engage in the therapeutic conversation in such a way that clients will be invited to share her 'curiosity' and to take up an observer stance in relation to their own participation. A systemic therapist will, in line with Von Foerster's (1990) definition of ethics, try to act so as to *increase* the number of choices, while maintaining 'a healthy disrespect toward any idea which restricts therapeutic manoeuvrability and creativity' (Cecchin et al., in press).

The struggle for increased understanding, better ways of working, more effective and more ethical approaches will continue. Despite constructivist assumptions about the elusiveness of 'truth', family therapists will likely continue to feel partisan towards their own preferred theories, and attempt to establish the validity of such theories in the face of others. In the mean time Bateson's dictum may help to hold these endeavours in some perspective: 'We are all deeply ignorant; and there can be no competition in ignorance' (1978b, p. 40).

CHAPTER 2　Working in teams

BACKGROUND

When family therapy was first practised it was common to use co-therapy, that is two therapists working together in the same room with the clients, for training purposes and also on the basis of assumptions similar to those held by psychoanalytically oriented marital therapists. That is, therapists assumed that the presence of a male and female therapist in the room would be useful to the building of therapeutic relationships, the management of transference, and the making of alliances. This was largely abandoned as it was realized that a team using a one-way mirror or screen could cooperate in a way that retained many of the benefits of co-therapy, while adding some new dimensions. As has already been mentioned in Chapter 1, the therapist in the room with the clients conducts the interview, asks questions, and is involved in the relationship and the emotional 'tone' of the meeting. The consultant (one person or more) observes the interview through the one-way mirror while being invisible to the clients and therapist, and is able therefore to stand back somewhat from the immediacy of the interactions between family members and therapist, and thus to add a different perspective.

One-way screens were first used for supervision purposes (Montalvo, 1973); the original Milan team in the 1970s was the first to use the screen to enhance the work of family therapists working together as clinical teams. The advantages and disadvantages, and the evolution in the uses of team and screen will be discussed in detail in this chapter, but it may be useful here to make the point that not all systemic therapists work with either teams or screens, even though this way of working is so powerfully associated with the approach.

RATIONALE

Why do we work in teams? And why do we, for the most part, place the team on the other side of a one-way screen from the therapist and family? The answer relates back to Bateson's views on the value of 'double description': he postulated that obtaining more than one view of an event would enable us to achieve the cognitive or emotional equivalent of binocular vision, thus gaining, in a metaphorical sense, perspective on our observations and experiences. The use of the screen additionally seemed to offer an answer, in the thinking of the original Milan team, to the problem of how to join a system while continuing to make a 'difference that makes a difference' (Bateson, 1978a).

When therapist and clients join together for the purposes of therapy, they inevitably over time form a new 'client-therapist' system. In the view of the Milan team (Selvini et al., 1978) it was important to find ways of slowing down this process, of enabling the therapist to retain enough difference in relation to the clients to make it likely that her contribution/intervention to their system would lead to change. One of the ways that this could be achieved was for the therapist to have simultaneous membership of *two* systems, that is of the therapist/client system on one side of the screen, and of the therapist/team system on the other side of the screen. This would enable the therapist to function comfortably in the position of someone who belonged to the group but was not wholly part of it, and thus to be of maximum benefit to clients.

In addition, an assumption is made that occupying a different *position* in relation to clients or events enables us to have different *views*. Thus the team members[1] behind the screen

---

[1] The use of the word 'supervisor' for the person(s) behind the screen indicates that the context is one of supervision. When the work of peer teams is being discussed, the word 'consultant' is used. The rationale for this is well discussed in Cade et al. (1986). In a consultant/therapist interaction the relationship is one of hierarchical equals, and would be seen as such even if there were a difference in experience, organizational status and so on between team members. For the purposes of the therapeutic work to be done the members of a consultation team have agreed that their

will have a different perspective from that of the therapist in the room. It is important to bear in mind that neither of these views is the correct one, and neither is superior to the other. For example, being behind the screen and observing aspects of the interaction not noticed by the therapist, who is involved in all the hurly-burly of relationships, affect, and complicated communication, does not mean that the consultant is cleverer than the therapist—she is merely in a different position. It is when these different perceptions are put together in the team discussion that, in Bateson's metaphor, binocular vision leads to a perception of depth. This can be compared to the way in which systemic therapists assume that an 'orgy of lineal hypothesizing' (Pirotta & Cecchin, 1988), as the team's mixing together of many different punctuations and attributions is sometimes called, leads to a circular, systemic description of client functioning.

APPLICATION

The classic application of team work in systemic family therapy derives from the work of the Milan team (Selvini et al., 1978, 1980b), although many family therapists working from different perspectives have contributed significantly to the use and flexibility of team work.[2]

Structure

Systemic therapy teams come in all shapes and sizes, although there is probably general agreement that there is an optimal

---

voices will carry equal weight. In a supervision team the members have agreed to meet for training purposes. Thus, even though trainees may be high-ranking and experienced professionals, there is an overt agreement that the supervisor holds the last word; in terms of agency requirements she is also likely to hold clinical responsibility.

[2] See, for example, the many and creative applications of team messages and team discussions behind the screen or in front of the family as described by therapists from the 'strategic' and 'brief therapy' orientations, such as Madanes (1984), Papp (1980), and De Shazer & Molnar (1984), to name but a few.

size for good team functioning, and that a mixture of genders, professional origins, ethnic and cultural backgrounds and ages or life-stages would be ideal, as it would provide the team with the built-in likelihood of different perspectives. Most workers express the view that five is a good size for team functioning: small enough to enable everyone's voice to be heard, and large enough to allow for diversity. In addition, five can be a safer number in terms of group functioning than some other configurations. Twosomes can become closed units, threesomes can become tense triangles with a constant threat that one will be excluded by the other two, and foursomes can break up into opposed twosomes. Ideally team members should be peers, that is, they should have similar levels of experience as family therapists, so that their agreement to give equal weight to each others' contributions (cf Footnote 1) can be authentic. In such a team it then becomes possible to allocate cases on the basis of the therapist's particular interests or expertise, and for team members to alternate regularly between the roles of therapist and consultant. On the other hand, looked at from the point of view of stability, it would seem that a team of two members only is most likely to stay together (e.g. Hoffman in Boscolo et al., 1987). For readers new to this way of working it may be useful to point out that the same therapist and the same team work with each client family throughout the therapy.

Those readers who work or have worked in the more usual kinds of family therapy teams, where team members with varying skills, interest in the work, theoretical orientations and positions in the organizational hierarchy are put together by fiat of management and told to be a team, will understand how important the peer composition of the team is. Where teams have been put together in the manner described above, the experience is often one of struggling against the odds not only to have space and permission to work well, but to overcome the obstacles created by the structure. For example, the person with the most status may not be the most skilled family therapist, or a group may be striving to work as a team of equals, valuing everyone's contribution, taking turns in front of or behind the screen, while never ever mentioning the fact that one team member earns three times as much as another. If the highest earner is also the family therapy novice (whether acknowledged or not) it only needs a tense or difficult therapy session to make buried resentments surface in the form of attributions to the clients, or hot disputes about the 'right' approach.

Working Rules

The pre-session

The team meets briefly before the session with the clients starts. The therapist presents the team with a summary of past sessions, and in particular with any hypotheses noted at the end of the previous session. The team discusses their ideas about the family and the therapist/team/client relationships. The concept of hypothesizing has been discussed in many systemic papers and books (and in Chapter 1). Arguably its main rationale rests on the idea that we cannot but hold values, assumptions, prejudices, stereotypes and pet theories, which will influence our work with clients. Spelling these out in the company of the team means that we lay them on the table, where they are visible to all. Thus they become available as creative resources to our work, rather than functioning as invisible organizers of our perceptions and actions. In addition, the participation of the team in hypothesizing means that several likely explanations and perceptions of the meaning of clients' problems and patterns of behaviour become available to the therapist. This ensures flexibility, and guards against the likelihood of becoming convinced of the absolute truth of one's own view. Milan therapists describe this as marrying one's hypothesis. The therapist decides which of these ideas, generated by the team discussion, to hold in the forefront of her mind as she starts the meeting with the clients. She knows that the team will hold on to the other ideas, and will generate further hypotheses or elaborations of existing hypotheses, while she is talking with the clients.

It must be admitted that the above is an ideal description of the hypothesizing phase of a therapy session. Busy teams, or teams that have been working together for a long time, may make do with a starkly abbreviated version of the above procedure. This may work well if they know each others' thinking well enough to get by with a kind of shorthand communication, in which brief phrases convey a wealth of associations. Such a team would need to be alert to times when these brief consultations are inadequate, so as to organize a longer period for themselves in which to hold a fuller discussion. On the other hand, skimping on the hypothesizing stage of a session may well be a sign of boredom, staleness and burnout, which will display itself in the way in which the team and therapist resort to stereotyped and familiar ways of viewing each new family's unique situation.

Introducing the setting

The therapist now joins the clients in the interview room. In a first session the therapist will deal first of all with explaining the existence of the team and screen to the clients, even though this information is also likely to have been sent to them in written form beforehand, or to have been explained in a telephone call by the therapist. It is necessary for all clients to agree to this way of working before it can be used. All teams will have their own tried and true methods of doing this. An example of a way of introducing the setting is given here,[3] with comments about phrasing and choice of language in the second column:

'Before we start talking about what brings you here/about how I may be able to help	Note: not simply 'before we start', since therapy started the moment clients first

---

[3] This is an approximation of a form of introduction used at the Family Institute, Cardiff, at the time of writing. As with the written consent form, the phrasing of this introduction is subject to constant change, as therapists respond to feedback from each other, from clients, trainees, colleagues and research (cf for example Kassis & Matthews, 1987, Killick, 1986, Wood, 1990, Young, 1989/90).

you, I have to tell you about how I like to work.'

started thinking about coming for therapy. The second phrase, including the word 'help', may be useful as it acts as an embedded suggestion that help is likely to come from the meetings; on the other hand, more democratically inclined therapists may shy away from the 'Lady Bountiful' associations of the word.

'As you already know, I work as part of a team; the rest of my team are behind this one-way screen, which looks like a mirror. They are there to help me to think more clearly about the things we discuss here; if they think that there are important issues I am not hearing clearly, or ideas that may be useful for you and me to discuss, they will call me on this intercom telephone.'

It is important to emphasize that the team exists in the first place to assist the *therapist*, since this is the simple truth, although a therapist experienced in this way of working will also convey in her manner that she is convinced of the potential benefit to the client.

'In our experience this is a useful way to work—it's like the saying 'two heads are better than one'. I will go out before the end of our meeting to talk with my colleagues, and hear what their thinking is, and I will then come back and share those ideas with you.'

In many teams it is the usual practice go out for a discussion about 40 minutes after the beginning of the session, which in general lasts between 1 and $1\frac{1}{4}$ hours. In other teams the regular consultation may happen closer to the midpoint of the session. In addition earlier consultations may happen at either the therapist's or the team's instigation.

'In addition I do not like to take notes while I am talking to you, because that interferes with my being able to concentrate on our discussion, so I like to make a videotape of our meetings, which I can look back at after our meeting. I need your permission to keep this videotape, and there is a form here which explains about the confidentiality, and the use I would want to make of the videotape. I will give this to you to read today when I go out to talk with my colleagues, so that you can look at it when you are private, and discuss it with each other. If you are happy to give me permission to keep the videotape I will ask you to sign this form, which I also need to sign.'

The signed form acts as a form of contract between clients and therapist. It usually contains (a) a request for therapist and team to be able to look back at the tape, as well as (b) a request for material from the tape and the sessions to be used by the therapist for teaching, research and publication, with an explanation of the confidentiality assurances that can be given. Clients can agree to (a), or (a) and (b), or neither. In addition it may contain information about the agency's open access policy, which allows clients to examine their files in the agency's records. Clients may have been sent the video consent form before the first appointment, to enable them to think about it, and if necessary, discuss it with others.

Therapists will continually hone this apparently simple statement over years of practice to ensure that it contains the maximum necessary information as briefly as possible, while taking care to phrase and time what is said in such a way as to increase the likelihood of clients at least being willing to give this odd way of working a fair trial. The vast majority of clients readily accept this way of working. There are many possible explanations for this. They may be keen to get on with discussing what brings them to therapy, and not interested in the therapist's agenda of explanation. Coming to therapy may be so stressful and strange anyway that the additional strangeness of the working method makes no difference. They may be cowed by the therapist's power, and that of the setting, and may not feel able to object. The agency's reputation may be such that they are willing to give the therapist and team the benefit of the doubt, or they may already know that the agency works like this. As family therapy has become more common within the mainstream of therapeutic approaches, many agencies have found that clients increasingly refer themselves, having perhaps been told about this way of working by friends, family, other professionals or neighbours. In addition it may be that clients who have decided to attend therapy as a family, whether at their own instigation or at the invitation of the family therapist, already demonstrate a degree of comfort with the idea of 'private' matters being discussed in 'public'. In other words, having shifted from the idea of an individual client to that of a family group, it may seem logical that the therapist should also belong to a group.

Nevertheless, it is important for the therapist to consider what negative reasons there may be for clients to be silent about objections to the screen, so as to present herself in such as way as to facilitate clients' questioning of the working method. Therapists should be aware that they are accustomed to the screen and the team and convinced of their benefits, and therefore may rush through the explanation, impatient to get to the 'real' reason for the meeting. If the therapist picks up a hesitation on the client's part, a non-verbal suggestion of unease, etc., this should be explored before going any further. Sometimes clients simply want some more information before assenting, sometimes they want an agreement to meet the team or see the consultation room. At other times clients' objections may be to being in therapy at all. Clients referred by other professionals sometimes disagree with the referral: discussion of their objections to the working method, if pursued sensitively, will give them the opportunity to discuss also whether they choose to go along with the referral or not. When clients' reasons for rejecting the use of videotape, or team behind the screen are persuasive to the therapist, these may be dispensed with. Sometimes the therapist will then work with a consultant in the room (Smith & Kingston, 1980, Kingston & Smith, 1983) or without any live consultation.

It can also be useful to seek access to the views of clients when they are not in the therapy setting. For example, research done at the Cardiff Family Institute (Killick, 1986) indicated that most clients accept the use of the team and screen. The detailed feedback on their comments served both to support and correct the team's practices. Recent changes in the theory and practice of systemic therapy, however, mean that the ethics and desirability of working with teams and screens has once again become the focus of attention; this will be discussed in more detail in a later section of this chapter.

The therapeutic session

While the therapist is conducting the session, the team have a number of agreed tasks behind the screen. It has been said that working with a team is like splitting the usual lone therapist in two: one half is free to engage intensely in the conversation, relationships, feelings and 'atmosphere' of the therapeutic encounter; the other half is sitting back and thinking in a more free-ranging, less immediately focused way, noting the kinds of hints and communications that must, for the therapist in the room, remain in the corner of her eye.

What the therapist particularly requires of her team is that they continue to examine the team hypotheses in the light of her continuing exploration with the clients, that they note down information about the family structure and history (i.e. a genogram or family tree), including dates, transitions, alliances, and descriptive phrases, that they pay particular attention to the telling use of language or metaphor by family members, and—most crucially—that they observe her relationship with family members.

At the heart of systemic therapy lies the assumption that human beings, in their interaction with one another, extend invitations to join with one another in a 'dance' of mutual adaptation ('structural coupling', according to Maturana & Varela, 1988). The therapist does not stand outside this interaction—she extends and accepts invitations. To the degree that her behaviour becomes organized by the habitual patterns of interaction between family members, and perhaps particularly by their problem-determined patterns, she offers first-hand information to herself, the team and the clients of the effects of their patterned behaviour. However, the team is likely to be in the best position to observe this, because least directly affected. There is a similarity here to the way in which psychoanalytically-oriented therapists might use the concept of countertransference to gain a better understanding of client dilemmas. The therapist needs to think carefully about herself, and what aspects of her own personal and family history may be being triggered by the therapy, before she attributes changes in her own behaviour to the effects of her interaction with the clients. Here, again, the team perspective can be a crucial one. There is an obvious implication for the role of the team in helping therapists distinguish between the above aspects: the team members need to know and trust each other.

Example

Mrs A was a widow with two young children. She had been almost continuously in psychiatric hospitals since her husband's sudden death two years previously; all previous professional help had been offered to her individually, but all had now stopped, since in the view of the professionals involved she should now have dealt with her grief over her husband's death, and was at risk of becoming overdependent on the helping services. She had been referred for family therapy by a social worker, familiar to her over the previous two years, after she had telephoned Samaritans and threatened to kill her children, without, however, being willing to accept social work help.

The session was, for the therapist, a difficult one, as the level of tension in the room was extremely high, with Mrs A speaking in a pent-up and hyperventilating way of her inability to accept her husband's death, her guilt over that as well as over her mistreatment of the children, her rage because they would not 'mind' her as they had minded their father, and the falling away of all her previous support systems. It seemed to her that everyone was now fed-up with her. The children were quiet and very obedient, displaying all the signs of 'frozen watchfulness' that those working with abused children are taught to look out for.

Nevertheless, the therapist had managed throughout the session to maintain an even-handedness towards all the different experiences and points of view represented in the family, including that of the late Mr A, who was a palpable presence. She felt that she had joined supportively with mother and daughters without taking sides, or leaping in either as the children's rescuer or as the champion of parental authority.

Just before leaving the room to join her colleagues for the consultation the therapist asked the children a would-be bland question about how they were getting on in school. It was hoped that this would introduce a more ordinary everyday note on which to leave them for a few minutes, after the fraught atmosphere of the previous 45 minutes. Instead, the question opened the chamber of horrors. Mrs A's previous descriptions of her negative behaviour to the children had mainly related to beating the 11-year-old, as well as Mrs A's fantasies of joining her husband in death, were she not impeded by the children. Now she described, while prompting the 7-year-old to join in telling the story, how she had two nights previously threatened to cut the little girl's fingers off as punishment for spelling mistakes in her homework, 'I'm telling you, if you get one more wrong I'll have a finger off for every one wrong. And there I was, Mrs J., with the freezer knife, and the two of them on their knees begging me Mummy please don't cut our fingers off. I'm telling you I would have done it too.' Throughout this narration the 7-year-old wept and wrung her small fat fingers together, while the 11-year-old stared stonily at the screen.

The therapist left to join her colleagues behind the screen with her composure shattered and her neutrality abandoned. She wanted to cry, she wanted to protect the children and take them away from their mother, and most of all she wanted to blame and punish Mrs A. Colleague A immediately took up the opposite position, taking the view that the children were playing Mrs A up, behaving provocatively, and needed to be brought into line. The therapist's fury at Colleague A thus apparently taking leave of her senses, and A's angry criticism of the therapist's 'better-mother' position was allowed to run on for a few minutes, at which point Colleague C joined the conversation and enabled the whole team to begin to think like professionals again.

Although there was some grounds, in the family's presentation, for the positions that the therapist and Colleague A took up during their angry interchange, these are nevertheless not views they would normally hold, either as professionals or in their private lives, though their personal and professional histories no doubt made these positions more or less available to them. Both were reacting to the stress of the session. Being able to feel very angry with Colleague A enabled the therapist to express some emotion, but not at Mrs A. By stating the position opposite to the obvious one Colleague A enabled the therapist to begin to remember that Mrs A, too, had a point of view and that she needed to be open, as she had been throughout most of the session, to the mother's experience as well as that of the children. The subsequent discussion between the three team members then enabled them to begin to formulate a broader systemic understanding of what was happening in the family, and of how they might be able to help, so that when the therapist went back to join the family she was able to behave in a containing and hope-giving manner, while not minimizing the risk to the children. With the watchful cooperation of social services staff she was able to work with Mrs A and her children not only to prevent the recurrence of any violence, but to help Mrs A to place her mourning for her husband in perspective, to become an adult in her interactions with her children and her extended family—a role she had never previously occupied—and to create a safe and loving atmosphere in which her children could resume their interrupted childhood.

A safe team is a place in which absolute realities can be suspended for a time, so that the unsayable can be said, and team members can risk expressing partial or unreasonable views or feelings in the certain knowledge that these will not be acted on immediately, nor be suspended around the team member's necks like a label of identity forever after. In dealing with the complexities of the grief, distress, and extremes of behaviour and experience that clients bring to us, therapists need such a safe place in order to think creatively and fully about all the potential realities available. A therapist seeing the A family above without a team, would have had to work very carefully and conservatively in order to try to control the effect of their experiences on herself. This would make it much harder to have been as useful to them.

Not all therapy is as fraught as the above example, of course, but the different perspective available to the team is frequently useful to the therapist. A more common example, representative of many team interactions, will illustrate some of the everyday functions of the team.

Example

A male therapist is working with a family consisting of two parents and three young adolescent children. The team notice that as the therapist talks animatedly with Ms B and the children, Mr B becomes more and more silent and looks angry. The team speculate, on the basis of their knowledge of the family's background, that Mr B, like many men in his situation, feels somewhat uncomfortable in the world of relationships, communication and emotion represented by his wife, who has hitherto been seen as the person responsible for the maintenance of these family functions.

Although Mr B has been making efforts to get more involved with the children, it is still a new world for him, and the team thinks that perhaps the therapist's ease and pleasure in talking with the children and with Ms B is contributing to Mr B's sense of alienation in the session. Although the therapist is a man, his choice of profession, and his training make him more comfortable than Mr B in 'women's territory'. A team member calls through to the therapist, points out briefly that Mr B has become very silent, and suggests that while exploring his current line of questioning the therapist should be sure to include Mr B. The team colleague further suggests that the therapist should alter his posture (which is mirroring that of Ms B, so as to mirror that of Mr B. (Adopting identical postures can often act as a signal, not necessarily in conscious awareness, of closeness or similarity.) Following this Mr B becomes more actively involved in the discussion again.

In talking with the team afterwards the therapist said that the call had been very useful to him. He had not noticed Mr B's withdrawal; uppermost in his mind had been the wish to engage the children fully in the discussion, for reasons to do with the problems that had brought the family into therapy. Changing his posture had contributed to a greater awareness of, and empathy towards Mr B on the therapist's part. It is particularly useful to bear in mind that such lapses in awareness do not only occur with inexperienced therapists. As with the previous example, it is possible for a skilled therapist to lose their usual level of even-handedness or alertness; it is then that the team proves its worth.

Team communication during the session

It is important for teams to work out their own rules for how communications will be conveyed. Teams, as well as individual team members, will have different priorities. A number of general rules are usually evolved, as well as specific rules that relate to particular therapists' styles. Some general rules for team action are discussed below.

Timing of calls to the therapist

In general the team is unlikely to call the therapist on the intercom telephone before about 20 minutes of the session have elapsed. This enables the therapist and family to settle into the rhythm of the session, and to determine on the themes they will be exploring. Exceptions to this rule would follow exceptional events. For example, a therapist new to the team may be asked a factual question early in a session, e.g. about the range of services of the agency, to which she does not know the answer. The team might then immediately call to give the therapist this information.

Frequency of calls to the therapist

On the whole the team will not call the therapist more than approximately three times during a session lasting about an hour. Too many calls affects the relationship between the clients, the therapist and the team, often giving the clients the impression that the team does not trust the therapist, or that the real power lies behind the screen. In response the clients may start defending the therapist against the team or, conversely, directing their communications at the screen and disqualifying the therapist's functioning. The therapist also is likely to begin to feel irritated with the team, which will interfere with her concentration on the clients. As systemic practice over recent years has moved away from a more interventive style towards a style in which the focus is on the co-developing narrative constructed together by clients and therapist, far fewer calls are made from behind the screen.

Increasingly the team's function is that of an added layer of observation of client and therapist relationship, rather than an active, interventive role in the moment-to-moment therapy.

Who represents the team?

During the course of any one session only one team member will call the therapist. Any call from behind the screen, no matter how carefully timed, will disrupt the therapist's thought processes, even if only momentarily. To cope, in addition, with a different voice, style of speech, and relationship each time the phone buzzes or there is a knock on the door is likely to act as an unnecessary distraction to the therapist. Moreover, teams which allow all the team members to call the therapist at various times during the session are vulnerable to competitiveness creeping into the decisions about what call gets made, so that the hapless therapist may become the intermediary in a behind-the-screen battle around whose ideas are most brilliant.

Timing and the group mind

Telephone messages must be succinct and clear, and should not be made on the spur of the moment, but rather emerge from a team discussion. It is important to remember that, because of the effect of the different positions of therapist and team, the team will always want to move a little faster than the therapist. This is because the therapist is *directly* engaged in the process of relationship and communication with the clients, and the team is not. It is therefore worth while, for the team members, to wait a little before calling the therapist. Quite likely, in a well-connected team, the 'group mind' will operate and the therapist will say what the team wanted to phone through to her—only a few minutes later.

Clarity of messages

A therapist who is absorbed in the complexity of a family session cannot understand a garbled message, or three hypotheses combined with two instructions for change of direction. Nor is a criticism of what she is doing useful without a suggestion about what to do differently. It is therefore important that team members should check the intelligibility of phone messages with each other before calling the therapist; a consultant working alone could rehearse the message through from an observer stance before calling.

Therapist's acceptance of team messages

The team agrees that the therapist will always use the team's suggestions. Failure to do so disqualifies the team's work, and is likely to cause considerable tension in team relationships. Unless the call contains a verbatim team message, the therapist should integrate the message in response to her own sense of timing and style. As a fail-safe rule it can be agreed that, if the therapist completely disagrees with the message, or cannot make sense of it, she should treat it as if it had been a request to come out for a consultation, which gives her the opportunity to clarify the team's thinking behind the screen. Telephone messages are about brief suggestions, sharing of observations, or clear changes of direction.

Example

A woman (mid-twenties) was being seen on her own, and in this session was discussing the forthcoming visit of her mother, with whom she had had a somewhat distant and tense relationship as far back as her childhood. She very much wanted her mother's visit to be a success, but dreaded that they would not find a way of 'clicking'. She had considered many possible ideas, but continued to feel 'stuck'; that is, stuck in her current view of the problem, which did not admit of any changes, and stuck with a sense that it was her responsibility to make the visit a success. The consultant called the therapist to say that bearing in mind the fact that the client was a dance teacher, the therapist should explore whether that could be used to help her find a way out of her dilemma. This made sense to the therapist, who said to the client: 'If you had to dance your relationship with your mother, how would you do it?' She was amused by this idea, and started to describe her own (metaphoric) dance style, as compared to her mother's wholly different style. As she described them both, dancing away in their own corners of the room, to different music, her amusement and her professional skill started coming together to help her envisage some new possibilities. She started describing ways of combining, contrasting and integrating the different musical and dancing styles. This led, during the session as well as later at home, to her feeling much more flexible and optimistic about the options for relationship with her mother, so that the visit was, indeed, a pleasant one for both. One explanation of what happened is that the move to a metaphorical level which drew on her skills, as well as a different mode of action, enabled her to leave the realm of wrong/right, self/mother, problem/solution, in which she felt immobilized, and to move, wearing her dancing shoes, to a realm in which all rhythms and styles are equally valid and creative.

Unscheduled in-session consultations

If the team wants to suggest exploring a different hypothesis, elaborated without the participation of the therapist, or wants to discuss aspects of therapist/client relationship which puzzle them, or wants to speak to the therapist about anything that requires more than three brief sentences, the team asks the therapist to come out for a brief in-session consultation. The therapist, likewise, may decide to come out at any time for an unscheduled consultation.

Calling conventions

Some teams use the convention of a knock on the door to call the therapist out for a brief consultation, and do not use the intercom telephone. Choice of either method will depend partly on preference and habit, and partly on facilities. The advantages of the telephone are that a call can be timed very exactly so as not to interrupt clients in mid-sentence. There are also teams who use an 'ear-bug' through which a consultant (or, more frequently, a supervisor) communicates with the therapist. This would require an exceptionally sensitive consultant not to interfere with the therapist's thought processes and autonomy; there are also implications for how clients adapt to the repeated experience of observing the therapist listening to 'voices in the head'.

The 'End-of-session' consultation

The therapist normally comes out for a consultation with the team shortly before the end of the session (40–50 minutes after the start of the session). In some teams this consultation may occur earlier. While the therapist is with the team the sound and video systems are switched off, and the clients told that they are in private during that time. This consultation is crucial if the therapist and team are to give the clients a task or a message at the end of the session, but is always important, even if no formal communication is to be used to end the session. It enables the therapist and team members to exchange their views of the content and process of the discussion with clients in order to decide what the therapist will say to clients before ending the session, as well as what the time interval before the next session will be.

The usual rule followed by most teams is that the therapist should have the first say during the consultation. It is necessary for her to say what the 'flavour' of the session has been for her, what thoughts and feelings she has carried with her, what her hunches are. Unless she does this she will not be receptive to the new and different thoughts and suggestions that may come from the team. Having done this, she then listens to the team's discussion of their ideas.

Ways of using the team's discussion will vary from therapist to therapist. One therapist may prefer to listen quietly to the team discussion, take from it what resonates for her, and then return to the clients to share her view of the team's views with them. Another may listen for a while, and then join the team in the elaboration of hypotheses, tasks or rituals. A therapist, on coming out for a consultation, may have a clear idea of what she wants to say to the clients on her return, and may only wish to check this out with the team. Another may feel that she has no specific ideas, and wants the team to make suggestions to her.

Similarly, therapists will differ in how team input can best be of use to her. One therapist will prefer to hear the team's views expressed through a spokesperson, after which she will want some quiet time to put her ideas in order before going back to join the clients. Another will find that the hurly-burly of many team ideas jostling with one another, disagreement, opposing views, even argument, will for her catalyse her own creative thinking and enable her, with the team, to arrive at a new synthesis in her views of the clients' dilemmas, and consequently in her subsequent discussion with them. The question of the delivery of team opinions and messages, or the setting of tasks and rituals, will be discussed in other chapters, as will the question of the careful use of language. However, one of the team's tasks is to help the therapist to be alert to client language use and metaphor, to enhance the likelihood of her making a fitting connection with family members in the way she speaks with them when she returns from the consultation.

CHANGING VIEWS OF TEAMWORK

Selvini and Selvini (1991) point out that little has been written in recent years about teamwork. They postulate that this relates to the presentation of family therapy at international conferences by 'mega-stars', who appear alone on the platform; they also cite Tomm's view (1984b) that teamwork is unnecessary once a therapist has achieved sufficient skill, i.e. there is an assumption here that teamwork is essentially supervision, rather than peer collaboration. Whether or not this is an adequate explanation, it is true that little has been published by systemic therapists in the last few years on this topic (but cf for example the many excellent chapters in Campbell and Draper, 1985). Some of the advantages and disadvantages of teamwork, as it has been traditionally practised, will be discussed before looking at new developments, and considering some future possibilities.

Advantages and Disadvantages

There can be little doubt that working with peer teams, the screen and video has been influential in enabling systemic family therapists to work more effectively, with wider categories of diagnosed problems, in a shorter time span than before. This statement can be made with confidence on the basis of clinical experience and client feedback; nevertheless it is significant that very little research about systemic work has been done (Carr, 1991, Wynne, 1988). What there is, is by and large regarded as unsatisfactory by clinicians and researchers who continue to search for an investigative and evaluative approach that will fit with the clinical and theoretical stance of systemic therapists (Fruggeri & McNamee, 1991, Roper-Hall, 1991, Steier, 1991).

The reasons why a changed method of practice should have such enhanced effects are complex and at best speculative. It might relate to the idea that 'the whole is greater than its parts'. Two therapists working as a team, regularly over time, constitute a different entity from two therapists as individuals. Everyone who has worked in this manner has experienced the phenomenon of the 'group mind', that is the almost mystical experience of thought, feeling and creativity existing not within one or other individual head, but in the space between therapist, team and clients (cf Bateson, 1980). Out of this entity a new narrative, with infinitely new possibilities, can be constructed, in a way that is often more far-ranging, and discontinuous, than the solutions or insights striven for by therapists working in other modalities. This is not to say that this way of working always or automatically produces these effects, but that beginning to work like this has enabled systemic therapists to tap into human capacities for change in a way not available to us before.

The method of working also has benefits for therapists (and therefore for clients) in that burnout may be less of a problem. This is because the therapist does not carry sole responsibility for the clinical work—though she will do so administratively. She does not have to look to clients for direct acknowledgement of her value, but can expect the team to praise her, criticize her and support her. Her creative range is extended, not only because of the input of team ideas, but because interaction with the team stimulates her own thinking. She alternates between being in the therapy room in face-to-face contact with clients, and behind the screen as consultant. All this forms a considerable contrast to the work of, for example, the lone individual therapist, drawing on her own resources in clinical hour after clinical hour, or the hard-pressed hospital or agency worker who is expected to make life and death decisions under pressure of time, overwork and hostile scrutiny from without.

There are many possible reasons why family therapy in general has been found to be economical of time despite the use of multiple therapists. One speculation that is relevant to the use of teams is that there is something about the therapist's membership of a team that makes it possible for her to make *assumptions* about the course of therapy, which then have an influence on the duration of therapy. That is, as a member of an autonomous group with a life of its own which continues before and after the therapy session, it may be easier for her, overtly and by implication, to recognize the equal or greater autonomy of the client family. This will lead her to make longer intervals between sessions where appropriate; to convey, whether by tasks or by her conversation with clients, that she assumes they have the resources to continue the therapeutic work in her absence; and to be on the lookout for indications that they are ready to continue without her.

The presence of male and female team members can be of great benefit in addressing gender issues within therapy. Team messages are often used to address perceived imbalances within the therapist/client group. For example, a female therapist may pass on a message to a male client, saying 'My male colleague says that as a woman I am perhaps not able to appreciate how you view this situation'; or a male therapist may say 'My female colleague thinks that there may be things that are difficult for you to say, since the rest of us in this room are men'. This enables clients to have a broader experience of gendered sensitivity without having to tailor the therapist's gender to the clients' situation—something impossible to predict, and even less possible to carry out when clients are both male and female. The question of whether teams should always consist of both women and men is a difficult one, and team members may not always have complete choice in the matter of new appointments. Experience suggests that a good gender balance in a team might be a crucial factor in its effectiveness, not so much because of the responsiveness to clients suggested above, but because of the implications for the team itself of a predominance of men or women. The gender politics of teams, the capacity of team members to help each other to work in a gender-sensitive manner, and the tendency to fall into gender-specific role patterns will all be affected by the balance of the sexes in the team.

One of the questions frequently asked by newcomers to teamwork is: 'But doesn't it make the therapist more dependent?' The assumption is that independence is of necessity an unqualified good. This proposition seems to me a dubious product of our culture, and could bear questioning. Most centrally, it seems to me strange that we should encourage clients to seek help from interaction with the ideas, experience, questioning and alternative perspectives of others, without regarding these same processes as beneficial to ourselves.

Nevertheless, teamwork is open to question. It may turn out to have been merely a phase in the development in the systemic therapies. As systemic therapists start working more frequently with individual clients (cf Chapter 6) the acceptability of the screen and team becomes more problematic. What has seemed a balanced situation, with a group on either side of the screen, that is family plus therapist, and team plus therapist, begins to feel overwhelming and intrusive when therapist and lone client are observed by a team. This is even more the case when the client is a survivor of childhood abuse, who may be particularly sensitive to issues of loss of control, voyeurism and so on (cf Chapter 7). In these situations increasing numbers of therapists, who are keen advocates of the use of the screen, are beginning to work without live team support (Speed, 1991b).

In the last analysis, teamwork is only defensible if it works. What makes it work? Whether a team works depends crucially on the mutual respect of members, which makes it possible for them to support *and* challenge each others' practice and thinking, so that they will continue to evolve. They need to share a coherent theory within which variations in style can become the source of difference, innovation and mutual learning. They need to work together sufficiently often and regularly to have a shared experience of a body of clinical work, as well as of each other's range and variability of functioning.

Ad hoc teams, eclectic teams, and teams with hidden or overt conflicts not amenable to resolution are more of a burden to the therapist than a help. When irritation, competition, miscommunication and lack of feedback characterize team functioning, this withdraws the therapist's energy from the work with clients, and adds an extra burden to her work. When she is more aware of the team behind the screen than of the clients, when consultation becomes an exercise in 'ego massage' and group dynamics, it is time for the team members to seek consultation (cf Chapter 8) or cut their losses and disband.

DEVELOPMENTS IN TEAMWORK

The most innovative changes in the use of teams have been stimulated by the work of Tom Andersen and his team (1987, 1990). His use of a 'reflecting team', members of which discuss ideas with each other while therapist and clients listen, is coherent with the evolution of ideas about co-construction, 'the second cybernetics' and empowerment, all of which are current in the field at present, as well as with his and his team's particular style of quiet respect for others.

This is not in itself a wholly new idea. In the early days of co-therapy in family therapy, therapist discussions were common in front of clients. For example, in the early seventies, a technique called 'gossiping' was used by some therapists. This consisted of one of the co-therapists, at a certain point in the session, declaring a 'gossip time'. The therapists would then talk with each other for five or ten minutes about their perceptions of the family's statements, dilemmas, and the relationship between family and therapists. Following this the family would be given equal time to 'gossip' about similar topics while the therapists listened.

Similarly techniques for 'live supervision in the room' (Smith & Kingston, 1980; Kingston & Smith, 1983) mean that the consultant or supervisor, sitting in the same room as therapist and family, but somewhat outside the circle, addresses remarks to the therapist which act both as directions to the therapist and as perturbations to the therapist/client system. This technique may be used for preference, or when the screen cannot be used, either because clients have refused permission for it, but are willing to work with a consultant in the room, or because the therapists are working in a setting other than their usual consultation suite. Because, in this situation, the consultant is to a degree less intimately involved with the clients than the therapist is, she can be in a position to say things or suggest topics that are less easily mentionable by therapist or clients, thus helping to place them on the agenda.

Andersen's work with the reflecting team is likely to have major implications for the practice of systemic family therapy. It is important that it should not be thought of as yet another technique, to be used strategically in order to manipulate the clients' responses with a show of openness. Whether teams adopt this way of working or not will depend on many factors; what is important is that systemic therapists should consider the *meaning* of this different way of working, and the implications it carries for relationships of power between therapists and clients.

It is impossible to predict whether systemic therapists will continue to work with consultant teams and one-way screens or not. Nevertheless it is certain that this revolutionary way of working has made a significant and probably enduring difference to the way that systemic therapy views the functioning of therapists and their interaction with clients.

CHAPTER 3   Working with families: 1

Although family therapy is still a relative newcomer in the psychotherapeutic field as compared with, for example, psychoanalysis, it is no longer considered revolutionary to meet with a whole family when one of its members is experiencing emotional or behavioural problems. From the first tentative moves to include mothers in the treatment of children, to the daring step of remembering that children tended to have fathers as well, to including families even when the person designated as the problem-carrier was an adult, family therapy has now become one of the standard approaches in the mental health field.

What do we mean by family? This may seem an obvious question, but it is one that has received different answers over the course of time. Is a family a household, in which case does it include non-related individuals who live in the household and participate in daily interactions, while excluding biologically related individuals who live elsewhere? Or does it mean only those who are biologically related or in some long-term relationship (heterosexual or homosexual) which society would recognize as a partnership? The answer to such questions would partly depend on culture; for example, in the Welsh valleys a maternal grandmother would be seen as more intrinsically a member of the family than she might be in, say, a metropolis. For the purposes of this chapter I shall assume that a family consists of at least two generations. This may include parental figures who are of the same or different genders, step-parents, divorced parents who live apart but participate in the therapy (in shared or separate sessions); it will also include a child generation, whether these children are adult or under age, genetically linked to one or both parents, or adopted or fostered.

As discussed in Chapter 1, the field of family therapy itself has diversified considerably, and continues to develop, so that different models of working have both become more distinct from one another, and have at the same time become more flexible and less exclusive; for example, a Milan-systemic therapist might well be seen also to include thinking that derives from psychodynamic or structural ways of working in her approach.

While much of this thinking has filtered into general awareness, via the media, clients' accounts of therapy, and so on, it is still likely that a family, on first arriving in the therapy room, will characterize their difficulties in a way that the therapist will describe as lineal. That is, the family members are likely to see one person as constituting the problem, and to explain the antecedents of the problem in a way which attributes a cause-and-effect responsibility to some person or event or intrapsychic state. It is the therapist's task to introduce flexibility and curiosity, and above all a possibility for circular attributions, to the client–therapist discourse, without attempting to convert the family to her own points of view. The therapist attempts to talk with the family members in such a way that her questions, the way she directs her attention, her persistence on certain points, her lack of response to others, begins to suggest to them the possibility of a 'multiverse' (Mendez et al., 1988), in which one person need not necessarily be fixed in the role of the mad or bad one, in which different, equally valid, meanings may be attributed to the same behaviour, and in which curiosity about the possible explanations for problems and their solutions can lead to creativity, where previously people may have felt that there were no options other than those already tried. If the therapist's task had to be summarized in one phrase, it would be said to be the search for flexibility and new options; a search, together with clients, for different attributions of meaning which alter the significance of behaviours, for alternatives to habitual and rigidified interactions or rules, for occasions when negative or hopeless or symptomatic descriptions of the situation did not apply, for future options that offer the opportunity for different outcomes and meanings from those hitherto regarded as inevitable. While this description would apply to work with individuals or groups, what characterizes family therapy is that this search occurs in the presence and with the cooperation of the symptomatic individual's 'significant others'. In this chapter and the next, work with several different referral problems and family configurations will be used to illustrate typical aspects of systemic work with families.

In this chapter a first session with a 'reconstituted' family, where the father has been designated as the person who 'has' the problem, will be analysed in some detail in order to tease out aspects of the therapist's way of thinking and working. This analysis will serve to demonstrate how problems which have been 'located' within one person may be contextualized within the wider family and social system, without simply shifting blame and pathology from one person to another, and how the referral problem may be found to be part of a wider interlocking web of family difficulties. It also demonstrates how the family's own way of thinking about difficulties may change so as to enable them to consider and discuss their relationships in a form which begins to offer new perspectives and the possibility of different outcomes. While the emphasis in this, and many of the other case examples, will be on the therapist/client interaction, it must be stressed that the therapist's thinking is in all cases a product of team interaction. The team is therefore implicitly present in all this work, even where team discussion has not been highlighted.

Example

Mr G was referred by a local psychologist, who had seen him at the request of his general practitioner (GP). She described him as severely depressed and suicidal, given to aggressive outbursts, and excessively strict with his step-children. He had previously approached other helping agencies to discuss his fear that his strictness with his oldest step-daughter might have a sexual element to it. He had a history of alcohol abuse, which seemed to have contributed to the breakdown of his first marriage. The idea of family therapy had been raised by the psychologist, and Mr G, after discussion with his family, had indicated that they would all be willing to come to a meeting. The psychologist had also referred him to a psychiatrist for investigation of a possible 'bi-polar' disturbance. The first session was attended by Mr G, Mrs G, and her three children Mary (18) Sharon (14) and Wayne (13).

Before the first meeting with the family the team discussed the information available in order to construct some preliminary working hypotheses. At this stage it is unlikely that a whole systemic hypothesis will be within the grasp of the team; nevertheless, before meeting the family for the first time it is important for the therapist and team to structure their thinking, declare their assumptions, and place the referrer's information in context (cf Chapter 2). Elements that went towards the construction of preliminary hypotheses, and therefore also to the guiding of the therapist's attention in the early stages of the session, were the following:

Mr G occupied a clearly defined position as 'designated patient'. The team wondered whether these descriptions of his behaviour came from him, from the referrer, or from the other professionals (including the GP) whom he had consulted, and what his family's views of these descriptions would be. In the light of his apparent 'patient status' his and his family's readiness to attend a family meeting was interesting.

The team was struck by the violent nature of the suicidal fantasy as reported by the referrer; 'he thought about driving into the docks with the family's eight dogs locked in the car with him'. This seemed like a very unpleasant form of death for him and the dogs; we wondered about the significance of the dogs for him and for the rest of the family, i.e. what was the coded meaning of this image?

The team were aware that they had almost no information about family members apart from Mr G, e.g. they did not, at referral, know the names or sexes of the children. In terms of Mr G's first marriage, the only information was that his children ranged between the ages of 19 and 13, i.e. the same age range as in his current family.

Since the referral information concentrated more or less exclusively on Mr G, it was not possible to know whether other family members also behaved in ways considered problematic by themselves or others; it might therefore be that, on meeting the family, the picture of Mr G as central problem carrier would be confirmed or altered.

In view of the children's ages, and the report of excessive strictness, the difficulties complained of could be related to family problems in facing a life-cycle transition as the children reached adolescence and, perhaps, prepared to leave home. Confirmation of this view would depend on what the family's assumptions were about when and how children attained maturity or left home.

Many remarried (or 'reconstituted') families experience certain typical difficulties in negotiating the losses and transitions implicit in leaving one set of relationships and entering another, in negotiating new rules and assumptions, e.g. about strictness, which may have been dealt with differently in previous families, in working out appropriate closeness between children and step-parents, or in making room for a step-parent in a family which may have been organized around a single parent for a while. Closeness and distance between a step-father and an adolescent step-daughter may present particular difficulties. Whether any of these transition factors would prove to be relevant would depend partly on how long the couple had been together. For example, if this family had only recently come together, Mr G's depression, doubts about his feelings for his step-daughter, and excessive strictness might be seen as his attempts to find his place in the family. If they had been together for some while it might be that these ideas were not relevant, or that they had become relevant again because the oldest daughter was at an age where, in the local culture, she might be expected to be leaving home— emotionally, if not physically.

Mr G's hypothesis about the potential sexual nature of his strictness towards his oldest step-daughter would certainly have to be borne in mind, even though the referrer's phrasing suggested that this was a concern that now lay in the past. Whether it was a live issue or not, what did such ideas tell us about the family? Perhaps this was a double bluff concealing a sexually abusive relationship; perhaps this was a family who thought and talked openly about difficult feelings, and were open to exploring many alternatives. Was this Mr G's fear only, or did other family members think that his relationship with his step-daughter had a sexual flavour?

Why was there so little information about Mrs G? Did this reflect how little information Mr G had given the referrer about his wife? If this was the case, how might it be explained?

The referrer (who worked in a psychiatric hospital) had, shortly before the referral, invited the therapist to speak to her colleagues about doing family therapy with adults who have been given psychiatric diagnoses. It seemed that this referral might be in the nature of a 'test case'. It was important, therefore, to bear in mind the alternative psychiatric referral which had been made at the same time by the referrer—was this a safety net, a responsible professional action, or a challenge? The team would help the therapist not to become too organized in her thinking about the family by the history of the referral— e.g. she might feel that therapy had to succeed to prove that she could work successfully with such cases.

Why was help being sought now? Had something changed recently, or threatened to change, to take Mr G to a number of professionals in quick succession? Was this to do with the family's life-cycle stage, or with other internal or external events?

When the family first seated themselves at the start of the first session, the therapist noted that the three children sat at one end of the semi-circle, although this was preceded by a brief and silent scuffle between Mrs G and Mary as to whether Mary would occupy the seat in between Mr and Mrs G. It was not possible to deduce which of the two was in favour of this position, but Mary ended up sitting next to her mother, who sat next to Mr G. He was at the extreme end of the group, and immediately pushed his chair back, so that he seemed comparatively separate from the group of mother and children, all of whom sat close together. As the introductions were made, the therapist was surprised to be told that the sophisticated-looking young woman, whom she had taken to be the 18-year-old, was in fact Sharon, the 14-year-old, while Mary looked shy and younger than her age. After the introductions, and obtaining permission for the presence of the team and video (cf Chapter 2), the therapist acknowledged that she had received a referral letter from the psychologist, and continued:

Therapist: 'I think it would be useful if we could start from scratch. Could one of you begin to tell me what the issues are that have brought you here today?'
Mr G.: 'Well, it appears that I'm the one at fault.'
Ther.: 'It appears like that to you, or to other people?'

Mr G's response indicates that he sees himself as the cause of whatever difficulties he and his family are experiencing; this, together with the seating arrangement suggests the possibility of a family pattern in which he regards himself, and is seen by others, as an outsider, who may be ill or bad. The therapist's question, on the other hand, begins to suggest that an idea such as 'being at fault' exists in an interactional context, that is, that it can be seen as an *attribution*, which has been made by one or more people. This is a small example, and occurs literally a few seconds after the question of problems has been broached, but it is one of many such attempts the therapist will make, by the careful and sensitive use of language, to begin to offer alternative perceptions and constructions to family members.

Mr G responds to the therapist's question by outlining his contacts with a variety of helping professionals, whom he saw on his own, that is without the participation of family members. In his view all these experiences have confirmed for him the idea that something is wrong with him.

Mr G: 'So . . . I don't mind, if it helps at all. But I seem to make no headway at home. I just seem to make matters worse.'

It is by now clear to the therapist that Mr G not only sees himself as 'the problem', he also sees himself as the main spokesperson for the family. Although the therapist has attempted to invite comment from the others Mr G is the only one who has spoken so far. The therapist is interested in Mr G's apparent centrality in the family, and begins to wonder whether this is related only to his 'problem-identity', or to wider issues. She therefore decides to go along with the family's willingness to let Mr G speak. She is careful to maintain eye contact with all the other family members, partly because this is her only way so far (apart from the introductions) of engaging with them, and partly to be alert for indications that they might be willing to take the conversational ball from Mr G. Therapists working in a different orientation might seize this opportunity to begin to push for change in the family structure, e.g. by insisting that Mrs G should speak, or by commenting on the way that Mr G dominates the conversation; however, the behaviour (including silence) of family members constitutes communication about themselves and their relationships with each other and with the therapist and therapeutic context. Respecting this, while remaining curious about it, is a useful stance for the therapist. She therefore decides to stay with Mr G's offer to discuss his behaviour.

Ther.: 'So what happens?'
Mr G: 'You name it, it happens. I'm too strict, in their eyes, and we're always rowing and fighting and arguing. Usually it's me that's shouting and bawling and whatever.'

Mr G's phrase 'in their eyes' could be used by the therapist as a cue to move to the other family members and solicit their views of the difficulties; however, she decides to stay with Mr G's definition of the situation a while longer, and therefore asks him who he rows with most. This is an example of the sort of question that introduces ideas of difference into the conversation, and elicits a more complex and diversified picture of relationships than the therapist would have had, had she merely accepted a global statement like 'we're always rowing'. He describes a situation in which he rows with all three of his step-children from time to time.

Ther.: 'So it could be you and all of the children, or you and one of the children. [To Mrs G]: At which stage do you get involved then?'
Mr G: 'Can I answer that? When I pick on him [Wayne]'.
Ther. (to Mrs G): 'Do you agree?'
Mrs G: 'He seems to think I do. I don't think so.'
Ther.: 'So he thinks you protect Wayne more than the girls?'
Mrs G: 'He thinks that, yes.'
Ther.: 'What is your view about what the difficulties are that bring you here?'
Mrs G: 'It's just the way he is. He's just so strict.'

It is noticeable to the therapist that Mrs G speaks in a soft, hesitant and almost inaudible monotone. Mr G's insistence on speaking, and Mrs G's hesitancy in speaking begin to look like a 'complementary fit'; however, the therapist cannot at this stage know what such a 'fit' might mean to the family members.

Mrs G, and subsequently Mary, Sharon and Wayne all describe the rows and Mr G's excessive strictness as their major worry. Mary offers an exact dating of the beginning of rows in this family: when she, five years previously, had asked to attend a disco at school.

Mr G: 'My first reaction was 'No way!' I got quite niggly about it.'
Ther.: 'So before that, had things been different amongst all of you?'
Mr G: 'Well ever since I've been here [he reminds the therapist that this is a second marriage for himself and his wife, and that the children are his step-children—Mary was six years old then, she had just gone six. I've had her since she was six years old. I've nursed her, I've mollycoddled her, and what have you, because she's always ill. I think they'd all agree to that.'
Ther.: 'So were you two especially close during that period?'
Mr G: 'We still are.'
Mrs G: 'They still are.' (Everybody laughs.)
Mr G: 'I had her out of bed at 3 o'clock last week, nursing her on my lap till we got her to the hospital.'

Remembering the information given by the referrer about Mr G's concern about the appropriateness or otherwise of his feelings for Mary, the therapist's attention is certainly caught by this description of control and closeness. Even without the referrer's statement the therapist would have been struck by both the language used ('I've had her'), the image of a man nursing an eighteen-year-old young woman on his lap in the middle of the night, and the analogic communication from all family members, in the form of laughter and sideways looks. However, it seems to her too early in the session (6 minutes) for questions designed to elicit more detail about a relationship which might be sexually abusive; in order for such difficult matters to be discussed safely both therapist and clients would have to feel that they had established a trusting relationship with each other and the context of the therapy. Also, while it is important to pay attention to the information and hypotheses passed on by referrers, it is equally important not to become overwhelmed by such information to the detriment of responding to what is happening in the here-and-now interaction between therapist and clients. The referrer's hypotheses represent merely another point of view, which may derive from a brief meeting with only one member of the client system, or which may be the product of long knowledge of the clients and—depending on the nature of the referrer's role—may be part of a relationship that has become 'stuck' and failed to resolve the client's difficulties, therefore necessitating a further referral. Whatever the case, it is not useful for a therapist to 'carry a parcel' into the therapy session; she is more likely to make sense of a situation, in cooperation with the family, if she is attentive to the cues they give as well as to the referrer's views and her own team's hypotheses. She therefore takes a side-route and gathers some information about Mary's illnesses; these have been many, and are described as non-specific aches and pains: 'I'm always ill.'

From here the therapist decides to gather some more general information about the family's history. In any first session enough three-generational information will be sought to enable the therapist, at least tentatively, to place the family within their background and history. Since the family are offering a great deal of information about some of their problematic patterns of relationship, and it is still very early in the session, looking to fill in the background will both enhance the therapist's understanding of the potential meanings of information, and may help to slow down the pace somewhat. When clients come into a first therapy session they are likely to have been thinking about their difficulties for some time, to have rehearsed in their minds what they want to say, what it is important for the therapist to know about, and so on. They may therefore want to get stuck in straightaway. While being respectful of this, the therapist is also entitled to slow the pace down to where she can absorb the information she is being given, and has time to think and to get to know the family. Her task is not merely to be told about difficulties and then to give a solution; it is, rather, to help create an atmosphere of trust in which family members will feel safe enough to explore their situation in a way different from what they have been able to do previously.

Ther.: 'So how long have you two been together?'
Mrs G.: 'We've been married ten years this year. . . together about twelve years. All I can remember, before it started—the rows with these [indicating her children]—we rowed about his children. It's been rows all the time.'

Ther.: 'What . . . you two rowed over his children, or he rowed with his children? . . .' (Therapist has been unable to hear Mrs G clearly.)
Mrs G: 'We rowed. I say his children—he's got four—but it's the eldest girl really. So it's always been arguing over children really. It's never been plain sailing.'
Ther. (to Mr G): 'Is that your view also?'
Mr G: 'Well, yes . . . her and my eldest . . . since the eldest girl was about twelve i think there was a bit of jealousy between her and my eldest girl over me. I'm not being big-headed, but my eldest girl tried to stir a bit with me and her.'
Ther.: 'Is that what also happened when Mary turned thirteen, that she was stirring it between you two?'

Since Mr and Mrs G have again returned to a theme which suggests a blurring of generational and sexual boundaries in relationships between adults and their adolescent children, the therapist now decides that it would be appropriate to do some more exploration about the nature of closeness, in particular that between Mr G and Mary.

Mrs G: 'No.'
Ther.: 'No . . . what do you think?' (to Mr G).
Mr G: 'What it is, I still suffer from it now, is I'm overprotective.'
Ther.: 'So when you [Mary] got to the age when you said I'm beginning to want to do teenage things, and to push the limits a bit, that's when you [Mr G] put your foot down, and that's when things started going wrong here.'
Mr G nods.
Mrs G: 'And from then on he didn't let her do anything. I mean she couldn't even go anywhere—could you? [To Mary, who nods.] When I was young we were given a chance to do something, even if it went wrong, dating and so on.'

An increasing amount of detail is now elicited about the nature of the 'strictness' and the rows, as they apply to Mr G's interaction with Mary, Sharon and Wayne, with particular attention to differences amongst these. Sharon is seen as the one who defies Mr G, so that confrontations between them escalate considerably, and do not really get resolved; Mary, on the other hand, tends to back down and give up.

Mrs G: 'All our rows are about the children. We haven't had an argument about ourselves for years.'

Mr G: 'That's true.'
Ther.: 'It doesn't sound like you have time!'

Mr and Mrs G both laugh and confirm this.

The therapist risks a small quip here, partly because it seems to her that the family, despite the difficult and serious issues they are discussing, show some signs of liking to laugh, and partly because she wants to put out a small feeler about the marital relationship, which seems almost invisible in their presentation of their situation, to test out how possible it may be later on to talk more directly about this. The issue of humour is important, and has been discussed by many family therapists (e.g. Cade, 1982). Suffice it to say that we all know, from our own lives, that while pain may sometimes be unavoidable, it is often easier to be flexible when we are laughing.

Ther.: 'So is it different when you [Sharon] and Uncle Brian [the step-children's name for Mr G] have a row, than when you [Mary] and Uncle Brian do?'
Both Mary and Sharon agree with this.
Ther.: 'How is it different?'
Mary: (she looks at her mother) . . . 'I don't know.'

The systemic assumption that behaviour can 'show' or mean many different things, and that different attributions by different observers may be equally valid, means that the therapist should not be in too much of a hurry to attribute a definite meaning to Mary's look (Scheflen, 1978). Mary's look could mean that there is a family secret that she is not at liberty to mention, or that she is behaving like a little girl and wants to cue her mother to speak for her, or that she could not hear the therapist clearly (one of her many illnesses is chronic earache) and hopes some family member will tell her what the question was. The therapist notices the look but does not speculate too much about its meaning at this point.

Sharon: 'He's always apologetic after, with you.'
Mrs G: 'But Mary's got a conscience as well, she knows he cares, deep down, he's not just spiteful; because I've always thought he's

just spiteful. Why I don't know, it was just my thoughts. But Sharon just sees him as pure spite, don't you? Whereas this one [Mary] she decides, O.K., if it's going to cause a row I won't do it. That's why she's never done anything.'
Ther.: 'But he will apologize more after a row with Mary, but not after a row with Sharon?'
Mr G: 'If I'm in the wrong . . . yes?' (to Sharon, who nods).
Ther. (to Sharon): 'But you think he apologizes more when it comes to Mary?'
Sharon: 'Yes he does.'
Mrs G: 'Yes, she's the apple of his eye.'
Sharon: 'Yes, because he favours her the most, and she favours him the most.'

It is noticeable that at this stage of the session (11 minutes) family members are using far more comparative descriptions than flat statements of predicates (he/she *is* so and so). They are making statements about their own perceptions which, overtly or by implication are being labelled as perceptions, in comparison with other points of view, rather than as indisputable truths. My assumption would be that, since we are all capable of thinking in absolutes or in flexibilities, it is the therapist's offer of a style of conversation that is curious, comparative and exploratory, that acts as an invitation to family members to join her in the general question: 'How can we explain that this is how it seems to x at this moment?'

The theme of who is whose favourite is now explored for a while; there is a clear pattern of Mr G and Mary being closest to each other, and Mrs G and Wayne (Mr G: 'If I say two words to him—boom!—she's like a lioness') while Sharon, by common agreement, is not particularly close to anyone in this nuclear family. However, she has been much closer than the other children to her maternal grandmother, who died recently, to various aunts and uncles, and in particular is the only one of the children to have kept contact with her biological father. She has indeed used the threat of her father's intervention to negotiate more relief from Mr G's 'strictness', e.g. in the form of being allowed to stay over with a friend, than Mary has.

The family's view is that Mr G is less strict in relation to Wayne partly because he knows that Mrs G will intervene to defend him, partly because of his age, which means that he does not yet want to do the things that activate Mr G's 'strictness', and—perhaps most importantly—because he is a boy.

Mr G becomes quite agitated as he elaborates on his suspicions of boys' intentions in relation to girls, his certainty that youngsters will get drunk, and the fact that he has been more worried since they moved to a new neighbourhood three years previously. In the old neighbourhood all the boys knew him and therefore would not 'try anything on'.

Mrs G: 'I understand why he's worrying, but because I don't go along with him he thinks I don't care. If they're going to be wild they will be. If he hadn't been so strict in the beginning he wouldn't be finding it so hard now. They're not allowed to say, 'I'm going into town with my friends'. He wants to know why, who will be there, what will they be doing? It makes them want to cram in everything they've missed out on.'

It emerges that Mary missed out on large parts of the last year or two of her schooling. She left school at 16 and since then has never looked for work—indeed, she has never even signed on as unemployed. She has never been out with friends of her own age. Since the original débâcle caused by her request to go to a school disco, she has only once recently been allowed to attend a school disco with her young brother. She stays at home with the eight dogs, who are seen as being her special responsibility. She says that she does not make any effort to get permission from Mr G to go out, as she can't stand the ensuing arguments.

Because it is clear from the discussion that the word 'strict' has a rather extreme application and consequences in this family, and bearing in mind the referrer's use of the word 'aggressive', the therapist now explores the meaning of the 'rows' further.

Ther.: 'When you start rowing, how far does it go? What is the worst that it gets?'

This question, like the opening question about what brought them to therapy, is asked of the group in general, while looking fleetingly at all of them. This means that the therapist may gain more understanding of the family by noticing who responds; in addition, since it is likely from the preceding discussion that Mr G will be described as the one who behaves aggressively, the therapist wants to offer him the opportunity to volunteer this information, without, so to speak, placing him in the dock by asking him directly. He does indeed take the opportunity to answer the question. This means that violence can now be discussed in a context where he gains dignity from expressing his own concern about it, and where the family are not placed in a situation of being divided into accusers and accused.

Mr G: 'The worst was recently. I actually hit her [Sharon]—I slapped her across the head and perforated her eardrum. Then me and her [Mrs G] were fighting—I'm told this is what happened, because I was drinking. Sharon tried to butt in and I elbowed her away, and hurt her ribs.'

The whole family are distressed as they contribute further to telling the details of what happened.

Mr G: 'I did not remember what happened. The next day I was scared of what I might have done to them—to anyone who'd got in my way. I've never done that sort of thing before. I've shouted and bawled and I've thrown things at the wall and so on.'
Mrs G: 'Mind you his shouting goes on for five or six hours.'

Therapist and family discuss their view that Mr G's use of 'words and noise' is experienced by the others as violent and intimidating, but that this is the first time he has been physically violent, an event which frightened them all considerably. Mr G is determined that it should be the last time, and Mrs G says that if it happens again she will leave him, in which she is supported by the children. However, they do not see the violent incident as directly connected with Mr G's search for help, which predated the incident.

Mr G: 'This all started a year ago, and I went to see my doctor because I just got really depressed about things, you know? I would

just come home, and I'd just sit there crying for no reason. I didn't
know what the reason was then.'
Ther.: 'Have you sorted it out since then, got clearer about the reason?'

It is important at all times to pay attention to the hypotheses
of family members about their own dilemmas. Just because
they have not been able to find solutions without seeking
professional help does not mean that they do not have a fuller
and wider-ranging understanding of their own situation than
a therapist can hope to build up in the short time she spends
with a family. Thus eliciting the family's explanations is for
the therapist *both* a way of finding out which hypotheses and
attempted solutions have not been helpful (yet) *and* a valuable
addition to her understanding of the situation. In addition
asking questions like 'How do you understand that?' or 'What
is your explanation for that?' are part of the process of inviting
the family's own curiosity about actions or meanings they
may have been taking for granted.

Mr G: 'I think . . . I've had so many things told to me by the other
people I've gone to see, and my doctor. And one of them said it's
because I'm losing control, or I feel I'm losing control. That could be
a reason why.'
Ther.: 'Losing control of yourself, or losing control of your daughters,
or . . .'
Mr G: 'I've noticed a few times—there would be an amazing row, and
then she [Mary] would faint on the floor, and the whole lot would just
stop. I'd see to her and get back in control.'

Not only is this idea fascinating in its own right (and coherent
with theories propounded by family therapists about the
intricacies of the power of apparent helplessness), but it
suggests to the therapist that Mr G himself is beginning to
think in a more 'circular' way about the interconnections
between various behaviours in the family.

Ther.: 'So when you start losing control over yourself she can get you
back into control by fainting . . .'
Mr G: 'Quite easily, yes. What I try to do is browbeat them, I think.
Thinking about it afterwards when I've calmed down—I try to browbeat
them into submission. Once they admit that I'm The Big I Am, I think
. . . I think that's why I do it.'

Ther.: 'Do you have an explanation why this is so important for you?'
Mr G: 'Well . . . I had a weird childhood—though I don't think it was
any worse than any one else's.'

It might have been appropriate and productive, in the section
above, to ask other family members for their views about
why, for example, this was so important for Mr G. However,
the therapist decides to stay with the sequence of direct
questions and answers between herself and Mr G. There are
a variety of reasons for this: all the family members are
showing distress at this point, but particularly Mr G. What
he is saying is in the nature of a 'confession', and the therapist
has a strong sense, based on non-verbal cues, that none of
the others has heard him speak so frankly before, so that
there is a possibility that they might change some of their
views of him, in hearing him talk with such openness about
his own behaviour. In addition there will be less risk of a
blaming and pathologizing discussion if the therapist later
hears the views of the others, having given Mr G the
opportunity to put it on the agenda himself first.

Both Mr and Mrs G now fill in some details of Mr G's
childhood, and describe a situation in which he, as the oldest
of six children being brought up in violent and deprived
circumstances, was particularly frequently beaten up by his
mother. This still continues, and Mrs G describes a recent
incident after he and his mother had both been drinking,
where his mother punched and slapped him around the face
and head while he stood there and cried. The therapist frames
this as indicating that Mr G has enough control, even when
drunk, to refrain from returning his mother's blows.

In response to further questions abut the meaning and
importance of control in this family, Mrs G suggests that Mr
G's 'strictness' may be linked to her own 'softness'. She tries
to shield the children and keep the peace, which in her view,
makes him consider her a careless mother, so that he then
intensifies his attempts at control. This again is an example
of a family member considering events, previously labelled
as belonging to one person's individual problem, as being
explicable within an interactional context.

While exploring Mrs G's 'softness' and attempts to shield the children from Mr G's excesses, the conversation returns to the family's hypothesis about Mr G's sexual feelings for Mary.

Mr G: 'At one time it was a case of—she thought at one time, until I went to see this marriage guidance counsellor, that what I was feeling for Mary was not a father-feeling. You know, that I fancied her and all this.'
Ther.: (To Mrs G) 'That was what you thought?'
Mrs G: 'I wasn't really sure, but . . . I didn't really believe it, but I wondered why he didn't want to let her go . . . I asked him and he wasn't sure—he couldn't say yes and he couldn't say no.'

This idea is now discussed with all family members, and particularly with Mr and Mrs G and Mary. The consensus is that the family does not accept a sexual explanation for Mr G's behaviour; the openness with which they discuss this goes some way towards convincing the therapist that she may not be dealing with a case of sexual abuse, although the relationship between Mary and Mr G is clearly highly charged, and implicated both in Mary's apathy and failure to seek more independence, and in Mr G's desperation at the thought of losing control of and closeness to the children. He puts forward the hypothesis, garnered partly from his previous therapeutic work, that the significant factors in the situation are his own tendency towards overprotectiveness, and Mary's position as the oldest in the family, combined with her frequent illnesses. Mrs G adds her observation that Mr G became stricter with her daughters when his oldest daughter became pregnant at the age of 15.

Mr G: 'You see what I do, I'm so overstrict, especially with her [Mary], that I try and overcompensate by catering for all her whims, like "go and buy me four gerbils", or "get me eight dogs one by one", or whatever.'

Something about Mr G's poetic image of the four gerbils and the eight dogs, and the rhythmic language he uses (reminiscent of the song 'The Twelve Days of Christmas') triggers a picture in the therapist's mind.

Ther.: 'It sounds, Mary, like in some ways you're kind of like the princess in the tower: you're locked in, you can't go out, but if you want strawberries at two in the morning he'll get them for you.' Mary confirms this with a rather smug smile at the rest of the family.

Ther. (to Sharon): 'Do you think she more likes it or more doesn't like it?'
Sharon: 'She likes it.'
Mary: 'I don't!'
Mrs G: 'You do when it suits you.'
Mary: 'Well, I like being spoiled . . .'
Ther.: 'Might she stay home for ever?'

The therapist's last question is intended as a challenge and deliberate attempt to perturb the system. This is followed by a variety of hypothetical future questions exploring how things might conceivably become different in the future, as well as what the consequences might be if certain problem-related patterns were to remain unchanged (Penn, 1985). Future hypothetical questions are enormously valuable for a variety of reasons. A client may feel unable to move towards actual change, but exploring a 'merely' hypothetical change has the effect of making that change possible in the mental sphere, and therefore much less impossible in the sphere of action. Once we have imagined something we have, in a way, already done it. However, this imaginary action feels safer, and allows us to play with possibilities, and examine the feared consequences of change, without having to make a dangerous commitment prematurely. Contemplating an unchanged future may also have the effect of changing the way in which the present is accepted.

Ther.: 'Do you think Mary is going to try and get out of the enchanted tower one day, or do you think she's going to stay?'
Mrs G: 'I don't know. I think she'd like to, but she hasn't got any friends even. With not going to school, and never having worked, she's only ever had one friend in all her life anyway. Unless she goes out of the house with Sharon she doesn't go anywhere anyway. If she was given the freedom I can't see . . . she doesn't want to work either.'
Ther. (to Mary): 'How do you see the next ten years?'
Mary: 'I don't.'
Ther.: 'Do you think anything's going to change or do you think it's going to stay the same?'

Mary: 'It will stay the same.'

There is a marked change of tone and affect in Mary's responses. She looks and sounds extremely gloomy and even despairing. It is as if the future-oriented discussion has allowed her to show an aspect of herself which is very different from the sweet child or the triumphant favourite. For the therapist the sense is, for the first time, of speaking with an adult Mary who sees her situation with a bleak clarity.

Imaginary futures are now explored in relation to all three children. All family members can clearly envisage both Sharon and Wayne as finding work, independent lives and partners in ways coherent with their culture, but all agree that Mary is likely to stay home, although there are shades of difference as to whether she would stay happily or unhappily. The therapist also asks questions of various family members about the potential effect of Mary's presence, after the departure of the younger children, on the relationship between Mr and Mrs G. Sharon thinks that her mother will (and maybe does now) feel a little jealous and resentful of Mary.

Mrs G: 'It's not so much jealous. . . . A bit jealous that she doesn't make the best of her time, go out and have a life. I think—if I could have *my* life again, you know. It's not that I'm jealous of *her*.'
Mr G: 'Yes you are because I fuss around her more.'
Sharon: 'That's what I mean.'
Mr G: 'Ever since she was six years old she always sat next to me on the settee or wherever we sit.'
Ther.: 'So she comes first.'
Mr G: 'It appears that way, yes.'
Ther.: 'So if she stayed with you for ever and ever, would she always keep the place next to you on the settee—would you [Mrs G] have to sit somewhere else?'
Mrs G: 'I've never sat by him on the settee anyway.'

The therapist's intention, with this line of questioning, is to explore and, to some extent, challenge the marital patterns. Is this a marriage which was—on Mrs G's part—entered into for financial security when she found herself alone with three young children and little earning capacity; and might Mr G's reasons for the marriage have had more to do with replacing his own lost children, and with his love for Mary, than with a wish for a close relationship with Mrs G? If this is the case, it would be crucially important for both marital partners that Mary should remain home and in between them ('on the settee'). If her pleasure in being 'spoiled', and her ignorance and fear of the world outside the home do not combine to keep her housebound forever, it is likely that Mary and Mr and Mrs G will have to make significant changes to accommodate her departure. Or will one of the other children, for example Wayne, 'volunteer' to take her place?

After consultation the team decided that a formal end-of-session message would be redundant. A large amount of ground had been covered, and it was likely that 'curious', wide-ranging and sometimes challenging conversation would have the effect of introducing sufficient alternative views and diversity into the family organization ('perturbation') at this early stage of the therapy. The session therefore finished with a general comment on the open way in which the family had discussed their lives and views of problems, an appointment for the whole family for another meeting, and an agreement, at Mr G's request, that the therapist would support him in asking the referring psychologist to postpone the appointment with the psychiatrist to allow time to see whether the 'talking treatment' might be sufficient. (The appointment with the psychiatrist was eventually cancelled completely, as neither Mr G nor the psychologist considered him to be depressed or otherwise in need of psychiatric attention by the end of the therapy.)

Twelve sessions in all followed. After the second family meeting Mary asked her parents' help in acquiring the social skills she lacked in order to venture into the world, following which she found work and friends of both sexes. Wayne and Sharon also took the opportunity to negotiate more age-appropriate social rules for themselves, and Sharon left the family to live with friends after she completed her schooling. Mr G changed his overcontrolling and aggressive behaviour, partly as a result of his own efforts, and partly because Mrs G became much more active, both in discussing his anxieties with him and in blocking his attempts to constrain the children. The therapy then moved on to focus on Mr G's concerns about his abusive childhood and the way this continued to affect him; this was done in individual sessions with Mr G as well as in couple and extended family meetings, which included many of Mr and Mrs G's siblings. Only at the end of this period did the couple decide to tackle the question of whether they had a marriage outside of their joint concerns with the children's upbringing.

While the intention here is not to give a detailed outcome report, but merely to give some sense of an ending, it is important to state that, for both therapist and clients it may be impossible, in looking back at the work done, to give a single explanation for any one of the symptoms complained of initially. Rather there is a sense of the way in which the history of both spouses, in their families of origin and their first marriages, fitted with each other to give both shelter and the context in which problems would be maintained; this combined with the idiosyncratic histories of the children and with random events, with the influence of cultural patterns and with deeply held fears and myths to produce the family configuration seen in the first session.

CHAPTER 4   Working with families: 2

In this chapter aspects of family therapy will be considered, in contrast with the previous chapter, by looking at extracts from work with families where children, of various ages and life stages, are presented as the focus of difficulties by families seeking therapy.

Sometimes families present themselves as unable to resolve their problems, and needing professional help in order to deal with issues they regard as problematic. However, on exploring their view of the situation, the therapist might conclude that their perceptions and attempted solutions seem highly relevant and likely to lead to the resolution of problems, although the family perhaps lack the confidence to carry these to their logical conclusion, or have not yet persisted sufficiently with new patterns of behaviour. Such a lack of confidence could be attributed to the response of others to previous problem-solving attempts, or to factors unique to the particular family. Thus the therapist may characterize her role as that of validating the family members' understanding of their situation, and amplifying or expanding the new patterns they have begun to explore. Her position as expert acts as support to family members whose own resources, creativity and thoughtfulness can provide an adequate response to their dilemma. Other families seem to be more tangled up in long-standing patterns of action and meaning, to the extent that symptomatic behaviour on the part of one member may be understood in terms of many and ambiguous myths, legacies and attributions over several generations. This type of dilemma may occur particularly in those families where a member presents with serious and sometimes life-threatening behaviour, which acquires a label of psychosis. In working with such families the therapist's thinking and actions will need to fit with the complexity of the family patterns: this may be where the assignment of ritual tasks becomes particularly appropriate.

VALIDATION AND AMPLIFICATION

Example

John and Mair Jones approached therapy because of worries about their son Meurig (aged four-and-a half). John and Mair were both teachers; Mair returned to work, through financial necessity, when Meurig was 7 months old. She gave up full-time work about a year before coming to therapy because she felt depressed and overwhelmed. According to the parents Meurig had always been difficult and wilful, but his behaviour had deteriorated drastically since he started school. He threw major tantrums when Mair fetched him from the school bus, which caused her embarrassment as well as hurt. She was inclined to blame herself for her son's bad behaviour, saying that she had been possessive and over-close to him since birth, and that this accounted for his assumption that he could always get what he wanted. She felt very rejected by him, said that she spent most of her time screaming at him, and had been reduced to a sense of helplessness. She sometimes used John's return from work as a threat to establish some control over Meurig.

Recently, at Mair's request, John had become more involved in disciplining Meurig; he had also smacked him, at the suggestion of their doctor, although neither parent felt happy about this. Both John and Mair had had a very strict upbringing, with their fathers as the disciplinarians. They said they wanted to be more lenient with Meurig, so that he should not fear them, as both of them had feared their fathers.

John had always been on the periphery of the mother–son relationship and described them as having a sort of cocoon around them. He had not tried to enter this cocoon as he said he considered it normal for a mother and child to be this close. In any case he was away a lot during the early years of Meurig's life, because of his work and his semi-professional involvement in sport.

This is a classic pattern which many couples experience, particularly after the birth of the first child. The close bond between the marital couple is altered and interrupted by the arrival of the child—and indeed even earlier during pregnancy. What has been called the 'primary maternal preoccupation' focuses the mother's attention on her changing body, and later on the relationship with a small and dependent new being, who requires intense nurturing in order to survive and grow. The father's response to this may be to back off, both in order to allow the mother–child closeness to flourish, and also because he may feel rejected, unwanted and jealous. The less he has to do with the infant, the more incompetent he will feel if called on to care for it. As John said: 'This was the first baby I'd ever been near.' In addition financial stress may make it necessary for a father to work harder and longer, if the child's arrival means that the mother's income is lost or diminished. The less the father is involved, the more the mother will feel obliged to stay closely involved; the child will feel more attached to the mother than to the father, and may express this in ways that make the father back off more. There is therefore a circular, mutually reinforcing pattern, which, depending on other influencing factors, may then evolve into problems which begin to defeat the family's coping skills.

The evolving patterns between the couple and their child are also influenced and organized by the dominant gender discourse of their culture (Hare-Mustin, 1991b), that is, by the assumptions and role attributions about gender which underlie apparently individual choices. These assumptions and attributions may be out of awareness, so that decisions which are organized by them may be seen as spontaneous or natural. It can therefore be helpful for the therapist to ask questions which allow these assumptions to be laid bare, so that clients can examine them with increased awareness and choice. Examples of such questions would be: 'How was it decided that Mair would stay at home full-time with Meurig after his birth?' 'If anyone had questioned this decision, who is it likely to have been?' 'Did you discuss any other possible arrangements?' 'Once Meurig arrived, did you rearrange the distribution of other household tasks?' 'How had you worked out who does what before Meurig arrived?' 'How was it decided that Mair would be the main parent?' 'How did you negotiate about John's absences from home?' 'Where does the idea about the primacy of the mother–son "cocoon" come from?' 'Who in your family would most support/dispute this idea?' 'If you could do it over, with hindsight, what would you do differently?'

John and Mair had, from the inception of their marriage, shared ideals about equality, and the equal distribution of tasks and privileges within marriage. It was valuable for them to realize, as they discussed these issues with the therapist, that their ideals had given way, after Meurig's birth, to a series of more rigid assumptions about role division, which neither of them liked. It is likely that a combination of the stresses of the period, the influence of patterns from their own families of origin, as well as the powerful pressure of cultural convention had allowed them to fall into a way of life that they had neither freely chosen, nor really noticed as they were settling into it.

Meurig's birth and infancy coincided with a number of events in Mair's family. Her mother, who was said to have been depressed and dependent on Mair since her husband's death some years previously, was diagnosed as suffering from a deteriorating and genetically transmitted disease. This placed an added burden of care on Mair, in addition to the worry caused by fears for herself and her child in relation to her mother's illness. She received a promotion at work, which, since she described herself as a perfectionist, led to severe overwork. Although Meurig was looked after by John's mother during working hours, Mair continued to breastfeed him for some time after returning to work, which made her already busy days even more complicated. She said that this decision related to her fear that Meurig might prefer John's mother to her. As said above, this was also the time when John was away a lot, often for a week at a time. To Mair all this felt 'like a snowball rolling down on me'; her eventual decision to leave work was therefore taken because of her stress and 'depression', rather than being experienced as a free choice.

While these idiosyncratic stresses pertain specifically to Mair's life history, it is not unusual for the arrival of children to coincide with other events in the wider family's life-cycle. The time when one generation is having children may well be the time when the older generation begins to suffer illness and loss. Just as the child's arrival will have meaning for everyone in the extended family, and will change their relationships to themselves and each other (e.g. the new parents' parents become grandparents), similarly changes and stresses throughout the families of the child's parents will affect how the child's world deals with him. One could therefore speculate that when Meurig arrived, Mair was having to be very supportive to her mother, at the same time as she was preoccupied with being a better parent than her mother had been, and while worrying whether her mother's genetic flaw had damaged her new baby. John's absence and withdrawal left her without significant support, whereas his mother's support was experienced by Mair as a threat. It is not surprising that she clung to Meurig in a protective way then, while also feeling guilty, and blaming herself for being over-possessive, tired, irritable and depressed.

While John said that he was not as worried about Meurig's behaviour as Mair was, he nevertheless indicated, verbally and non-verbally, that he was less than happy with the distance in his relationship to his wife and his son, but felt helpless to change it. In the session it was noticeable that, while Meurig related easily to the therapist, and participated usefully in the discussion from time to time, he also at times demanded considerable attention from his mother, and tended to shun his father's attempts to play with him.

Like Mair, John had seen his own father as overstrict and hard to like; he was therefore reluctant to step into the same role. His mother was described by them as dominant, loud, warm and easygoing, and John had, as an only child and only grandchild, been close to his mother, and held the view that an exclusive relationship between mother and son was normal and not to be interfered with. This left him with no comfortable role in the family.

As Meurig's behaviour got worse John had been under pressure from various advice-givers to adopt a disciplinarian role, which he had done with reluctance. This in turn increased Meurig's angry and close attachment to his mother, and Mair's appeals to John to become more involved with their son, as she felt unable to deal effectively with his angry attacks and disobedience. At times John would respond to these calls and act the 'ogre' in relation to Meurig; at other times he would dismiss the seriousness of the problem. He saw such dismissiveness as an effort to calm things down and avoid the ogre role, but Mair saw it as a lack of support and a confirmation of her own unreasonableness.

At the same time Mair and John dreaded creating a relationship similar to the ones they had had with their fathers. John had found shelter from his father's rages in his close relationship with his mother, while Mair had developed a habit of conscientiousness and perfectionism in order to try to avoid punishment. Mair linked Meurig's bedwetting with her own childhood enuresis, saying that it seemed to her, looking back, that wetting the bed at night, after a day spent in fear of her father, felt like the only way she could express control over her own life. She worried that it might have the same meaning for Meurig.

Although Meurig coped very well in school, and was seen as more advanced than his classmates, he complained that school was 'too long'; Mair saw this as a comment on his absence from her, and therefore as another indictment of her possessiveness. They had discussed with teachers the possibility that Meurig might be understimulated at school, and had also considered moving from their isolated cottage to a house in a street so that he would have easier access to playmates. They were, however, reluctant to do this, not only because they loved living in the open country, but because it would mean that 'he's winning yet again'.

Legacies from the past, patterns and beliefs about family structure and relationships learned in the parents' families of origin, as well as idiosyncratic circumstances, combine to form a context in which a problem may become embedded, and may begin to feel intractable. In such a context it can become hard to distinguish the ordinary complications of life from more significant problem indicators. For example, Meurig's complaint about school being too long is not unusual in a lively four-year-old; indeed John said that he, as a teacher, found school too long too! However, given Meurig's other difficulties, Mair feared that he might not be able to cope with schooling because she had kept him in too close a relationship with her. Both parents felt, as did their extended families, that things might have been very different if they had had more than one child. However, the diagnosis of Mair's mother's illness, combined with Mair's subsequent feelings of depression and inability to cope, had made them decide against having another child, at least for the time being.

In addition to the focus on Meurig's behaviour, and the question of how to cope with this, it seemed that another request underlay the decision to come to therapy. Both Mair and John gave the impression of yearning for more closeness to each other. The exigencies of child-rearing can allow spouses to drift apart; a request for help to get a child out of the centre-stage position may also therefore be a request for the parents to find time and emotional energy to be with each other again in a new closeness.

Before coming to therapy Mair and John had done a great deal of thinking about the possible causes of Meurig's difficult behaviour and their problems in coping with him. They had read books and talked to their families and friends. They saw their own childhood influences as being significant, and clearly described their current 'stuck' pattern. They had tried many solutions, from their own repertoire as well as those suggested by others; for the most part none of these had made a significant difference.

The one success they had had occurred in the week before the first therapy appointment (after the referral had been made). On collecting Meurig from the school bus Mair had been very distressed because he had beat her with his fists. She had followed her usual style of reasoning with him; however, because she was very angry (and it may be assumed that her anger gathered weight from her childhood history of being beaten) she said to him very firmly: 'Daddy doesn't hit me. You don't hit me. Nobody hits me.'

On John's return from work Mair related this instance to him, in Meurig's presence. John was outraged, and spontaneously jumped back—away from Meurig—reiterated that his behaviour had been unacceptable, and sent him to his bedroom. Since then Meurig had not played up at all, and he had also pointed out to both parents that he was not doing so. John and Mair felt that something about the handling of this incident, in which they had not resorted to verbal or physical violence, but had nevertheless made an impact on Meurig, was significant.

It is important for the therapist to get a clear picture of a family's beliefs and hypotheses about their problems, and to know what they have tried as solutions, including what has or hasn't worked, and what the explanations might be for such successes or failures. Families have far more knowledge and understanding about themselves than a therapist can hope to achieve in a few hours of contact. In addition, if the richness of their creative repertoire is respected by the therapist, the solutions they come up with are more likely to fit well with the whole pattern of their lives than any prescriptions offered by a therapist. It is not unusual for families to begin to find new solutions after referral, and before seeing a therapist. It may be that the decision to go for therapy acts as a sign of commitment to change, and thus enables new ways of behaving, and of looking at difficulties, to emerge. The therapist's task then is to search for, and to amplify, such new patterns.

At the end of this first meeting, after consultation with the team, the therapist offered a brief summary of the topics that had been discussed, using this opportunity to offer a normalization of some aspects which worried them, as well as slightly different perspectives on their situation. She described the mother–son closeness, and John's relative distance as a fairly usual pattern in the culture they lived in, while agreeing that its perpetuation was not desirable to them. Similarly, she commented on the fact that aspects of Meurig's wilfulness could be seen as age-related, while agreeing that the time had come to sort things out. As Mair said: 'If he's like this at four, what will he be like at fourteen?' The therapist discussed the new pattern they had found in the previous week, when Mair had invoked John as a good example to Meurig, and the parents had stood together, so that both of them were able to express themselves forcefully and clearly, without either being seen as 'the ogre'. The therapist suggested that they could experiment, in the period between therapy sessions, with demonstrating their collaboration to Meurig in whatever ways seemed relevant; their feedback from this would then be discussed in the following meeting.

This is a simple and minimalist message from the therapist. The therapeutic skill consists in facilitating, in an hour, the sort of discussion which enabled the couple to express all the components of their situation that seemed most relevant to them, as well as having a new experience of the coherence and 'fit' of these components as they explored them with an outsider. Since the parents had achieved a success, shortly before therapy, which was coherent with their child-rearing values, it was important to amplify this, while remaining in an experimental framework, so that any failures of this new approach could be treated as providing information, rather than proving the parents or the solution to be worthless.

The family returned to the second session a fortnight later feeling very happy with developments. Both parents had acted in a consistent and united way throughout, and there had been no incidents of the sort they had complained about previously. Meurig had been slightly more attention-seeking at school. The parents had discussed this with the teacher, explaining that they were adopting a new style with him, and speculating that he might therefore be 'trying it on' at school. They and the teacher mutually agreed tactics to deal with this.

It was clear from the behaviour of all three in the room that changes had occurred. John took a much more active part in relation to Meurig, and Mair was less indulgent; Meurig responded with warmth and ease to both of them. Mair, in particular, seemed much more animated and less self-blaming. John and Mair had continued talking with each other after the previous session about the patterns they had begun to observe in relation to their families of origin, as regards closeness, discipline, and so on. They had made new connections with their own lives, and expressed the feeling of having more clarity and choice about what to carry through from their heritage, and where they were free to choose their own values and styles. John also 'confessed' to more jealousy of Meurig and desire for closeness with Mair than he had previously admitted to. It was obvious from the way they discussed this, and the warmth, amusement, and erotic spark between them, that this topic had already received a good and satisfactory marital airing!

At the therapist's suggestion it was agreed to have no further meetings. It is my view that it is usually preferable to stop slightly before the end, rather than to try to tie up every loose thread for clients. This ensures that they close the circle, so to speak, for themselves, and therefore feel a clearer sense of ownership of the solutions and new behaviours and meanings arrived at. Clients are told that they can consult again, whenever this, in their view, is necessary; having had a good experience which did not pathologize them, or drag on forever, makes it more likely that they will seek appropriate help, if necessary, in the future.

LEGACY AND RITUAL

The Clarke family came to family therapy as part of their search, over the previous two years, to find some treatment that would help Lance who had been diagnosed as schizophrenic. The family consisted of Paul (54), Roberta (47), Arthur (23), Lance (21) and Pauline (17). Lance had experienced his first 'psychotic episode' at the age of eighteen. Since then he had been admitted to psychiatric hospital on section numerous times, was on heavy medication, and had also had spells in 'alternative' treatment centres adopting approaches based on the ideas of R.D. Laing, or on spiritual values. None of the various approaches had made any significant difference either to his well-being or to his suffering. The parents were continuing to explore alternatives, while keeping all the options open. The first two therapy sessions were therefore framed by the therapist as consultations in order to explore whether family therapy might be useful. A detailed exposition of a long and complex piece of work will not be attempted here; rather, the Clarke's family story, and aspects of the work with them, will be used to examine the kinds of pattern and meaning that may be involved in serious difficulties (like the behaviours which we label as schizophrenia) and to illustrate systemic thinking about work with such families (Selvini et al., 1978, Boscolo et al., 1987, Jones, 1987).

Both Paul and Roberta came from families where they had experienced abrupt and influential losses of family members, and where a meaningful distinction was observed between artistic endeavour on the one hand and discipline and conformity on the other. The unexpected death of Paul's artist father in his early thirties had plunged the family from wealth into poverty. During World War Two Paul and his siblings were evacuated to different places—his older brother and sister to relatives, where they remained after the war, and Paul, aged 7, to strangers. He repeatedly tried to run home to his mother, and was repeatedly returned to his temporary home. After the war he found himself the only child at home, and soon, thanks to money made available by a family benefactor, was sent off to boarding school. After his schooling he went straight into the army at the age of eighteen, first to do his national service, and then as a career. In his mid-forties he left the army to set up a craft workshop with his wife. They continued to work together at that.

Roberta was the daughter of a wealthy businessman, described as strict and cold, who 'threw his wife out of the house' when Roberta was eleven. After this neither she nor her siblings saw their mother again. Roberta left home at seventeen, and saw herself as having to be tough and independent. She had, in recent years, developed an increasing interest in spirituality, which Paul did not share.

Arthur, the oldest son, had always been characterized by the family as disciplined, hard-headed, and ambitious. He lived away from home, and was making a success of a commercial career in the Arts. Pauline, like Arthur, was seen as similar to Paul, in being active, outspoken and independent. Both she and Arthur had, in conformity with the family's circumstances and values, attended boarding school from an early age.

Lance had always been the exception in the family. Seen initially as the brightest of the children—in that his early development was quick, and that he had presented himself as a bright, lively and imaginative child—he started to change at around the age of four, becoming, in his parents' eyes, dreamy, incompetent, unhappy and dependent. When he was two years old a baby sister was born but died after a week in intensive care. Lance had missed his mother's active presence during this time, and clung to her. Roberta remained very ill, as well as sad, for some time after the baby girl's death. She continued to express guilt about not having been fully available for Lance during this period, while suggesting that Paul had been less than emotionally available to her. Two years later, when Pauline was born, and needed special care initially due to her extreme frailty, Lance expressed concern as to whether she would die as well, and attempted to engage a great deal of his mother's attention. The parents pushed him towards his older brother Arthur at this point, and encouraged him to grow up more quickly. Paul remembers a conversation at this stage, when walking the children to school. Lance said that, since it was a lovely day, they should not go to school. Arthur countered that if they did not go to school they would not learn things and get work and be rich. Lance's response was that he did not want to work or be rich—he wanted to enjoy the day. Paul's view of this conversation, at the time and later, was that the children here were already demonstrating their essential personalities: the practical go-getter and the artistic dreamer.

Lance never liked any of the schools he went to, and his parents repeatedly responded to his complaints by trying to find new and better schools; it can be speculated that their responsiveness was fuelled by guilt (since they believed that pushing him to grow up fast after Pauline's birth might have harmed him), by their ambivalent beliefs about the care due to artists, as opposed to go-getters, and by their own childhood experiences in which the adult world had not seemed to care much about their feelings. In discussion during the therapy Lance said that he had not really been that miserable at any of his schools, but that it had been lovely receiving repeated acts of indulgence from his parents. By the age of fourteen he had stopped going to school altogether and had been provided by the authorities with a tutor. The tutor was of the opinion that he had considerable artistic talent, and decided to concentrate only on developing his skills in this area.

On leaving school Arthur had travelled around the world for two years, supporting himself and making a 'rite of passage' into adulthood that fitted with the family's beliefs about independence. He returned home on Lance's eighteenth birthday, when the latter for the first time showed the fearful, distressed, violent and 'irrational' behaviour which was to result in a diagnosis of schizophrenia, and which had continued intermittently over the subsequent period. He had very confused ideas about being a genius, which linked with strange versions of things his father had said to him. He feared for his life, often became abusive and violent towards his parents, and talked wildly about death, his destiny, and visions he had seen. Since that time he had remained at home, not working, and losing the social relationships he had had. He had been admitted to psychiatric hospital from time to time, always under section, as he would not go voluntarily, and tended to regard admission to hospital as part of his father's conspiracy to get rid of him. He had become very clingy in relation to Roberta, but was also hostile to her, blaming her for babying him. At times he allied with Paul, particularly in opposition to Roberta, but would also be very aggressive and suspicious towards him, seeing him as a rival for Roberta's attention and that of other women, especially in what the family regarded as his less lucid periods. In the fortnight preceding the first session he had spent much of the time crouched naked behind the piano in an apparent state of great fear, and had tried to throw himself out of the car at high speed.

Therapeutic meetings included many different configurations: the early sessions consisted of Paul, Roberta, Lance, Mary (an assistant in the workshop who lived with the family and was said to be Lance's girlfriend), and the family dog, whose friendliness and trust went a long way to helping Lance (and probably the other participants) to relax in the strange and new family therapy setting. Later Arthur and Pauline, who were both abroad when therapy was first started, joined some of the meetings, and Mary left. At a later stage of therapy Lance was seen individually, and Paul and Roberta attended together to work on couples issues (cf Chapter 5).

The family's communication style was one of great ambiguity, and fitted the sorts of communication patterns described by the Milan team (Selvini et al., 1978) in describing 'families in schizophrenic transaction' (cf Chapter 1). Both Paul and Roberta spoke in mutually and self-contradictory ways. Paul frequently used a style of oblique humour, which was not accompanied by any of the more usual analogic signals indicating that a statement is not to be taken literally. Roberta would sometimes close her eyes in the middle of conversations, and seem to disappear, and many of her sentences had a kind of transparent quality, so that it was difficult to assign clear meaning to them. They often exchanged apparently mutually exclusive positions; for example, in an early session Paul spoke eloquently of his mistrust of psychiatric intervention, and his dislike of having to see Lance on heavy doses of medication, while Roberta insisted that the doctors were their only hope, and clearly knew what they were doing. Later in the same session the therapist referred to Paul's statement, quoting one of his phrases. He protested with surprise that he had great faith in his son's doctors, while Roberta took up a position that mirrored that previously held by Paul. Attempts to clarify such confusions inevitably led to further complexity.

It is important for the therapist not to assume that such a style of communication is based on malice, insanity or intention to mislead, but rather to retain her curiosity as to the meaning of such acts within the family system. It was noticeable that Lance's response to communications like these was often an escalation of those behaviours most likely to be seen as deviant or nonsensical; that is, he would be quite likely to resort to metaphorical actions or utterances that served, on the one hand, as clear meta-communications regarding the situation, and on the other could be ignored as psychotic. For example when the baby sister's death was alluded to obliquely for the first time he placed his fingers in his ears—this was taken by the therapist as a signal to ask for more detail about the oblique remark, which she might otherwise have missed. These phenomena have been discussed extensively by others, notably by Bateson (1978a) and the Milan group (Selvini et al., 1978); I shall confine myself here to looking at a way of making sense of the specifics of these patterns as they were shown by the Clarke family.

Most of the work done with this family followed the pattern described in other case examples in this book, that is, an emphasis on the mutual exploration of pattern and meaning, and the assumption that the family members are active agents in the reconstruction of their own lives. However, a ritualized task, given at the end of session three, will be discussed in some detail, as it serves to highlight hypotheses about the meaning system in which 'psychotic' behaviours may be embedded.

There have been many attempts to explain the aetiology of the group of observed and reported behaviours described, in psychiatric typology, as schizophrenia. To all these, whether biological, psychological or whatever, a non-partisan assessment must accord the verdict 'not proven'. I follow Bateson in choosing to think that the behaviour of someone like Lance could probably be explained, if we understood more, as a vulnerability, perhaps genetic or neurological (which means that he will have greater difficulty than others, e.g. his siblings, in decoding complex or ambiguous or paradoxical communications), combined with the influence of patterns and events over the course of family life. The question for the therapist is not which, amongst mutually contradictory explanations is 'true', but which offers most opportunity for flexibility and therefore for alternatives. Lance's birth position, the meanings assigned to his birth and gender, the name he is given, and other events in the family, together with his interpretation of these events and relationships, may heighten this vulnerability, so that he begins to seem designated to be special.

The combination of all these factors may make him more sensitive to relational stresses, so that he makes himself more available than other family members to involvement in family coalitions, triangles and tangles. Just as his environment moulds him to fit his role, so he also reciprocally moulds his environment to fit his role. Whatever the origins of the disturbance of the family member designated as psychotic, the concern of systemic therapists is not to engage in a search for aetiological explanation, but to interact with family members in such a way that those family patterns, maintaining and being maintained by the designated person's symptomatic behaviour, and by the meanings assigned to it by family members and professionals alike, can be disrupted and altered to allow new relational and meaningful configurations to evolve.

> Human beings are in the habit of attributing meaning to behaviour, and the joint construction of new meaning

> . . . enables the participants in the therapy to attribute
> an explanation of the situation which does not necessitate
> assumptions of incurable illness in one member or blame in
> another, but enables changes in organization to be made
> (Jones, 1987, p. 14)

In attempting to understand the family's communications about their situation, the therapeutic team speculated that the theme of response to loss was significant. Both Paul and Roberta had had extreme experiences in their families of origin which taught them that family members could be lost unexpectedly and permanently, with major effects on the survivors. Both had learned, in the face of such loss, to present themselves as independent, while indicating, by choosing to highlight this theme in their discussion, that loss, and the way in which one could protect oneself against it, was an important ingredient in their own understanding of their family style.

> The therapeutic conversation is a mutual search and exploration
> through dialogue, a two-way exchange, a criss-crossing of
> ideas in which new meanings are continually evolving toward
> the 'dis-solving' of problems and, thus, the dissolving of the
> therapy system and, hence, the *problem-organizing, problem-*
> *dissolving system. Change is the evolution of new meaning through*
> *dialogue.* (Anderson & Goolishian, 1988, p. 372, original italics).

In searching for 'problem dis-solving' conversations with client families, the therapist treats the hypotheses of family members with respect, and attempts, by the kind of responses and questions offered, to link these to current interactional patterns, and to expand the meanings attributed to them so as to facilitate increasing flexibility, and a shift from lineal attributions of blame and responsibility to a more speculative standpoint which looks at pattern and meaning as being in continual negotiation and evolution.

Roberta and Paul (and via them their children) may have formed a belief that the overt display of love, dependency or vulnerability was dangerous. Their communication styles, in which it was very hard for them to be pinned down to one particular stance, could be linked to such a fear. Such a pattern could then be understood in terms of the Milan group's description (Selvini et al., 1978) of communication styles in which the underlying message can be interpreted as an invitation to remain in interaction without ever clearly defining a position which, once defined, could then make its representative vulnerable to rejection, defeat or disqualification.

Any attempts by the therapist to discuss the spouse relationship were met with mutually disqualifying jokes about abandonment. It seemed that Lance had the view that he was the cement that kept his parents together; it was certainly true that it needed both of them to care for him, and that both spouses indicated uncertainties about the future of the relationship without a child at home. The theme of the polarity between the artistic life and the regimented one, starkly symbolized by Paul himself in his two careers, had also been significant in the designation of family roles. Both these choices (artistic eccentricity or regimented success) were described by the family in ambivalent terms.

The family presented themselves as close and relatively undifferentiated, so that, for example, apparently contradictory views could be claimed alternately by any one of the protagonists. The physical organization of their house (designed by Paul) reflected this. It was built in such a way that no private spaces existed: any conversation could be overheard by anyone else in the house, and there was therefore also nowhere that the marital couple could exercise any claim to a private relationship. At a later stage of the therapy Paul said that he realized this design for a house (and for relationships) reflected his own ideal of 'dormitory life', as experienced at school and in the army. Roberta's view was that this style of functioning had suited her very well in the early years of the marriage, when the children were small, and when the warmth and closeness of this way of living offered a contrast to her own early family experiences. However, she said that, in retrospect, she had been struggling for her own independence for some years before coming to therapy; she saw Lance as offering her an example of this struggle, and subsequently arrived at a point where she could overtly engage in a redefinition of relationships between herself and Paul. Also in retrospect she described her habit of closing her eyes and drifting out of the conversation as a way of entering a 'room of her own'.

At the end of the third session, following a team consultation, the therapist presented the family with some ideas distilled from the team's hypotheses, built on the foundations described above, and on the ideas which had been explored with the family in the preceding sessions. The first two sections were addressed explicitly to Lance. The therapist indicated that she and the team were, at this point, considering several hypotheses offering potential connections between the past and his present situation.

These were, in summary:

1. That, given the impact of his first sisters' death and his second sister's frailty, his parents' distress, and the subsequent understandable decision to push him to grow up quite quickly to catch up with his brother Arthur (two years older), he may have continued to feel that he had been cheated out of part of his childhood. Consequently he had dragged his feet all through his growing-up time, having learned ways of organizing those around him into looking after him; this came to a head when Arthur returned from his trip around the world on Lance's eighteenth birthday. It was as if the implicit message, in the minds of all the family members, was that the time had now come for Lance to grow up and leave home. He, however, had demonstrated quite spectacularly that he was not ready to do so, and had compelled his parents and others to continue to take care of him. If this explanation fitted, then—taking a developmental view—it would mean that he was now at the point where he was ready to grow up, since two years had elapsed since that date.

2. On the other hand, it might be that Lance's own view (offered during the session) was relevant, namely that he had become accustomed, in early childhood, to making his parents 'spoil' him, so that he was committed to a life in which he would not have to face the boring alternative, as set out by Arthur so long ago, of having

to learn and work. Expanding a double-edged metaphor presented by the family during the session—of Lance as a coddled but helpless slave-owner—the therapist then talked about the advantages and disadvantages of slave-owning. This metaphor was used to suggest that Lance might have a choice about whether to remain in his current situation. As things were he received considerable attention from others, was not required to carry stress or responsibility, had the perks of a potential genius, and could make others jump to it by threatening to become distressed. However, in return he gave up his freedom, relationships with his peers, and—over time—his own belief in his capacity to stand on his own feet, as well as losing out on the age-related socialized learning which his peers were becoming skilled at, while he lagged behind with ever-increasing consequences in terms of self-confidence.

3. However, it was also possible that a complexity of factors had led up to Lance's disturbed and disturbing experiences; this was accompanied by a summary, from the therapist, of the relevant history as detailed by all family members. These factors might no longer be active or relevant; nevertheless the fears and habits of relationship built up around them acted as present constraints on all family members. Because of what all of them had said in this session, the therapist accepted that each of them individually felt that it might now be possible to change, and to resume normal life where it had been interrupted two years previously. However, they were constrained from doing this because Lance, on the one hand, and the parents on the other, found it hard to believe the other's protestations of readiness for change. When Lance expressed his impatience with his parents' constant anxious monitoring of his behaviour, and declared his readiness to stand on his own feet, they saw this as further signs of his disturbance; when his parents talked of their impatience with having their lives, work, time, and their own (perhaps shaky) relationship frozen in place by the need to put him first, Lance saw this as a threat of abandonment and panicked. From the

therapist's outsider perspective it seemed likely that each side might be ready, though fearful, to attempt some shifts, and therefore a task was suggested.

As in the first case described in this chapter, this task was carefully framed as experimental. Its structure owes much to the Milan team's thinking about 'odd and even days' (Selvini et al., 1980c). What is particularly significant about tasks of this kind is the idea that the introduction of time, that is of separating out the interwoven strands of contradictory and paradoxical patterns by introducing variations which follow one another rather than coinciding, can undo the binding nature of the pattern. It can also, of course, allow participants to observe themselves in a way not possible when actions are governed by unexamined and taken-for-granted premises.

The task required the family members living at home at that point (that is, Lance, Paul and Roberta) to alternate their behaviour from week to week, based on two opposite premises. In one week the parents would behave as if they were certain that Lance was independent, and that it was not their job to look after him; Lance would reciprocate by behaving as if he was sure that he could look after himself, and would not send signals to his parents asking for babying. In the following week Lance would do everything he could think of to show his parents that he still needed looking after, and they would do this to the fullest of their ability. It was up to them to decide whether to start with a 'baby' week or an 'adult' week. The two weeks would be alternated again (making four weeks in all), and on the fifth week they would simply behave as normal. The suggestion to revert to 'normal' behaviour after such an experiment may of course be experienced as ludicrous, as it implies that one can step into the same river twice, and all members of the discussion made it clear, by their smiles, that they were aware of its nonsensicality.

It is not suggested that changes following on the giving or carrying out of such a task are caused by the doing of the task. (Indeed, whether or not a task is carried out is not of primary significance within this framework; its hoped-for effect lies in the communication of meaning in which therapist and clients engage around the task.) Rather, there is an assumption that the kind of conversation in which therapists and clients engage has several likely effects: the making overt of that which is covert or latent; the linking of aspects of meaning and behaviour which have not previously been juxtaposed; the 'lifting out' and exploration of the logic of the meaning systems which the family and professionals have previously constructed. The technique called circular questioning is highly useful in pursuing this aim, but it is not the only way of doing this. Indeed, it is important for therapists not to treat 'circular questioning' as a new orthodoxy with rules and set pathways; what is necessary for the therapist is to allow her way of *thinking* to suggest whatever therapeutic behaviours (that is, conversation, stance, curiosity) will be coherent both with her thinking and with the client group's exploration of the logic of their own system.

A few of the family's responses to the giving and doing of the task will illustrate the above points. After the therapist had outlined the task, Roberta asked: 'But what should we do if he goes and stands in the road stark bollock naked?' (This was something he had done before.) The therapist responded that in an 'adult' week (which was under discussion at that point) they would have to assume that he knew the consequences of his action—namely that an adult behaving in this manner was inviting agents of social control to remove him to hospital—and was choosing to do this for reasons of his own. In the past, an orthodox systemic view may have regarded such a question as an attempt to disqualify the therapist's 'intervention' (cf Chapter 1). Instead, it was treated simply as a request for clarification. Roberta then said that she foresaw some problems with money during the 'adult' weeks, as Lance had a small legacy which they were currently administering for him. Paul responded to this by suggesting that, in adult weeks, they would simply have to accept that Lance had free access to his money, and contain their anxiety about the consequences; in 'baby' weeks they might give him pocket money.

On return to the next therapy session five weeks later the family reported considerable interest in observing their own responses to the task. Lance had 'cheated' by remaining in adult mode throughout, while Paul and Roberta had stuck to the pattern of interpreting his behaviours alternately through 'baby' and 'adult' lenses. They were particularly struck by how easy they, as parents, had found the 'baby' weeks, and how the 'adult' weeks threw up considerable anxieties and issues of control for them. These changed perceptions then led to fruitful further explorations.

Families may present to therapists with difficulties which, at first sight, seem fairly straightforward, or which come festooned in daunting diagnostic labels and extreme relational and behavioural patterns. It may well be necessary for the therapist to react with different levels of skill and theoretical complexity to different problem patterns. However, the same stance towards interactional patterning, meaning and change underlies all the therapist's responses, regardless of how simple or complex they may seem to the observer.

CHAPTER 5   Working with couples

BACKGROUND

Traditionally family therapy and couples therapy have been seen as distinct, so that marital (*sic*) therapy is often regarded as a separate specialism, requiring different skills and training than that required for work with families. In contrast many family therapists have been reluctant to acknowledge this distinction, and see systemic theory and technique as being equally applicable whether a family is being worked with or an adult couple. Even within family therapy, however, work with couples who live together in an intimate relationship (usually including sexual intimacy) is seen as having distinct characteristics and difficulties.

What then are the factors that stand out in work with couples which persist in leading to a distinction being drawn around them by therapists? Two aspects will be discussed here which contribute to the delineation of couples therapy as presenting special difficulties for therapists: the nature of the couple bond and the place of a third person (therapist) within it, with its concomitant pressure to act or be seen as arbitrator; and the highlighting of gender roles and difficulties. In addition clinical examples will be used to illustrate various stages in the life of couples, and particular questions which tend to get highlighted in couples work.

TWOSOMES AND THREESOMES

The strength and intimacy of the couple relationship has been celebrated (and execrated) in story, song and myth. In some ways it is seen as more mysterious than the perhaps equally powerful mother–child bond, since the latter has a biochemical and physiological explanation which acts dormitively (i.e. putting one's curiosity to sleep! (Bateson, 1980, p. 146)), and thus seems to be 'natural' and beyond question. However, the search for sexual, physical and social intimacy with a chosen other seems universal: most people engage in this search at least at some stage of their lives, and the family (the usual consequence of heterosexual coupling) is regarded by most societies as the cornerstone of the social fabric.

The creation of family is not, however, a sufficient explanation for the intensity with which adulthood is characterized by the search for an intimate partner; this is evidenced by the fact that many couples, whether heterosexual or homosexual, do not seek to extend the boundaries of their closeness to include children. The intensity of meaning attribution in couples can in many respects be seen as distinct from the meaning conferred on the relationship by its participation in the construct of the family. The family has many functions, which differ to some extent from culture to culture; in Western post-industrial society it is seldom a unit of economic production in itself, as it was in the past and continues to be in many parts of the world. The functions the family is expected to fulfil in any society may add to the stresses placed on the couple relationship; for example, economic responsibility, difficulties with children, inability to bear children, care of elderly or sickly members, will impinge on the relationship of the adult couple in ways which may become complexly looped with more specific couple difficulties.

In addition, as many of the social tasks of marriage have changed or fallen away, and the nuclear family becomes the dominant Western pattern, it can be seen that couples turn more intensively to each other for the fulfilment of numerous personal desires. Although homosexual partnerships are not nowadays, in many societies, regarded as outside of the norm, such couples may nevertheless find that they are subject to extra stresses which derive from the model of the normative family which continues to be dominant (Ussher, 1991). Such couples, like other unmarried couples, childless couples or single-parent families, may then feel obliged to 'prove' their viability, even to the extent of denying problems for fear that any acknowledgement of difficulty will reflect not on the themselves alone, but on their sub-group.

When working with couples the impact of wider family relationships and societal expectations cannot be ignored. Nevertheless there is that in the nature of the bond—what Rilke (1929) calls 'two solitudes (that) protect and limit and greet each other'—that brings its own major satisfactions and problems. This means that in a cultural context where intimate relationships are engaged in for reasons of love (a word which probably has as many definitions as there are people using it) disappointment with the chosen partner can be severe, and not as easily remedied as dissatisfaction with children (who are expected to grow away), other family members (from whom less may be expected) or workmates (who can perhaps be endured or left without major personal impact). Thus couples seeking therapy are likely to bring intense emotion to the situation, to have invested considerable self-esteem in the success of the relationship, and to think badly of themselves and the other for what may be seen as personal failure rather than a problem requiring solution. Moreover, the intimacy of the relationship—and perhaps particularly the intimacy of sexuality and vulnerability—means that the couple's relationship may carry meanings which are not always overt or open to rational analysis, and which refer to the real or imagined safety of the mother–child symbiosis, and the longing of individuals for a 'haven in a heartless world'. An additional stress factor, which is often seen as one of the triggers for family and marital stress and violence (cf Frude, 1991) is the level of irritation and expectation which comes with propinquity.

A therapist who joins a couple in a therapeutic relationship will be required to respect, and help to restore if at all possible, the particular meanings invested in their partnership, and will at the same time easily be seen as an intruder in the privacy of this most personal bond. For therapists it is couples work that most often brings problems of alliance and coalition; it is as if, when working with families, it is easier to respect the systemic whole, the many interlinked relationships and the independent life of the family away from therapy, whereas, when working with individuals a therapist may feel more at ease with seeing events mainly from the point of view of the client. With some couples, however, therapists report a constant 'pull' to take sides—sometimes referred to as 'playing courtroom-courtroom', i.e. the therapist can experience herself in the role of the judge who by turns is presented with the case for the prosecution by one or other partner. It is for this reason that family therapists, like therapists of other theoretical persuasions, have often seen it as important to work with an opposite-gender colleague, in the room or behind the screen. Alone in the room with an embattled couple, a therapist may find that the mere act of listening to one partner's account is seen by the other as taking sides. Therapy then becomes, perhaps more than with any other client configuration, a balancing act of even-handedly shared attention and empathy. It is here that the two cornerstones of systemic interviewing take on crucial importance: increasing options and flexibility by the constant search for polyphonic discussion which recognizes the validity of many different points of view, and finding common ground, even if this common ground consists only of a mutual acknowledgement that the relationship is in trouble. Therapists working with couples will know from experience that some partners cannot even agree on this!

It is also important for therapists working with couples in troubled relationships to remain open-minded and 'curious' about the outcome of the work—that is, whether the relationship will improve or be broken up. Family therapists have at times been accused, particularly from a sociological or feminist perspective, of being in the business of keeping the institution of marriage going at all costs. Systemic neutrality in such a situation will therefore test the therapist's ability to help the partners find their own preferred outcomes, without imposing her own views about the desirability of their relationship or of relationships like theirs in general. Thus the therapist's own life experiences, experience of and views about intimacy, sexuality, hetero- or homosexuality, and relationship with a partner are likely to be central to her thinking, and she will have to ensure that these do not intrude unacceptably into the therapeutic work.

THE ROLE OF THE THERAPIST'S GENDER

Just as the therapist's personal values and life situation take on more prominence than usual in working with couples, so the therapist's gender becomes relevant, to herself or himself and to the clients. In working with two adults whose beliefs, values and learning about their own gendered sense of self, and roles within the relationship, will be intrinsically part of their difficulties with each other and of their search for solutions, therapists cannot avoid bringing their own values and life experience in this area to their perception of the therapeutic task. Because gender is an overarching concept (Goldner, 1985, 1991b; Jones, 1990), and we are all men or women, couples therapy is bound to touch more directly than many other therapeutic concerns on the private identity of the therapist. The solution to this difficulty is not to deny that it exist, but to ensure that the therapist is aware of this and has the opportunity to make these concerns overt, for example by working live with a consultant or by having access to other forms of consultation.

In addition to the way that the therapist's perception of clients, and ability to understand their points of view, will be influenced by her own and the clients' gender, the clients themselves will bring attitudes and expectations related to gender to the therapy. This applies to their views of each other, their expectations, disappointments, blind spots and so on, but also to how they will perceive the therapist. Fear of not getting a fair hearing, because the therapist is of the 'wrong' gender, or 'wrong' sexual orientation; feelings of rivalry, contempt, inferiority, or flirtatiousness; these may influence the clients' views of the therapist, and moreover these influences may be outside conscious awareness.

It is also useful for therapists to be aware of how language and speech patterns may be gendered (Spender, 1980; Cooper,

1990). In most societies men and women use gender-typical speech styles. While individual variation may override gendered style, and while therapists in general will attempt to notice and adapt to clients' individual speech patterns (e.g. the use of visual or kinetic imagery, rational language or feeling language, etc.), it is worth considering what general gendered speech patterns may be present, and how the therapist's use of language may complement or breach these. In English-speaking cultures there is a general tendency for women to use relational and feeling-tone language, and to speak in ways which facilitate the entry of other speakers; this is referred to by linguists as 'tagging' (Cooper, 1990). Examples are sentence endings which trail off, and use invitations to the other speaker to come in, such as 'isn't it?' or 'all right?'. Thus two women speaking with each other are likely to create a fugue-like pattern, where their statements overlap or weave in and out of each other. Men are more likely to speak in declarative sentences with clear endings. Thus two men speaking together are likely to create a pattern of clear turn-taking. In mixed-sex conversation men are more likely to interrupt women's speech, and women to allow this. A female therapist trained in circular questioning, and holding the assumption that it is her job to direct the conversation, is likely to breach many of the male client's speech norms: she will interrupt him, is less likely to tag her sentence endings, and will act in general in a confident if not dominant manner (cf Chapter 7). This may offend the man and his woman partner's sense of normality, without them necessarily being able to put their fingers on what is wrong, since all these speech habits tend, most of the time, to pass unnoticed. Similarly a male therapist may display himself as someone who is at home in 'female' territory, that is, the world of relationships and feelings, and his speech patterns, for this reason, may be more 'soft-edged' than his male client's; cf for example the characteristic reactive style of circular questioning (Cooper, 1990). This may then cause him to be seen as allied with the female client, or ineffective and wishy-washy (because like a woman); the reasons for these judgements in the minds of both clients may once again not be overt.

Example

Mary (45) and Peter (64) Smith had found their relationship becoming very tense following a number of life events and changes, which included his retirement from a powerful international position, and her taking on of part-time work which had, in recent years, become more absorbing and prestigious. He had found himself on several occasions playing second fiddle to her on social occasions—as she had once done at his business-related social events.

After a fruitful first session, in which they had discussed their long history together, and offered the female therapist their thoughtful appraisal of the difficulties they now faced, a second appointment was arranged. The first date offered by the therapist was not suitable, as Mary had to be away from home for an event related to her work. The second appointment offered was on a Thursday, and Peter joked that he was superstitious, and in the past had never made important business deals on Thursdays. The couple accepted this appointment without further discussion.

Mary arrived twenty minutes early for the second appointment, and Peter arrived half-an-hour late. In consultation with her colleagues the therapist had decided not to start the session without Peter. On arrival in the therapy room Mary immediately started apologizing on her own and Peter's behalf, sitting on the edge of her chair, and saying—with many anxious glances at Peter—that she had made a mistake about the time of the appointment, and thus had been early. Peter looked morose, did not speak, and with great deliberation placed himself on a chair as far as possible from both his wife and the therapist.

Fruitless attempts to take up the therapeutic discussion where it had been left after the previous session made it clear that Peter's angry attitude had to be dealt with first. He declared himself angry with his wife, because he had felt neglected and insignificant at his wife's work event which they had both attended (the one which had prevented acceptance of the first appointment offered). He was also angry with the therapist because she had accommodated to his wife's inability to keep the first appointment offered, but had not done the same for him. He spoke in a hectoring tone, with many angry jabs of the finger, frequently interrupting his wife and the therapist, and sometimes declining to respond, shrugging and turning away. 'I said explicitly and clearly that it did not suit me, and in spite of that you went ahead and made the appointment.' Subsequent review of the video recording of the first session made it clear that he had not said this; what also became clear, on further acquaintance, was that he had been accustomed, in his working life and also in his relationship with his wife, to the expectation that his wishes would be divined (especially by the women who served him) from small hints or none. Mary's anxious apologetic behaviour at the beginning of the session was her usual response to a failure to read his mind accurately, which had often in the past served to placate him after a time.

Peter: 'I had reasons why it was not convenient to me and notwithstanding that I was obliged to come. Being realistic and objective the fact that it was on a Thursday was irrelevant. . . . You did not know my reasons, but I did say at the time that it was not convenient. I did advance a reason which was actually not applicable, and with respect you dismissed that.'
Ther.: 'Is it the same pattern then for you. . . [as in Mary's business meeting] of feeling you weren't being heard but Mary was?' In response to this Peter shrugged and turned away.
Ther.: 'Because I agreed to change for Mary but not for you.'
Peter (folding his arms pugilistically over his chest): 'Well in the politest possible language I made it plain, even to a person with a modest amount of intelligence, I made it plain in very polite and tactful terms that it did not suit me to come today—and notwithstanding that we are at this meeting today.'

Peter went on to describe the similarity of this situation to another example where Mary had thwarted his wishes, concluding, 'I'm absolutely under her thumb and I object'. Mary started to say that she had always stood in the position Peter now occupied, but he cut across to reiterate his anger, and she subsided.

It was clear to the therapist, and this was confirmed by a consultation telephone call from her colleagues, that Peter had to be helped to find a way out of this situation in order to be able to participate in the therapy. He had, in the first session, shown himself as a sensible, warm and self-respecting man. He had also displayed his awareness of the impact which the reversal in their roles and relative status was having on his and Mary's relationship, and had described their desire to find a life-enhancing way of coping with it as a major reason for coming to therapy. If he were to leave the session having persisted in what, in a younger person, would be called a tantrum, he was likely to feel too ashamed to return. It was important, if he were to have enough respect for the therapist to be able to benefit from work with her, that she should demonstrate that she was not intimidated by him, and could take him on on his own ground without joining him in a symmetrical escalation of aggression. For the therapist to back down without losing her authority might serve as a model for him, just as

Mary might make good use of observing a woman who did not, in the face of Peter's bullying, either cave in, which Mary usually did, or lose her temper, which Mary sometimes did.

Accordingly the therapist responded to Peter by using a mixture of messages at different analogic levels. That is, she adopted the same body posture as his (arms pugilistically crossed, feet planted firmly as if ready to jump up), and then allowed this posture, during the course of her conversation, to ease and open up. She used the same sort of formal, cognitive language he habitually used, and offered an apology combined with a challenge to him to take responsibility for getting some work done in the session.

Ther.: 'I quite agree that I did not hear your objections that clearly. My colleagues think, and I also realize that I have not fully appreciated that it must have been quite an effort for you to come to the meeting today. . . . I may not have taken cognizance sufficiently of the facts you have stated today. . . . What do you want to do with the rest of today's meeting—do you feel it would be more useful to stop now and reconvene at a time when it is more convenient and we have time to talk, or shall we use the rest of the meeting for a specific purpose?'

In response to this Peter thawed, apologized for the fact that so little time was available for the meeting due to his lateness, and he and Mary together defined a focus for the rest of the work they wanted to do with the therapist and her colleagues.

GETTING TOGETHER AS A COUPLE

When couples first come together with the hope and intention of making a long-term commitment to each other they may be surprised by the impact this decision has on their families of origin and the other systems, e.g. friendship, in which they participate. They may also find that the influence of their families of origin, in respect of altered relationships, as well as the internalized values, expectations and self-perceptions they carry with them, may constitute obstacles to the smooth progress of their relationship with each other.

Example

Anne and Mark had lived together for ten years, and came to therapy because Anne had become increasingly depressed. They related this to long-standing difficulties with her parents. Anne had always seen her family as strict and rather harsh, the sort of family that was 'hard to leave or to enter', but while this had caused unhappiness and strained her relationship with her parents it had not, before getting together with Mark, seemed a major problem. Her brothers and their wives had found ways of coping with this ('They put a boundary around themselves') as well as with her parents' somewhat rule-bound style of doing things. Mark came from a family described as open and easygoing; this contrast caused them both, but Anne in particular, considerable sadness. She had begun to feel inadequate in relation to Mark, and it seemed to her that she 'was' her family. Anne's parents were described as unwilling to accept Mark. They would not let the couple share a bedroom when they visited, and described Mark as a negative outside influence on Anne. The couple saw this as the reason why they had not been able to decide whether to get married or have children.

They described themselves as having different styles of doing things, thinking and relating to others, and this complementarity had worked well in the past. Now their difference was being construed, by Anne, but increasingly also by Mark, as a sign of inferiority or superiority. Anne saw herself as neurotic, unable to cope with ordinary situations, depressed and unworthy of Mark. A metaphor generated between them and the therapist described this relationship as one which was originally entered into because of the attraction of difference, with no implication that one or the other was better—like a Scandinavian and a Mediterranean choosing each other—but now it felt more as if Prince Charming had found himself married to the daughter of notorious criminals, with the effect that he resented his tie to her family and the problems she carried because of them, and she resented the constant sense that she was expected to feel inferior and be grateful.

At intervals during the course of the therapy Anne arrived at a point where she could begin to accept that her parents were as they were, and that her own life and choices need not be governed by her parents views; however, at this point Mark's part in helping to maintain the problematic situation would emerge. He had, in childhood, been disappointed in his own father, and had admired Anne's father very much when they first met. He felt correspondingly hurt by this surrogate father's unwillingness to accept him, and moreover, given the beliefs and values of his family of origin, could not accept that family relationships could be distant but adequate. Anne's suggestion that 'this is how it is' or 'life's like that' would make him first incredulous and then distressed and gloomy. He would therefore urge Anne not to give up hope of bringing her parents round, and would make considerable efforts, at the cost of his own pride, to seek reconciliation. Anne then felt pressurized by his expectations of closeness with her family, and they would renew their efforts to achieve a better relationship. The failure of these attempts would then reconfirm Anne's sense that she came from a terrible family and was thus herself a terrible person; her lowering of confidence would detrimentally affect the relationship between her and Mark.

Using the couple's own thinking about boundaries, the therapist and team offered them ideas to add to their own thinking about their situation. These included the view that they had become stuck in a position where their identities were being defined by way of their relationships with the parental generation, as in adolescence; their relationship as a couple had lost its boundaries with other systems; and the balance and equality which had characterized their early relationship had gone out of kilter. Moreover these three components were interlinked in that difficulty in each of these areas tended to trigger the others. Since they were both computer experts they were also familiar with cybernetic concepts which then became useful in sharing the therapy team's views with them. For example, when Anne suggested that if she and Mark could change their actions in relation to her parents, then the parents—as the other parts of the system— would also have to change, the therapist agreed with this, but cautioned that this was not necessarily so, as there was no telling whether change on Anne and Mark's part would constitute a sufficient perturbation to invite change from the parents.

While discussing the patterns of two-generational belief and action which were connected with their difficulties, the therapist also speculated with them about the possibility of devising some ritual to be performed with Anne's parents to symbolize their togetherness as a couple, when this had been achieved, and the new style of relating they wished to establish. Mark and Anne devised such a ritual themselves, and carried it out, with the help of Anne's grandmother, on a Christmas family visit. They decided to stay in the grandmother's house, and formally invited her parents to meet them on 'neutral ground' for a walk on Christmas Day. Both couples treated the physical meeting half-way between Anne's parents' house and her grandmother's house as a symbol (mutually agreed but not overtly commented on) for 'meeting each other half-way'.

As the tension between Anne and Mark on the one hand, and Anne's parents on the other, began to ease and the relationship to change in a more satisfactory adult-to-adult direction, the couple began to confront questions which had perhaps been disguised by the decade of standing together in the face of a common external threat. They examined their commitment to each other—each went through a separate period of thinking they wanted to leave—and what they wanted from a relationship, whether they would choose to have children, and what their demands and hopes were of each other. The balance between them shifted so that their complementarity was now experienced as more flexible, with each feeling more independent as well as more able to be vulnerable and to expect support from the other. This point was not reached without a few ups and downs, but by the end of therapy, when they had just moved into their own house together, they talked of 'having our own boundary now', having 'drawn lines of distinction in the landscape of things', and of their increased sense of choice and flexibility. The end of therapy was marked by their advising the therapist (computer-illiterate) who had just acquired a word processor—perhaps an appropriate ritual to signify the restoration of their own sense of competence and autonomy!

The way in which couples choose each other may well contain components of a therapeutic wish for replication or reparation in relation to families of origin. This wish can be compatible with a satisfying relationship, but can also become a factor in a pattern which keeps the couple frozen at a point before actual commitment to each other can be properly realized. The task of therapy, then, may be to help dissolve this over-emphasis on the past and past relationships, to enable a couple to get on with their lives separately or together.

GENDERED PATTERNS AND PROBLEMS

As the twentieth century draws to a close the influence of feminism in Western post-industrial societies has meant that awareness of questions of equality between men and women, and of the shifting of gender roles, is widespread. This does not necessarily mean that a majority of women and men have changed the way they construe their own gender identities, or relate to each other, but rather that the language of feminism has become part of popular culture—watered down, to be sure, in the same way that psychoanalytic concepts have, since early in this century, become part of a general vocabulary.

Thus through the medium of television, newspapers, magazines and so on, gender roles are on the agenda, regardless of whether the ideas of feminism are espoused or lampooned. It is no longer unusual for clients to announce to a therapist 'I'm a male chauvinist pig', or 'I'm an old-fashioned woman, I'm afraid. I don't hate men'. Thus they signal identity, not through allying themselves with these cultural movements, but by placing themselves in the context of what they assume to be the shared social discourse.

As discussed above, factors of propinquity and intimacy must make any intimate relationship fraught at times. When gender difference is added, with its potential for complementary richness as well as for misunderstanding and mutual alienation (cf, for example, Goodrich, 1991, Hare-Mustin 1991a, Jones 1990), a couple's therapist has to expect to find 'gender on the agenda'. It should be unnecessary by now to say that the therapist is not entitled to press her own views, whatever they may be, onto her clients; it should be equally obvious that *not* discussing questions of gender, as they impinge on the couple's life in relation to role expectations, styles of functioning, relationships to each other and to family members, sexuality, work and the sharing out of responsibility, etc., etc., constitutes a failure of professional responsibility (cf, for example, the findings on the negative effects of sex-role stereotyping on women's well-being, Hafner, 1989).

Example

David and Caroline Martin came to therapy following an escalation of violent actions on David's part, directed mostly at Caroline, but sometimes also involving their four children, and usually triggered by incidents to do with Caroline's closeness to the children and David's sense of exclusion. The children ranged in age from 22 to 10; the oldest two had left home, and the two younger were away at boarding school for much of the time. Caroline had been occupied full-time with the house and children for most of the marriage, but had recently taken a part-time job. David was the head of his own successful business.

David came from a family in which his father had been largely absent, due to his work involvement, and his mother had been very close to his older brother, who was seen in the family as having been more successful than David. He bitterly resented the feeling of always having been 'second best', and saw this replicated in Caroline's closeness to the children, and her sharing of intimacies, particularly with her adult daughters. The fact that she had taken part-time employment at the point when the children no longer required all her attention proved to him that she had never seen it as important to be there for him; he had assumed that the children's growing up would herald a period of closeness and leisure for him and Caroline.

Caroline's mother had left her and her father in a violent and publicly scandalous manner when she was ten years old. The stigma of this remained significant to her, and she had devoted herself to 'making it up' to her father throughout her childhood. At heart she felt unworthy, particularly to the degree that she shared her mother's gender and might turn out to be like her; she could only disprove this by continual acts of devotion and self-sacrifice, especially in the service of a good man, which she saw David as being.

David was initially suspicious of therapy and had come only because Caroline threatened to leave him if he did not. This threat of divorce, while frequently uttered, was ambiguous, since Caroline also said that she would stick with David no matter what, in part due to her convictions about the inviolability of the marriage bond, and in part because she saw it as her mission to 'save him'. Thus her remaining with him did not reassure him that he was loved. Each saw the other as profoundly unstable. Caroline had become highly sensitized to the imminence of David's 'flashpoints'; if these were not headed off in time his subsequent violence was dangerous to her and frightening to all of them. Her vigilance to his moods, however, had in recent years often served to trigger a flashpoint, since her concerned attempts to draw him into the family circle, and to make him feel better, would exacerbate his irritation and his feeling that he was an unlovable outsider. Caroline's history, her conviction that she was responsible for David's emotional welfare, her sense of her own insignificance and obligation to serve others, meant that she did not take steps to ensure her own safety. For David his outbursts of rage were the only way he expressed emotion; he had never, before coming to therapy, discussed his own feelings, wants or relationships, and felt profoundly constricted and incapacitated in this regard. The aftermath of violence, for both of them, offered an emotional experience that was so significant as to act, in all probability, as a reinforcement: it was only after a violent attack that Caroline could comfort David and feel herself needed and strong and loyal, and that David could weep and express his fear of losing her (cf Goldner et al., 1990 for an invaluable discussion of this pattern).

They described themselves as having a conventional marriage. Caroline had always obeyed David, but now, because of her part-time job, she had in her own view gained confidence and had therefore become less likely to obey in all things. David saw this change as due to her having made the acquaintance of a 'strident feminist' at work, and to her discussions with her daughters, who had also become 'infected' with feminism at university. The daughters, the family doctor, David's brother and all Caroline's friends were said to be in favour of her leaving him; by remaining loyal to him she demonstrated her capacity for devotion beyond thoughts of her own welfare. David brought a computer print-out to the first therapy session on which he had charted, with minute attention to detail, all their ups and downs over recent months: this was partly intended to support his contention that Caroline was mad due to the menopause, an idea which had been dismissed by her doctor.

Their communication was characterized by ambiguity on Caroline's part, and a kind of rigid fragility on David's. It could be seen that each of these habitual communication patterns elicited the other in a circular fashion. For the sake of discussion the vicious circle can be punctuated from Caroline's actions: she gives messages which at one level offer reassurance, but at the other emphasize her perception of David's weakness. For example, Caroline would say that David need not see her small job as a threat to his preeminence in her life, since she had deliberately taken a mundane and low-paying job because she knew he could not stand competition. David's response to this statement (which could also be punctuated as the trigger for it) would be to insist on finding a four-course meal on the table five minutes after arriving home each evening, on the grounds that Caroline's taking a job was an indulgence and not a financial necessity, since he was the family provider; it was up to her to prove that she wasn't secretly moving away from him into a world of career, feminism and independence, by maintaining the home standards he had always insisted on. Any variation in the rigid rules and timetables of their lives could then become a 'flashpoint' for David; these flashpoints happened most often when Caroline attempted to make time for her relationships with the children. The more David was experienced by the family as violent, unpleasant, rigid and ungiving, the more the children sided with Caroline; the more she tried to spend time with them away from David (in order to shield them and him) the more likely this situation then was to provoke an outburst from David.

The saving grace of this beleaguered couple, for each other and for the therapist, was their robust sense of humour. This made it possible for the therapist to make humorous and paradoxical comments on, and occasionally to set tasks relating to, the ambiguities and sticking-points in their relationship. David talked constantly in terms of control and its major importance to him; Caroline described herself as responsible for 70–80 per cent of his aggression, due to her failure to placate him in time. The therapist defined this taking of responsibility as an indication of control, and teased and challenged David about his acceptance of such a situation. The therapist suggested to David that, in the face of the pressures from his wife, her colleagues, his daughters, and the late twentieth century, he should decide how many concessions, if any, he was prepared to make to 'strident' feminism. He agreed to read up as much as he could about it, so as to be clear about the demands made, and then to make a list of those concessions he was prepared to grant, and to give this to Caroline in the form of a 'housewife's charter'. This task afforded them both much amusement— neither was unaware of the impossible bind in being 'given' liberation— and led them to making changes to their joint satisfaction. The linking of David's violence to his feeling of weakness, and Caroline's 'martyrdom' to her desire for affirmation, enabled them to shift the rigid categories within which they had imprisoned themselves and each other, so that David could take responsibility for controlling his actions, and Caroline could take care for her own safety and well-being (Goldner et al., 1990).

Not all couples present themselves in such polarized and stereotypical ways. Nevertheless, the search for love and affirmation, for flexibility and choice, and the influence of learned roles on the options available to men and women are likely to be present to some degree in the situations that couples bring to therapy.

GETTING SEPARATE AS A COUPLE

Just as the forming of an autonomous unit in the early stages of a couple's life together can bring forth problems, so too the later stages of life together may bring new possibilities or obstacles. The stage in a couple's life when children grow up and leave home (literally or figuratively), when parents become frail or die, when retirement may approach, is often seen, in popular and in professional writing, as a problematic one for women in particular. It can be easy to exaggerate the difficulties of women, to ignore those of men, and to misunderstand both if looked at in isolation; that is, the context—familial, social, economic—within which this life-stage is negotiated has to be taken into consideration (Carter & McGoldrick, 1981, Walters et al., 1988). A woman who has devoted her life to the rearing of children is likely to feel bereft and redundant when they leave home; a man who has invested most of the meaning of his life in work will feel equally rudderless when retirement day looms. Couples often grow apart while their children are growing up; their differentiation and specialization of function (child-rearing, bread-winning) can mean that they have less and less in common as time goes on. Without the buffers and motivation of children and work they may feel uncomfortable when required to spend more time than usual with each other.

Even without the trigger of retirement from work or child-rearing couples may begin to re-evaluate their lives together, to long for more than they have with each other, and to ask the sorts of questions that belong properly in the second half of life—what have I done with my life? What shall I do with the rest of it? What meaning has it all had? Do I want/need to do more before it is too late? What about spirituality? Is this all there is?

Having been together for a long time, loved each other, brought up children, shared a life, does not mean that partners will feel the urge for change simultaneously. It is more likely that couples who come to therapy will have been changing asymmetrically, so that one may have been maturing or exploring in ways they find worthwhile, but which put them out of step with the other.

Example

Gillian (52) and James (56) came to therapy at James's request. He feared that Gillian would leave him, felt very depressed, and described himself as senile, old, boring and wet. Gillian was not sure whether she wanted to divorce James; what she was sure about was that she wanted more autonomy.

They had been married for 29 years, and had worked together for most of that time. Until recently two of their three children had still lived with them, in a large house which James had renovated to his own design, such that all rooms led into one another and there were no private spaces in the house. Gillian said that her major wish was for a room of her own with a door that she could close. For James, however, who had grown up in boarding school and then been in the army until he married Gillian, this communal atmosphere was delightful. Gillian thought it had probably suited her quite well when the children were younger—it was only in recent years that it had become a major irritation to her.

Gillian wanted no longer to work with James, wanted to have friends and journeys of her own; as she had pushed for this over recent years and months James had insisted, in ways that he himself found demeaning, that he should be allowed to share everything with her. The more this happened the more Gillian's desire to be alone became a wish to leave James altogether. However, her concern for his distress, his insistence that he could not cope on his own, and the way he counted the days when she did go away, combined to make her feel paralysed; she did not want to be with him like this, but felt unable to abandon him. James thought that his 'clinging' must be driving Gillian further away from him, but at the same time saw his 'dependency' as his only remaining claim on her.

Ther.: 'What, in your view, is the explanation for your feeling of dependency on Gillian?'
James: 'I suppose I've never really, since I came out of home and joined the army—and the army's another mother—I've never really stood on my own two feet. I had an odd sort of childhood [he lost most members of his family while very young, and had a very negative experience of evacuation during the war, when he was about seven] and I suppose I developed a fear of being alone.' After some discussion, the therapist asks Gillian for an explanation of her sense that she has become stronger and more separate during recent years.
Gillian: 'I think I've always been reasonably strong, even as a child. I had a tough childhood, because my parents divorced when I was eleven, and I lost my mother, but I don't know—I seemed to sort of get stronger on it.' (It is interesting to consider the different constructions these two people put on their difficult childhood experiences; for each it is of importance, but they see the influence in opposite ways.)
Gillian: 'I meditate a lot, I'm probably more spiritual in all sorts of ways than James—that side of me is quite important, and, I don't know, maybe it has helped me.'

James talks some more of his need for Gillian, his anger with her for not being totally available, and his self-contempt for being so 'wet', while he nevertheless remains convinced that he could not survive without her. The therapist asks: 'Is it her in particular or could it be anyone?' This question is intended to be provocative, i.e. to focus James away from Gillian's misdemeanours in changing, and onto his own current sense of inability to change.

James: 'I think it's particular, but I don't know—it's probably just looking for a Mummy.'
Ther.: 'And I guess this has been a particular Mummy for a long time.'

Throughout the work with this couple the therapist repeatedly asks questions to clarify what it is they are working towards: divorce, work separation, personal separation while continuing to work together, or more personal autonomy within a relationship which might continue, externally, to look very much the same. There are no clear answers to this, but the repeated consideration of these questions brings up more and more facets of their relationship and sense of themselves.

James: 'I can sympathize with and understand women, when their children have grown up, feeling we've got to make an identity and do something for ourselves. But I don't feel that, and I think this is a problem for a lot of men, because they don't feel that.'

The discussion leads on to Eichenbaum and Orbach's thesis (1983) that men appear more independent than women because they have the hidden support of women; thus one of the tasks for men is to become truly independent.

James: '. . . That is, if you want to!'
Ther.: 'Or if life gives you a hard push.'
James: 'That's right, but I don't know—civilization and families and living together is about dependency. We are a dependent species, a species that's intended to be dependent.'
Gillian: 'I think we all should—I know we're all very individual—but I don't particularly want to be dependent on anybody. I want to feel able to be just myself, and be able to look after myself without feeling frightened. I want to be able to face death. I feel very positive about . . . just being me, and I would just like for it to be so that everybody could feel like that, then maybe things would be a lot easier.'

For this particular couple the resolution lay in James taking the risk of letting go of Gillian—the experience of not being constrained by his clinging and her own guilt allowed her to clarify that she did want to be with him, and they negotiated a relationship which gave both of them space to be autonomous but connected. However, the more general issues with which they struggle are universal, and probably require to be tackled, in some form and at some time, by most adults, in or out of therapy, and not omitting therapists themselves!

While ritual, challenging, humour, tasks and so on all played a part in the work with couples described in this chapter, there are connecting themes that run through all these various examples. These are the attitude of curiosity, which questions any and all assumptions brought by clients, as well as those held by the therapist and her team, and the attitude of respect for the great variety of patterns and views, even if these differ from the views and values held by the therapist herself.

CHAPTER 6   Working with individuals

BACKGROUND

Family therapy can be said to have originated from the dissatisfactions of psychotherapists working with individuals (cf for example Bell, 1967; Boszormenyi-Nagy & Framo, 1965; Bowlby, 1949, 1951; or Selvini, 1974). Therapists working, in particular, with children, adolescents, and young adults with diagnoses of psychosis, became increasingly convinced that, although clients might change in the course of therapy, they were unlikely to sustain these changes over time when back in the milieu of their families and daily lives. The attempt to find a way of addressing the 'significant system', that is the relevant change-producing system, as well as the theoretical new ground broken by Bateson and others, led to early experiments in working with those individuals, designated as suffering from problems, together with their parents or spouses.

Family therapy, like other new ventures, initially placed a tight boundary around its territory. In order for fledgling family therapy and systems thinkers and practitioners to gain clarity about their new approach, and to establish its distinctiveness, it was important to emphasize the *differences* between the 'new' and 'old' ways of working. The same process can be observed wherever breakaway groups begin to found new approaches. The fact that many of the founders of family therapy had a professional grounding in the psychoanalytic individual therapies perhaps accounts for the intensity with which early family therapy practitioners refused to contemplate work with anything less than 'the whole system'.

In recent years systemic therapists have become increasingly willing to work with individuals, even to the extent of talking about 'rediscovering the individual' (Jenkins & Asen, 1992; Selvini, 1986; Steinglass, 1991). The Brief Therapy approaches (Weakland et al., 1974) have always worked with individual 'customers' or 'complainants' from a problem-solving stance. The greater flexibility in regard to the specification of the 'significant system' is generally seen as a sign of systemic therapy having come of age. To continue the metaphor, it may be that the approach is now sufficiently mature to relax, acknowledge the wisdom and contribution of previous generations and other systems-based approaches, and to open itself up to a wide range of influences. Furthermore, having become skilled and confident in a way of working, family therapists will be asking themselves questions about those clients who do not respond positively to their methods—thus individual therapy might, in this context, be seen as a new and appropriate response, rather than simply a return to the past. However, for systemic therapists working with individuals this does not mean an abandonment, or even a dilution, of systems ideas. It means rather that it now seems possible to work with larger interactional systems even though only one member of such a system attends therapy.

THE 'SIGNIFICANT SYSTEM'

It is important to remember that the description of, for example, a nuclear family living in one household as a system, is merely a metaphor. That group of people does not literally constitute an organic or cybernetic whole—calling them a system is a description used by an observer. Where the boundaries of a system are placed is equally a 'punctuation' decided upon by the punctuator/observer/describer, on the basis of her theory, idiosyncratic observation, purposes in designating a system, and so forth. Some examples of 'significant systems' might serve to illustrate this point.

1.   In the early days of family therapy most therapists insisted on seeing the whole family—this was usually defined as all

those family members living under one roof. If fewer, or even more, people than designated by the therapist arrived for the session, this was likely to become the focus for a protracted battle of wills. Families were sometimes sent home without being seen, and no matter how gently or harshly the refusal was framed, many therapists agreed that the struggle over who would come to the session was perhaps the most crucial part of the therapy. Therapists were sustained in sticking to their guns by the conviction that working with a group other than the 'family system' was unlikely to be beneficial to the clients. Sometimes the validity of this point of view was borne out by experience (cf for example Jones, 1987).

2. Milan-systemic therapists in particular became identified with an interest in the three-generational pattern. This therefore would often involve working with the family living in one household, plus previous generations living in other households. Once the therapist started asking herself questions about *who* constituted the 'significant system', the arbitrary boundary around the people sharing one roof became nonsensical, but the problem of who to see became one that needed to be decided each time. Were lodgers or neighbours parts of a significant system? (cf for example the 'networking' innovations by Speck and Attneave (1974) where very large groups of people—sometimes as many as a hundred—were considered to constitute the significant system). Should systems therapists continue, to all intents and purposes, to ignore the world of work, given that a majority of their clients probably spent as much time and emotional energy in the workplace as in the home?[1]

It is obvious, therefore. that once the therapist *thinks* systemically, rather than working to a rigid *technique*, different

---

[1] An innovative approach to some of these dilemmas has been taken by Gaćić and his colleagues (1992) in their work with alcoholics. They work individually with the drinker and with the drinker's spouse, with the marital couple, with the spouse plus friend/support, with the family, with members of the family's community, and with the drinker's colleagues and employers, as well as making educational contributions to the media. This may sound overwhelming, but in their view this is the minimum significant system, and their excellent results bear them out.

decisions will be taken at different times to determine which collection of people is most significantly involved in the problems for which help is sought, and which people might most usefully contribute to solutions. Thinking about the therapist (plus team) as part of the observing system, and thinking about problem-determined systems (Anderson et al., 1986 and Chapter 1) rather than about families or individuals as having or maintaining problems, helps the therapist to think more clearly about which group of people should meet together to maximize the opportunities for change.

WORKING SYSTEMICALLY WITH INDIVIDUALS

Under what circumstances do systemic therapists, convinced of the value of working with family groups, agree to see individuals instead? Some of the answers provided by therapists will depend on their particular context; for example, systems therapists working in adult psychiatric contexts may feel constrained by their working system, its history, beliefs and political situation, to work with individuals even when they would prefer to meet with a larger family group.

Family therapists working in a wide variety of agency contexts have, over the last few years, noticed emerging patterns in relation to those clients who are seen individually for part or all of the therapy. These will be discussed below.

Clients without 'Significant Other' Relationships

Some clients seek therapy in a situation where they experience themselves as cut off from all intimate relationships, whether of family, friends or workmates. They live alone, do not have social lives, do not work, or work in isolation. This situation is likely to be part of the problem they bring to therapy, so that it would be foolish, as well as cruel, of the therapist to insist on seeing the client only in the company of others with whom they have a more than casual relationship. Such clients bring special problems to therapists of whatever persuasion. What would a systemic therapist offer to a client in this position?

An individual in the situation described here will probably have been considering his problems from an individual framework: that is he will assume that he is solely responsible for bringing about desired changes, and, most likely, solely responsible for his difficulties. A systems therapist will consider it desirable for individuals to claim responsibility for their actions, rather than shifting motivation, blame and capacity for action onto others. However, she will also bring an interactional perspective to the unfolding of the client's story. Via the use of circular questions she will attempt to establish connections between her client's experiences, points of view, and actions, and those of others who exist in the client's milieu, though he may not have regarded them as significant. She will have a view that new narratives, co-constructed between therapist and client, will lead to new meanings and/or new actions, so that the client will find solutions to his problems in ways that fit with his own history, values and preferences. She will assume that patterns evolve over time, sometimes with unintended consequences, and that understanding how a situation came about, and how it may change, does not necessarily involve knowing what caused it, or require the attribution of pathology. For a client working with such a therapist the effect of the *process* of the therapy is likely to be one of making connections, in his mind and in his world. The experience of locating himself and the difficulties he complained of within a network of meaningful relationships with people, ideas and events is *itself* part of the change process for him.

While individual therapists working within the more tra-ditional individual modalities, whether behavioural or psycho-dynamic, will no doubt see much that is familiar in the work of a systemic therapist working with an individual, there are certain significant differences within the technique of the therapy and, perhaps more importantly, within the thinking that underlies it. Systemic thinking, and circular interviewing, introduce into the therapeutic discourse[2] certain possibilities. The therapist's questions, statements, hunches, or attention to some areas of discussion in preference to others, have the effect of suggesting to the client a particular world view, which includes an assumption about mutual determination and the relevance of context, multiple possible realities, connections between the past, the present and the future, and the presence and relevance of others even though they may not be physically present in the room.

Example

Mr E was a man in his late twenties who came to therapy wanting help with his social isolation. He had had a very difficult and harsh childhood, which he had apparently survived by taking refuge in his intellectual skills. He was a mathematician living in almost complete social isolation. He had been in therapy previously and talked scathingly of the uselessness of his previous (and his current) therapist, despite the fact that during his time in the previous therapy he survived a period of suicidal despair, sleeplessness and physical collapse. His description of this was: 'I happened to be seeing X at the same time as I solved these difficulties myself'. He insisted that everything had a rational solution, and demanded from the therapist and her team some formula to solve his loneliness. He dismissed attempts to 'talk therapeutically', and saw the problem as if it was a formula capable of logical solution: he was attractive and intelligent, so why could he not get a girlfriend? The instrumentality of his attitude towards others, the fact that he dressed like a ragged tramp, and his evident fear of any sort of emotional closeness were dismissed by him as irrelevancies. His style of relating in therapy was adversarial: every question or comment of the therapist was challenged, disqualified or dismissed

---

[2] Like Goldner (1992b) I prefer the term 'discourse' to 'conversation' when referring to the speech between therapist and client. Although 'conversation' is the term most frequently used, it can convey a sense of casualness that does not reflect the meaningfulness of the interaction, and which sometimes misleads newcomers to the family therapy field into thinking that 'being with' clients and chatting represents an appropriately 'non-instructive' stance. As Goldner points out, a conversation may well be a chat, and may have no significant consequences. Her preferred phrase ('deliberative discourse') gives some sense of the weight attached to such interaction, and of the awareness that it is likely or desirable that significant consequences should follow it.

with contempt. He was in the position of the proverbial porcupine who could not eat while his hackles were up, and so starved to death.

Therapist and client agreed at the beginning of therapy (unusually for the therapist's practice) to meet for a year to see whether they could get anywhere with problems that had proved intractable in previous therapy. In all ten sessions took place. Typically the therapist would engage with Mr E in an increasingly symmetrical interaction (that is, meet his adversarial style and flat statements of fact with a similar style of her own). For example she would, via questions or shared opinions from the team, posit a point of view about his dilemmas that took into account his many hurtful experiences in relationships with others, refer to his habit of avoiding vulnerability, make connections between his actions and those of others, translate his rational statements or physical symptoms into emotional ones, etc. He would vigorously oppose this, deplore the therapist's stupidity, or compare her detrimentally to his previous therapist, while visibly enjoying the interaction, and showing every inclination to allow the therapist to substitute for relationships in his real life. The therapist's willingness to engage in his usual patterns, with some relish, combined with her frequent abandonment of the struggle, signifying that winning or losing was in her view unimportant, meant that the process of their discussions began for him to constitute an experience of multiplicity of styles of action. Similarly the therapist's continuous attempts to explore explanations, other than his rigid ones, for his solitude, gave him the repeated experience of multiple descriptions; even though he would not accept these points of view, he had to acknowledge intellectually that they existed.

By the ninth session his desperate 'stuckness'—mirrored in the equal 'stuckness' between him and the therapist—was evident as the central dilemma. He had tried every solution that he could rationally accept. He knew rationally, on the basis of previous discussions in therapy, that other solutions, attitudes, feelings, and ways of relating were theoretically possible, but could not bring himself to abandon his mathematically logical and rigid way of functioning.'I have tried all the solutions I can come up with, and I repeatedly find myself back in the same place.' It was as if he needed to find a route that would allow him to incorporate other ways of functioning without having to abandon the important safety of his belief in the saving grace of his logical mind.

In the course of the session the therapist had asked him, in an aside, whether he was familiar with the nine-dot problem. This is a mathematical puzzle in which nine dots are placed in a square formed by rows of three dots each, vertically and horizontally. You are required to connect all the dots by means of four lines only, without lifting the pen from the paper. The point of the exercise is that the problem cannot be solved without going outside the parameters of the imaginary boundary which one tends to place around the square formed by the dots. He was not familiar with it.

At the end of this session, after consultation with her colleagues, the therapist told Mr E that she was faced with a dilemma. She had a view of what was imprisoning him within his solitude, and had stated this view to him in the past. At the same time she knew that this view was unacceptable to him. It seemed to her that if she was ever to be of use to him she had to be true to her perceptions, experience, and points of view, but at the same time she was aware that doing so ran the risk of disqualifying him, not seeming willing to respect and accept his perceptions, experience, values and so on. However, she could not confine their discourse to the frame posited by him, since this seemed to her so clearly to constitute part of the problem; she was sure that if she did this she would not help him to make the changes he sought. The therapist said that she would continue to think about this, and in the mean time would send him the nine-dot problem in the post. He replied that he would solve it immediately and send it back to her by return of post.

He did not do this, but had solved it by the time of the next session a month later. Part of the session was spent discussing the methods he had used to approach the problem. He also informed the therapist of a number of significant changes he had made in the practical arrangements of his daily life—he had applied for and accepted a prestigious job, bought new clothes, and reframed his attitude towards the search for a woman so that he was now able to begin tentatively to explore ordinary friendships, rather than his previous method of not considering it worth while speaking to a woman unless he could be sure she would end up in his bed! He had also decided to view his past failures as a consequence of his own choosiness, rather than what he now for the first time acknowledged to be his fear of his own complete unacceptability.

Of course the nine-dot problem did not 'cure' Mr E. What might be described as the 'mortal combat' of the whole of the therapy, including his work with his previous therapist, had led to a point where he held all the ingredients for change in his grasp, but needed some metaphor that would enable him to make use of these without denigrating his entire previous life and the survival strategies that had enabled him to cope with severe emotional hardship. This metaphor therefore had to speak to him in his own language; thus he could allow himself, within the mathematical solution to the nine-dot problem, to 'know' that in order to solve his own problems he had to move outside the parameters of his previous explanatory system.

The therapist's statement to him was not intended as a paradoxical intervention. The dilemma she described was a very real one to her, and had become explicit between herself and Mr E over the course of the sessions. It can be observed again and again that when therapist/team and clients arrive at an impasse like the one above, this can often signal that the moment for change—for the creative leap—has arrived. Knowing this does not prevent therapists from becoming, at such times, frustrated, convinced of their own incompetence, and angry with their team's failure to help. It may be that reaching this point is essential in certain difficult therapeutic situations. In retrospect it often turns out that the clients had reached a similar point. Something about the mutual experience of being backed in a corner, with nowhere to go, seems to be essential to the burst of creativity that, so often, lifts clients and therapist to a different level in relation to the problem situation (cf Bateson, 1978a, pp. 248/9).

Similarly, giving him the nine-dot problem to do was not intended as a strategic intervention, in the sense that 'strategic' is often used to signify trickery and manipulation. It seemed an apt metaphor for this particular client, containing as it were both the rigorous language of logical problem-solving, and the surprising discovery that he would have to 'leave the field' in order to succeed.

Single Clients, Relationship Problems

All family and marital therapists will have had the experience of a referral in which one member of a couple presents, saying that the problem they wish to work on is the relationship with their partner, but that the partner either will not come to therapy, or has not been informed of the referral. This may often be accompanied by a statement that either or both partners agree that the problem lies with the client who wants to be seen individually.

When agreeing to meet with such an individual client the first session may be described, in the appointment letter and at the beginning of the session itself, as a consultation to determine jointly whether it is feasible to work alone with this client, or whether the therapist and client should jointly work out how to make it possible for the absent partner to attend subsequent sessions. The therapist will urge the lone client to be sure not to discuss matters which would make it more difficult for the absent partner to attend in the future, and may check from time to time, e.g. as complaints or the absent partner's misdemeanours are raised, whether this is safe ground or not. Of course this may mean that the client is constrained, in this first session, from telling the therapist everything she may need to know about the situation, but the therapist will make it clear that she would rather be handicapped by ignorance in this first session, than risk the absent partner, when he or she attends a later session, feeling that the therapist has already sided with the partner who attended the first session.

If the therapist and client agree, by the end of the first meeting, that it would be possible to invite the partner to join in the therapy, a number of routes are available for doing this, depending on the situation. Often one partner has come as a sort of 'scout' on behalf of the couple. The therapist's accepting, containing and neutral behaviour will then have reassured the client that this is a safe place where the couple can risk tackling their relationship difficulties. Therapists need to bear in mind that life is always much more complex than it seems in the therapy room. If this seems a cliché, consider the following common scenario. A woman comes on her own and wants to talk at length about her husband's violence or drinking or other misbehaviour. Nevertheless, she gives some subtle signs of relief when the therapist cautions her against the kind of discussion that may make it hard for her husband to join the therapy. When he does subsequently take part in the sessions it becomes clearer to the therapist that the wife—given that she also loves her husband, is aware of his vulnerabilities, and in the habit of protecting him—was in part checking out whether the therapist could be relied on not to take sides. Only if the therapist can be trusted to be neutral can the wife stop protecting the husband at her own expense; then they can begin to work towards changes in their relationship.

In the example above the client who came to the first session will make the necessary arrangements for the couple to attend the next one. However, it may often be necessary for the therapist to write to the absent partner, having discussed with the original client what will be said, to issue an invitation, and to give some explanation for the *therapist's* reasons for wanting the other partner to attend. It is usually a good idea to offer the absent partner an individual session on their own, to balance that given to the other partner; even if this offer is seldom taken up, it indicates the therapist's awareness of the likelihood of the absent partner's (justified) fear of an alliance having already been formed.

Sometimes, after seeing one half of a couple individually, the therapist may agree that this is the most appropriate way to continue working. It is always worth while bearing in mind the warning (Whitaker, 1969) that working with one partner, where there are marital/relationship difficulties, may place the therapist in the position of co-respondent! Having paused to consider the warning, the therapist might go ahead, because it seems to her and her team that the issues the client wants to discuss are more related to individual than to couples concerns; because she has become convinced that the other partner, despite opportunities offered, will not attend, and she does not consider that the individual client should be refused the right to have therapy; or because the situation seems to her to be one of danger, and the risk of working with the individual is outweighed by the risk of doing nothing.

Example

Mrs G came to a first session wanting to discuss difficulties in her second marriage. Indeed it seemed to her that she had made a great error in getting married at all, having done so on the rebound from her first husband unexpectedly divorcing her and marrying a good friend. She felt she had chosen badly, but felt ashamed, both of the hurt she might inflict on her second husband, but even more so of the triumph she felt her first husband would experience if he saw her fail a second time. In the course of the first session it became clear to client, therapist and consultant that there seemed no point in considering whether or not Mrs G could make a go of her second marriage until she effected a divorce from her first husband. It was therefore agreed to see her on her own.

In the course of the therapeutic discussions Mrs G came to the conclusion that she did not know her second husband at all well, and that she had in fact prevented all exploration of intimacy and liking between them, as if to do so would constitute an infidelity towards her first husband. She therefore realized that she could not tell whether his behaviour, which caused her a great deal of aggravation, was a cause or a consequence of her own distance from him, and her frankly expressed dislike of him.

Most of the therapy (6 sessions) was spent discussing her 'perfect' first marriage, and its shocking ending. She arrived at a point where she felt that she could retain many good memories of the first marriage, which had lasted for twenty years, without remaining forever in the position of Patient Griselda, and while feeling able to be angry with her ex-husband as well as clearer about her own part in what had happened. She now started to turn her attention to her current marriage. She thought ruefully that he was not quite what she would have chosen had she not been on the rebound; nevertheless she also thought she ought to give this relationship a chance. She repeatedly got stuck at this point. It seemed to both client and therapist that this now was the central dilemma: if she decided to give her current relationship a chance, she would have completed her divorce from her first husband.

Mrs G was a keen gardener, and had occasionally talked of her garden as one of her few pleasures, one which she also shared with her second husband. As Mrs G and the therapist were both sitting in silence, having spent a large part of the session talking their way through and around her dilemma, the therapist started to talk of a visit she had made to friends over the weekend. They had just moved into a new house, and had consulted her about a dilemma facing them in their new garden; at the bottom of the garden was a huge and beautiful copper beech, which shaded the whole garden. Their choice, put starkly, either was to keep the glorious beech and do without a proper garden, barring a few mosses and ferns, or to chop the tree down and start a new garden. The analogy between the story and Mrs G's dilemma was so obvious that it did not require spelling out. However, the therapist's friends' dilemma was discussed at some length, weighing up the pleasures of a new and functioning garden against the great grief of killing such a wonderful tree that had been there for so long. Mrs G left the session in a thoughtful frame of mind, and when she next came to see the therapist, after about a month, it was to report that she had decided in favour of the new garden.

Anecdotes, stories, or hunches that occur to a therapist who is 'tuned in' to the client's situation are more likely than not to be apt to the client's situation or dilemma. Nevertheless, what the client takes from the story, which aspects resonate, if any, and how they use it will be determined by the client's 'structure-determined system'—that is, the therapist can only speculate as to which aspects of the story about her friends' garden were meaningful enough to Mrs G to become part of her decision about her second marriage.

Appropriate Individual Sessions within Family Therapy

At times during work with a family it may seem appropriate to have individual (or couples) sessions with one or other family member, while retaining the flexibility to return to family sessions at a later stage. It goes without saying that this can only be done if rules regarding confidentiality and sharing of information are carefully negotiated with all family members beforehand. The situations in which one might be most likely to see a family member individually for one or more sessions, during or after family therapy, would be when working with adult survivors of childhood sexual or physical abuse, or when working with a family member exploring their age-appropriate separation from the family.

Because of the wider recognition within the helping professions, and therefore in society in general and in the media, of the existence and prevalence of the physical, sexual and emotional abuse of children, many adults who were abused as children now feel able to come forward to speak to a therapist, with the hope, this time, of being heard. They may come to therapy initially for other stated reasons, for example difficulties with their children, and may only begin to speak of their own abuse later on in the therapy; on the other hand increasing numbers are referring themselves with a specific request to work on the effects of their childhood abuse (cf Jones, 1991).

If other family members are available a systemic therapist's preference would usually be to see clients, such as those mentioned above, in their family context. Nevertheless, at some stage in the therapy individual sessions may often be useful. The telling of the details of the abuse, where relevant, may best be done away from other family members, given the client's previous experiences of breaches of privacy. (The problems presented by working with the screen and team with these clients will be discussed below.) Similarly, family patterns of silence, protection and denial may be entrenched, so that the survivor may initially find it easier to lift lifelong taboos away from their family of origin in the 'safe space' of an individual session. On the other hand abuse survivors may have a strong preference to be seen on their own, without either family of origin or current family members present, and respecting this wish would be part of the therapist's acknowledgement of the client's entitlement to control her own life—it goes without saying that the establishment and encouragement of such a sense of entitlement is a crucial part of the therapy.

Much of the early focus of such work would be on enabling the client to relate her *own* story with the expectation of being heard and believed. However, while validating the client's retrieval of her own perspective on the events of the past, and the way in which they influence the present, the therapist will also introduce perspectives that make it possible to gain a larger systemic perspective on the participation of all members of the system in the abuse, its maintenance and its non-disclosure in childhood, as well as the continuing patterns of relationship within which the abuse was embedded.

Example

Ms F had been seen with members of her family and is now, in the second individual session, talking of her fear of her stepfather who had sexually abused her throughout her childhood, and of her habitual attempts to be good and avoid attracting attention or causing trouble.

She has described feeling bad and dirty inside and therefore cultivating an 'innocent outside'.

Ms F: 'I tried always to be quiet and not in the way—sort of like the angel, you know—and you know that was hard for Mary (her younger sister). Because . . . imagine having a sister that is an angel. She was never good enough, because I made damn sure I was the best. Not intending to do anything to her, but . . .'
Ther.: 'But to have that innocent outside . . .'
Ms F: 'So Mary, everything she did, Mum always made her feel bad about everything . . .'
Ther.: 'So Mary was protected by you in the sense that you took the worst of your stepfather, and she was more free of that, but what she suffered was that of the two little girls she was the bad one and you were the angel.'
Ms F: 'And she used to get upset, she'd call me The Angel, and I'd say I'm not an angel, and she's say yes you are you're a bloody angel. Because to live up to me was a strain, and to live as me was a strain. It was ridiculous, but that's how it was. Mary said to me the other day, because I happened to say, God, you know, I really worked at it (i.e. being 'good') and she said yes it was awful being in your shadow. When I think what she's been through! Imagine having people say: this is the good one. It was hard for her. Of course my action had an effect on her which I didn't see . . . but I don't feel guilty.'
Ther.: 'I don't think it's something to feel guilty about. It's something about how the pattern . . .'
Ms F: 'It formed—it just formed. It just happened. At one time I would sit there and think Oh, you've done that to your sister, and take it all on myself. I don't now. I think that's just life.'

This is the first time that this client has started to look at the wider systemic ramifications of her abused role in the family. It is significant that she can do this from a position of systemic curiosity, rather than feel obliged to attribute blame or guilt.

Later in the same session she has been exploring the theme —central for her—of whether her mother knew that she was being abused.

Ther.: 'So if you try to think, there you were as that 8, 9, 10-year-old, how old would your mother have been then?'
Ms F: 'Well, she's 61 now, and I'm 29, so what would that have made her—if I was 10, she'd have been 43, about that.'
Ther.: 'So what do you think. . . if you had to try and think your way back to that, if you could see through her eyes, what would she have seen, what would she not have seen?'

Ms F: 'Well, she should have seen a pretty unhappy child. . . mind you, I was a good actress, so there again . . . I mean I covered up, as best I could, I think.'

Ther.: 'So she would have seen the angel.'

Ms F: 'She would have seen the angel, yes. But she must have had a feeling, especially at that age, with me always hiding and covering my body. I mean if my kid did that I'd go what's the matter? I'd want to know.'

Ther.: 'So what about back to the time when you went to tell her that he was touching you in a funny way (aged 6). What do you think might have been happening for her at that point?'

Ms F: 'She'd just remarried, and she'd been through a lot—a hell of a lot—and she was looking for security, and for a home and everything for us kids. When I told her that she may have took it that I was just a child and ignored it . . . because she wanted to. She chose to run from it because she wanted to.'

This exploration of different perspectives was taken up again and again in different individual sessions, and later in family sessions. Given Ms F's lifelong role as her mother's protector, and her mother's extreme reaction to the faintest hint of criticism, it would have been impossible for Ms F to do this same work in her mother's presence at this stage of the therapy. Later, in family sessions, relevant issues from the individual sessions could be considered together. The question of whether Ms F's mother knew or not is a useful example of the rationale for the interspersal of some individual sessions. To explore this with Ms F's mother in the session runs the risk of turning the therapy session into an investigative battle: did she or didn't she? In my view, even if it were possible to establish beyond doubt whether she did or did not know, such a verdict would have little relevance for the problem Ms F is struggling with. Therefore it is more useful for her to explore the problem in relation to her desire for certainty, her fear of the consequences of anger with her mother, her assumptions about blame and the assigning of responsibility, and so on, in the absence of her mother. In Ms F's words: 'I don't think she can make it better. I think I've got to make it better.'

As with Ms F, clients in the process of effecting separation from their families of origin, such as late adolescents, or clients with diagnoses of schizophrenia or the eating disorders, may well benefit from a few individual sessions interleaved with the family work. The participation in an individual session acts, in itself, as a marker signalling that this individual, who until now has been defined primarily in the context of the family, also exists in his or her own right. In this sense the discussion and negotiation in family context of an individual session can represent a rite of passage.

We all carry internal representations of important relationships, meaning systems, family myths and constraints. 'Significant others' exist not only within the corporeal reality of the family, but also within the minds—and on the shoulders!— of individual family members. The contributions and influence of these others can be made a part of the therapy even when they are not physically present.

Problems in Working with Individuals

As mentioned earlier in this chapter, the important question for systemic therapists is whether the clients in therapy represent the part of the significant system most able to bring influence for change to bear. When working with individuals this question becomes crucial, and the work may often be harder than it would have been if the therapist had thought more carefully about who to convene. Now that the individual has been 'rediscovered', there is a temptation for family therapists to climb on the bandwagon, and to forget why it was that therapists started working with families in the first place.

Systemic therapists in general tend to do brief work. Although sessions—also with individuals—are likely to be further apart, so that therapy may, for example, extend over six months or a year, sessions are usually few in number. There is an assumption, when working systemically, that clients will continue to do the major part of the work in the period between sessions. The job of the therapist in the session is to work in such a way that the client's system is most likely to be perturbed to a significant extent, thus enhancing the likelihood that clients will find new patterns and adaptations which will eliminate the necessity for organization around problems. This may be harder for an individual to effect than for a number of people, living together day in and day out, responding to one another and to the effects of the previous therapy session. In my experience individual therapy tends to take longer. This may be because clients and therapists share a cultural assumption which expects individual therapy to consist of frequent sessions and to last a long time; it may be that the kinds of situations or problem systems, where a decision for individual therapy is made, are particularly difficult to shift; or it may be, as early family therapists speculated, that when seeking change, rather than self-knowledge, this is best done in natural groups.

When working with individual clients a therapist, regardless of her own systemic assumptions, will have to take into account those relationship phenomena more thoroughly explored by psychoanalytically-oriented therapists. The systemic therapist may not choose to work actively with transference,[3] but given the greater intimacy of the one-to-one relationship, the absence of 'significant' others from the session, and sometimes the greater frequency and duration of meetings, the client's feelings for and expectations of the therapist may well require more attention than they usually receive in systemic family therapy. To put this more ordinarily, the sessions can become very cosy, and therapist and client can become overly attached to the meetings. It may also be harder for the therapist to retain a systemic perspective when working with one member of a system over time. Thus the therapist allies herself with her client's perspective, is no longer able to value her team's different perspectives, and finds herself in the position of her client's champion.

While the team can be invaluable in helping a therapist to retain multiple perspectives on her work with individuals, the presence of the team and the screen can also constitute a major difficulty. Many individual clients accept this way of working with ease, but many—far more than in family

---

[3] 'Transference' is the transferring onto the therapist by the client of inappropriate emotions and relationship expectations deriving from the client's own background. An interesting paper by Papadopoulos & Saayman (1989) explores an attempt to reconcile Jungian views with systemic approaches to the use of relationship attributions towards the therapist.

therapy—express reservations or unwillingness to work in this way. The basis for concern is clearest when thinking about abuse survivors. These men and women have, in childhood, and often throughout the rest of their lives, experienced themselves as powerless in relation to the abuses of power by others (cf also Chapter 7). They may have actual experiences of voyeurism, but are in any case highly likely to be uncomfortable about being observed by unseen persons whom they might well see as censorious. In general, the intimacy of a one-to-one discussion sits uneasily with the presence of a team on the other side of the one-way screen. Bringing the team into the room, as an attempted solution, may make things worse, as the client now is outnumbered. Doing without the team may not be a solution either, as it leaves the therapist more likely to slide into the pitfalls of cosiness and alliance as discussed above. Until such time as the systemic field brings forth some creative innovation to deal with this dilemma the best solution may be for a therapist, working alone with an individual client (where permission for the team and screen has been refused) to ask for the client's agreement to regular consultation for the therapist outside the therapy sessions, and perhaps to the use of video or audiotape for the purposes of such consultation.

In summary, systemic therapists may at times decide to work with individual clients, for reasons that seem persuasive. They should bear in mind, though, that systemic therapy, developed while working with families, does not have a well-articulated theory of individual functioning, nor has much thinking been done about technique in individual systemic work. A simple extrapolation of theories and skills developed in family settings is unlikely to be good enough; it would imply that systems family therapy possesses a universal theory and technique, while disregarding the theories and skills of therapists much more familiar with individual work than systems therapists tend to be.

CHAPTER 7   The abuse of power

INTRODUCTION

Recent developments in the systemic therapies place the therapist and the context of therapy within the observing/observed system (MacKinnon & Miller, 1987, and Chapter 1). Implicit within this stance is the opportunity for therapists to consider the effect of wider social and political contexts, as well as of the therapist's own history, theories and biases, on the way that families in therapy are perceived. It is interesting, therefore, that therapists espousing 'second-order cybernetic' approaches have, by and large, been slow to scrutinize the effect of their own gender and power status on how they see the difficulties of family members.

During the nineteen-eighties many Milan-influenced therapists have attempted to incorporate ideas obtained from the work of Von Foerster and others (cf Chapter 1) in their work. This 'second-order cybernetic' or 'observing-system' stance implies that the therapist is part of the therapeutic system she describes and observes. The therapist and the family mutually construct a description of the family's situation, and of the potential different options open to family members as they explore new ways of being together or different. The search is to find a construction of family relationships which does not require or maintain the presence of symptoms and problems. The therapist recognizes that her construction or description of the family does not constitute an objective 'out-there' reality about them; rather, it constitutes a description co-constructed between therapist and clients, which attempts to fit the experiences of the participants, while introducing also some difference. This new description does not necessarily have greater validity than other descriptions, but may have more desirable consequences than those previously adhered to by family members and other significant persons, including professionals.

Furthermore, some of these therapists have rediscovered aspects of the work of Foucault, notably in relation to the concept of dominant and subjugated narratives. Foucault (e.g. 1967, 1972, 1979, 1980) analyses and 'deconstructs'[1] the ways in which some ideas, practices, and versions of history become dominant, so that other voices and perceptions in relation to the same event become marginalized and silenced. These ideas do not constitute a blueprint for better therapy (Luepnitz, 1992), but do offer techniques for calling into question one's own habitual practices, which may well, through the force of habit and unexamined assumption, be found to be in contradiction to one's avowed ideals and theories. Thus including herself in the (self)-observing system should imply, in the first place, that the therapist is aware of her influence in deciding which narrative may become dominant, and in the second place, that she recognizes that she herself, like her clients, is organized and inevitably influenced by the dominant narratives of the social structures within which they all live.

However, as the work of critics (Golann, 1988; Goldner, 1985, 1992a; Hare-Mustin, 1986; Howell, 1992; Jones, 1990, 1991; MacKinnon & Miller, 1987; McCarthy, 1990 and numerous others) of family therapy shows, these ideas have often failed

---

[1] The concept of deconstruction is associated in particular with the practices of the French post-structuralists, such as Derrida (cf for example Derrida, 1976, Norris, 1987). Since Derrida has vigorously resisted any attempts to define deconstruction as a method—'All sentences of the type "deconstruction is X" or "deconstruction is not X", a priori, miss the point.' (Derrida, in Norris, 1987)—I shall not be so presumptuous as to attempt to give a definitive description here, but will merely indicate how a deconstructive lens, applied to comfortable and familiar descriptions, may sometimes help us to see what has been left out or marginalized. 'To "deconstruct" a piece of writing is therefore to operate a kind of strategic reversal, seizing on precisely those unregarded details (casual metaphors, footnotes, incidental turns of argument) which are always, and necessarily, passed over by interpreters of a more orthodox persuasion' (Derrida, in Norris, 1987, p. 19). Thus deconstruction can enable us to consider what lies behind a dominant narrative: if one view is being highlighted or privileged, what other points of view or versions of an event have been left out, rendered invisible, marginalized or subjugated?

to be taken to their logical conclusion, or to affect the mainstream work of practitioners of the new systemic family therapy, which has presented itself as democratic, co-constructive, non-hierarchical, neutral and value-free (Hoffman, 1990, Boscolo et al., 1987). It is noticeable that the critiques come primarily from women family therapists who label themselves overtly as offering a feminist critique, rather than coming wholly from within the systemic field. Perhaps it was only by virtue of the double description (i.e. deriving from feminism at d family therapy) that enough perspective could be gained to begin to critique the applications of the ideas of second-order cybernetics. These critiques are now beginning to influence the mainstream of systemic theory and practice. Goldner (1991a) looks forward to the day, before long, when it could be said 'that feminism has generated a second-order change in the theory, practice and ethical structure of family therapy' (Goldner, 1991a, p. 342). Systemic therapists, whether primarily motivated by feminist critiques or by a thorough incorporation of the implications of the second-order approaches (e.g. Hoffman, 1990) may arrive at similar endpoints (thus demonstrating the systemic premise of equifinality), where good practice will routinely consider the impact of social structures, power and inequality on the interactions of clients and therapists.

THE QUESTION OF POWER

The dictionary (Chambers, 1988) variously defines 'power' as 'the ability to do anything: capacity for producing an effect: authority: rule: influence: control.' Family therapy debate about the nature and existence of power has focused particularly on the last of these meanings.

Family therapists have long referred the question of whether power does or does not exist in family relationships, and whether power inequities and abuses were the business of family therapists, to what is loosely referred to as the 'Bateson/Haley' debate. It would probably not be an exaggeration to say that most family therapists have not read the original works on which this debate was based; however, different schools of family therapy are regarded as being allied with one or other of the protagonists. Milan-systemic therapists are, in general, seen as aligned on the 'Bateson' side (1978a, 1980), where the 'myth of power' (Bateson, 1980, p. 239) is regarded as a risky delusion for family members as well as therapists. This myth of power refers to the idea that, within a system, it is not possible for one unit or participant to exert *unilateral* control over another. Bateson also held the view that belief in the myth of power was likely to lead those who held this belief to acting greedily and destructively. It could be said that his objection to the idea of power as a central organizing reality in relationships, as espoused, in his view, by Haley (1961a, 1961b, 1969) was in part a moral and aesthetic objection. This may be connected with his increasing interest, after World War II, in ethical and ecological questions, and with his reservations about the thoughtless application of ill-digested ideas by pragmatic therapists in a hurry for results. The attribution of ideas such as 'there is no such thing as power' to Bateson is therefore a gross over-simplification. Nevertheless, his (remarkably) few statements on the topic of power have acted as a severe constraint on the ability of family therapists to think about the occurrence, use or attribution of power in systems. In the view of Kearney (1991) this is because Bateson, like Freud, attained the status of a patriarch in the field (of family therapy), thus being regarded as beyond comment or critique. If this is true, then a systemic perspective would require one to look not only at the way in which the patriarch laid down the law (Kearney, 1991), but also at the way in which the recipients enshrined the patriarch's words as being 'beyond comment or critique'.

Current systemic attitudes towards the idea of power are connected with another theoretical contribution derived from Bateson's work (1958, 1978a), namely the concepts of complementarity and symmetry. Complementary interaction, put simply, would consist of reciprocity between protagonists whose actions are responses to, and elicited by, the actions of the other, but are of a different kind. Thus a relationship in which one person behaves protectively while the other behaves dependently would be described as complementary. Other such complementary patterns could be, for example, admiring and showing off, domineering and submitting, writing and reading, pursuing and withdrawing. In symmetrical interaction the behaviours of the participants would be of the same kind, for example competition and competition, love met with love, generous acts with generous acts, mutual striving for dominance, or the shared wish to be the one who gets to define the nature of the relationship. As is obvious from the few examples given, there is no intrinsic implication of desirability or its opposite in these behaviours; however, the one could not be sustained without the response of the other. Thus when contemplating a complementary relationship such as that between, for example, an abuser and a victim, the attention of systems thinkers has tended to focus on the interactionality and system-maintaining reciprocities of this relationship, and away from the differences between the participants, particularly as these differences relate to access to choice and influence.

In more recent years Maturana's (1988) ideas about structure determinism have also influenced the way in which ideas of power in relationships have been dealt with by systemic therapists. Because he argues that the structure of an organism is the main determinant of how it will respond to a stimulus, it therefore follows logically that instructive interaction is an impossibility, i.e. the action of the originator of the stimulus may trigger a response but will not determine its nature, direction, force, etc. While Maturana is careful to point out that his ideas apply most specifically at the level of biology— and thus perhaps to individual human beings, but not to families—there is similarity here to Bateson's point (1980) that, in interactions between living beings, the response of B to an act by A will depend on B's internal state as well as B's construing of the relationship with A. Thus, again, it is clear that the part cannot unilaterally control the whole. However, to conclude from this that A's act has no influence on B, or that responsibility[2] for the consequences of A's act rests solely with B, is again an unwarranted conclusion.

---

[2] 'Responsible: liable to be called to account as being in charge or control: deserving the blame or credit: morally accountable for one's actions' (Chambers, 1988).

It is well known that ideas, no matter how elegant or well founded they may be originally, will, in the course of their repeated pragmatic application, become blunted, reified, mythologized and misunderstood. This then makes it necessary, from time to time, to return to the source and reexamine the ideas upon which practice rests, partly to rediscover what was said originally, and partly to critique such ideas in the light of further experience and thought.

While the application of the ideas summarized above to the practice of family therapy has been invaluable, and has enabled therapists to work with clients in a way that is more respectful and participatory, rather than blaming and manipulative, nevertheless some of the conclusions drawn from the understanding or misunderstanding of these ideas have led to therapeutic abuses and absurdities. Some of these will be referred to briefly.

There Is No Power

An oversimplified version of the ideas discussed briefly above has led some family therapists to the view that power cannot be exerted by one person in relation to another. A quick glance at the daily newspaper will of course reveal this idea for the absurdity it is; nevertheless theories do not always rest on common sense, and thus this idea requires to be taken apart and examined. A second and related idea, incorporated into systemic family therapy, is that—since participants in systems are in complementary or symmetrical interaction with one another, and the actions and meanings of each is recursively responsive to and eliciting of the actions and meaning attributions of the other—all system members therefore have equal influence within relationships.

These ideas can be explored by looking at the example of the complementary relationship between torturer and victim. The torturer cannot torture without a victim to torture; the victim cannot be victimized without a torturer. Once they are engaged with one another it can be said that the actions of the victim—screaming, suffering, showing courage and determination, begging for relief—act as triggers which elicit more of the torturer's torturing behaviour, just as the torturer's actions trigger the responses of the victim. It would be absurd, however, to suggest that the victim is responsible for the torturer's actions, or has equal responsibility and power in the situation with the torturer, or even—in the sort of reversal beloved of family therapy strategists—that the torturer can be usefully described as the victim of the victim. It is clear that they do not have equal choice and influence in relation to being in the situation in the first place, or to terminating the relationship. The torturer has more choice, influence and power in regard to what can be done to the victim, and to remaining within or leaving the field of relationship. (There are factors relating to context which are of crucial relevance in understanding such a situation, which will be discussed below.)

One could say, here, that the torturer does not have 'real' or 'absolute' power, but only such power as is attributed to the position and person of the torturer by him or herself, by the victim, and by their social context. Personal as well as social upheavals show that those who have been in the 'victim' position can, sometimes, by a change in their attribution of power and invincibility to another, change that other's access to and use of oppressive powers; slaves sometimes overthrow their masters, battered women murder their violent partners, 'velvet' revolutions can, perhaps, happen. However, it is morally perverse, as well as socially blind, to conclude that victims are therefore co-responsible for their continuing victim status (cf also Goldner, 1985, Goldner et al., 1990, MacKinnon et al., 1987, Jones, 1991, for more detailed discussions).

When such claims are made at the social level (e.g. some of the more extreme anti-Semitic claims made in relation to the Holocaust) they find relatively little support; we therefore need to consider why family therapists have so often taken a position which has the effect of holding all family members equally responsible for events, even for those events in which some members are severely harmed or damaged, such as where children are abused. There are differences between individuals in their ability, within a particular systemic pattern, to influence the outcomes of actions and interactions in that pattern. The failure to recognize this may be partly due to therapists' good intentions, which will be discussed in the next section.

Neutrality

In the move away from individually-focused, intrapsychic theories and techniques, family therapists were in part motivated by a desire not to attribute blame or pathology to individuals. Instead, by understanding the wider system and the way in which everyone's behaviour fitted into this, systemic therapists were able to achieve the positive or logical connotation of the behaviours of all participants. At times this may have stretched the credulity, not only of the clients, but of the therapists themselves somewhat; nevertheless, by standing back and taking a 'meta-view', it was frequently possible to think about behaviours and the meanings attributed to them by family members as making sense when seen in the context of the history of the system members and their interactions over time. This means that when therapists are approached by clients who are apparently stuck immovably with situations that make the participants unhappy, cramp their development, or land them in hospital or prisons, it is possible to have a view of the clients' situation that does not have to lead to the pathologizing or blame of one or other member.

This attitude on the therapist's part, and the active avoidance of the semblance of taking sides, form some of the main constituents of therapist neutrality. The therapist maintains neutrality towards points of view, towards persons, towards outcomes, and towards the overall system itself. This stance of curiosity (Cecchin, 1987) is one of the strengths of this approach, but is also perhaps one of the greatest sources of controversy and criticism. Apologists for the Milan approach and the later 'second-order' developments from it (Cecchin, 1987, Green & Herget, 1991, Hoffman, 1985, 1990, Jones, 1990, McNamee, 1987) have argued eloquently that neutrality does not imply coldness, distance, inactivity or lack of therapeutic empathy. It can be observed in work done by these therapists that the approach lends itself easily to the intense engagement of therapists and clients in their mutual curiosity to understand how they come to be in the position they are in, and how they may get out of it.

However, it may be that systemic therapists, in attempting to avoid the crassly punitive, judgemental and pathologizing behaviour which flows easily from a first-order cybernetic perspective (i.e the assumption that the observer is outside and objective to that which is being observed) have trapped themselves into a stance of *moral neutrality*. A therapist who is required to work with a father who has had sex with his daughter needs to be clear about the differences in access to choice, influence, independence, power and responsibility between father and daughter. The therapist will recognize that the actions of the father and the child have been influenced by social attitudes (such as obedience to parents, the myth of ungovernable male sex drive, etc.), as well as by personal and family events, beliefs and so on. Nevertheless, father and daughter do not have equal influence and freedom for action in this situation. To approach the therapeutic work as if they were equal would guarantee the further abuse of the child. As MacKinnon and Miller (1987, p. 145) point out: 'it may be those who lack an analysis of power relations who most easily, albeit unintentionally, engage in oppressive relationships'.

One of the cornerstones of systems-based approaches to therapy is the idea, discussed by Bateson (1978a) that we cannot not communicate; that is, silence, the refusal to engage in a relationship, etc. are *also* communications about relationship. It would be useful to bear in mind that a similar rubric would apply to the recognition of inequities in relationship. For example, a therapist working with a black family living in an inner-city area, who does not include in her hypothesizing, and in her discussion with the family, the possibility that they may be subject to racist harassment, is not being neutral. Instead, she is likely to be experienced by family members as implicitly and powerfully condoning their experiences of persecution by her failure to consider them worthy of comment (Boyd-Franklin, 1989).

When therapists attend to experiences of inequity in the lives of their clients, they may worry that doing so constitutes taking a non-neutral stance; however, *ot* attending to such inequities is likely to have the effect of (silently) condoning them, of giving the stamp of the therapist's authority to the idea that such relationships are so normal that they require no notice. Taking these ideas on board means that therapists will no longer struggle with the idea of whether paying attention to power abuses in or in relation to client groups will compromise their neutral and even-handed stance; rather, therapist concern will be with the pragmatics of *how* to pay attention to such relationship events in a way that maximizes the opportunities for change and choice of all members of the therapeutic system, including the therapist.

The Impossibility of Instructive Interaction

This concept, and the related one of structure-determinism (cf Chapter 1), rests on the observation that an organism's response to stimuli are primarily specified by its structure, i.e. regardless of the nature of the stimulus, an organism can only do what it can do. Thus organism or event A cannot elicit a response from organism B which is not potentially within B's repertoire. This idea, explicated at the level of biology by Maturana and Varela (1988), and resting on much of Bateson's work (1978a, 1980), has been adapted by systems therapists to mean that person A's action cannot specify person B's response; it will depend on person B's structure (which must be seen to include physical, physiological, emotional, relational and meaning-construing components) what the response to A's action will be. Therefore if I ask you to open the window, you may or may not do so. Your response will depend on a host of factors, such as whether you are tired or full of energy, hot or cold, angry with me or in a compliant mood, whether you see it as a reasonable request or an attempt at dominance, etc. I cannot with certainty predict your response, although I could make a better or worse guess, depending on how well I understand our current relationship and your situation. The fact that I cannot fully predict or control your response does not mean that I should refrain from making my request; it means that I should respect the fact that you will respond to it in your way. It also does not mean that my request is irrelevant to your response; my request *triggers* and *influences* your response, though it cannot *fully specify* it.

Considerable confusion has arisen as family therapists have attempted to adapt these ideas to their practice. Some have concluded that all action and intentionality on the therapist's part must be futile. Others have concluded that the therapist holds no responsibility for the response of the client; this then leads to an amoral stance where the therapist feels free to do anything whatsoever—or nothing—on the assumption that it is up to the client to make what they will of the interaction. Such absurdities aside, some of the applications of these ideas have significance for the debate about power and responsibility.

The idea that instructive interaction is impossible has been used to bolster the belief that one individual cannot exert power over another. This is illogical, since it is clear that the psychological and physical nature of human beings does permit them to be dominated and abused; their 'structure' allows of a range of responses, from helplessness to counter-attack, to such triggers. The context provided by their history and relationship with the abuser will further specify their response. Submission in the face of dominance does not mean that either the dominating behaviour did not occur, was impossible, or is not the responsibility of the dominator. It is, once again, the oversimplification of complex ideas that leads some family therapists to take up a stance which suggests that there can be complete equivalence between the influence and consequences of acts by different participants in a system (Goldner, 1985).

Furthermore, it is clear, whether considering single cells or complex human beings, that the predictability of a structure-determined response varies with the nature of the trigger.

Hitting a porcelain cup with a hammer, or shooting a person with a machine-gun, allows for a limited range of responses which can thus be predicted with a fair degree of certainty. Such predictability rests on an understanding of the interaction between the nature of the trigger, and what the structure of a unit specifies as its possible range of responses to such a trigger. Telling someone else what to do opens a far wider range of possibilities of response, and the outcome is therefore less predictable.

Thus respect for the idea of structure determinism does not mean that therapists can avoid thinking about the possibility of coercion within relationships, nor about the need to take responsibility for their own actions in the context of therapy.

Context-blindness

One of the critiques of individual therapy proffered by early family therapists was the failure to address the wider context of the individual client's life, that is the influence and mutual patterning between family members which could be seen as linked to the origins and maintenance of the client's symptoms. Systemic therapists have, in particular, also been interested in a historical perspective, and have paid considerable attention to the generational transmission of patterns, myths, and beliefs about roles and relationships.

It is puzzling, then, that some systemic therapists have balked at the idea of considering the wider contexts in which families and individuals live, and have branded attempts to do so as political. It is as if family therapists at this point come up against an invisible taboo which specifies that, while it may be useful, therapeutic, and progressive to consider individual processes in the context of intimate relationships, it would be dangerous, 'non-systemic', and—dreaded word—'subjective' to do so in the context of any of the other meaning systems within which people live.

> In this way, they refer to the autonomy of the family system as if it existed out there, instead of, as second-order cybernetics

point out, as a construction or punctuation of a process by an observer. Thus, the family is reified. The process by which the observer draws the boundary is forgotten and Milan therapists make the same error as first-order cybernetics. (MacKinnon & Miller, 1987, p. 150)

Any consideration of the contexts within which the family and its individual members structure their sense of self, their relationships, and their beliefs about how they may or may not live, must include, interwoven with the family's unique meaning systems, an awareness of the social, ethnic, historical and political contexts which affect the construction of reality for family members (McGoldrick et al., 1991). A systemic therapist will, in the process of hypothesizing and exploration with clients, be curious about how these individuals and their ancestors have construed their beliefs about, for example, the roles of parents and children, men and women, loyalty, closeness, separation, love, violence, and so on. It is also necessary to consider the influence of the culture's ideas, rules, role-prescriptions, constraints, permissions and allocations of power and choice.

Once therapists allow awareness of the social/cultural context to become part of their thinking it will be impossible to look at family patterns as if they belonged only to those unique individuals, or to behave as if those individuals' lack of choice and power to change their situations were a matter only of individual responsibility. Thus the inclusion of wider contextual factors, including political-historical power structures, will be seen to be an intrinsic part of what assures a therapist's responsible attention to all relevant issues which organize and influence the lives and well-being of clients. Two examples may illuminate this idea.

Example

Mr and Mrs X and their three children have sought therapy, and complain of the rebelliousness of the 15-year-old son, and also of marital stress. Mrs X is close to her two daughters (16 and 13), and to her sisters, their children, and her mother, who all live within about three streets from one another in the same mining village. Mr X has worked underground in the coal mines all his life (as did his father and grandfather), has been made redundant by the closure of the mines, and is unemployed. Mrs X has started part-time work in a factory (which prefers to employ women for piece-work), and the couple have undergone somewhat of a role reversal, as Mrs X is now the main bread-winner, whereas Mr X is taking on more responsibility for housekeeping work.

It is likely that a therapist who is thinking contextually will avoid framing the family's difficulties only in terms of the narrow confines of nuclear family relationships. Thus there will not automatically be an assumption that the family's problems are necessarily due to Mrs X's excessive closeness to her female relatives to the exclusion of the males in the family, thus blaming Mrs X for her husband's humiliation and her son's rebelliousness. Nor will there be a narrow or exclusive assumption that Mr X's failure to fulfil his role as head of the family has led to confusion in his son, who is calling for more paternal discipline by behaving in a challenging manner. Sensitivity to cultural and community contexts, and thorough exploration with the family of their own perceptions and values, will clarify a picture in which therapist and family will be able to consider a number of factors. These might include awareness of family patterns in certain mining communities, where 'leaving home' is not necessarily a desirable event, and where sons and daughters remain close to their families of origin, physically and emotionally. In such communities 'women's culture' may be carried through shared domestic work and child-rearing, while 'men's culture' would be carried through a sharing of dangerous and difficult work, in fact and in anticipation. Where men and women share membership of such significant in-groups by virtue of their gender or their family origins, the primacy of the marital bond can not necessarily be assumed. An open-minded exploration of these beliefs in the clients and their culture may then lead to the idea that the family's current problems are linked to a necessity to adapt to changed circumstances which have affected the way in which they construe their relationships and ideas about themselves. Thus the son's rebelliousness may be linked to an implicit request to be helped to construct an adult identity without the automatic path which would previously have offered, not just work, and an adult role, but a model for relationships of closeness and distance to men and women inside and outside the family. Similarly the marital stress experienced by the couple could be seen as an expression of their attempts to work out satisfactory ways of reorganizing their lives in relation to work, self-esteem,closeness and traditional male/female roles, against the background of a community which is being forced, by economic and industrial events, to reconsider its traditional structure.

While the way of thinking in the above example may cast a somewhat wider net than is always employed by systemic therapists, there is probably little in the example to elicit dissent. Consideration of a different example may then highlight the way in which some contextual influences are easily integrated into work with families, while others cause therapists to balk.

Example

Mr and Mrs Y and their three children (16, 15 and 13) have sought therapy to get help with the 15-year-old son's rebelliousness and with marital stress. They describe a situation in which Mr Y often behaves aggressively—shouting, throwing things and threatening—and occasionally becomes violent. His violence is most often directed at Mrs Y, but sometimes at the children also. Mrs Y usually behaves in a fearful and placating manner, trying to anticipate his moods, and sometimes interposes herself between him and the children when she thinks he may become aggressive. She is close to her two daughters, and used to be close to her son before he reached puberty. The son now refuses to accept any discipline from his mother, and behaves in challenging and aggressive ways to her and to his sisters. Mr Y is sometimes called in to ensure his son's compliance with rules. Mr Y has recently been made redundant, and Mrs Y has in the last two years been doing part-time work.

In order to work effectively with this family it will not be enough to look, for example, for some circular pattern whereby it can be postulated that Mrs Y's nagging, or fearfulness, or greater financial independence, or sexual unwillingness, are, together with his loss of work status, making Mr Y feel impotent, leading to his aggressive behaviour. It is common in the family therapy literature to see descriptions of such work, where the therapist's conceptualization of the situation rests on an unacknowledged assumption that the two adults function from a base of equality, that is of equal access to choice and power. Such a view can only be sustained if the therapist confines her gaze to the interactions between the two partners alone, without taking into account the ways in which their actions, feelings and assumptions have also been influenced by social constructions of their roles and identities. If a therapist works with the couple and family from such a basis the end result will be, not neutrality, but an aggravation of the situation of inequality (Hare-Mustin, 1991a).

A therapist in this situation would have to explore with the couple and their children a number of levels of belief and behaviour that are pertinent to the dilemmas of the family. Briefly, these might include the following: How did Mr Y acquire the belief that violence (whether verbal or physical) is an appropriate response to situations of vulnerability or stress? What were his individual experiences, in his family and with his peers, that confirmed this belief? What are the cultural and social role ascriptions that make violence an acceptable or even an attractive option for him? How did Mrs Y acquire the belief that it is acceptable to be in a relationship with a violent partner? What were her individual experiences, in her family and with peers, that convinced her that she can neither defend herself nor leave an abusive relationship? What are the cultural and social role ascriptions that contribute to her belief that she should accept her partner's behaviour? What are the circularities of belief and action that organize Mrs and Mrs Y's continued participation in a destructive pattern? What have the children learned, from their parents and their culture, and how is this learning influencing their actions, now and in the future, in particular the ways in which they construe their gender roles?

In addition to these explorations, the therapist also needs to acknowledge and discuss certain extra-familial factors which are likely to act as considerable constraints on the choices open, in particular, to Mrs Y. Frustrated therapists, working with couples where battered women remain with violent partners, often blame the woman for her failure to look to her own welfare, either in terms of leaving or of using her own authority and that of outside sources to put a stop to violence within the relationship. Before a therapist can begin to struggle with the complexities of the emotional reasons why women may remain in life-threatening relationships (Goldner et al., 1990), the pragmatic circumstances have to be considered. Will Mrs Y have legal protection if she leaves, or if she stays? The answer is probably not (Edwards & Halpern, 1991; Jukes, 1990), and will partly depend on yet more extraneous circumstances such as class, colour, articulateness, neighbourhood, money and family and friendship networks—all of which are recursively looped with the degree of access an individual may have to choice and power. Will she have somewhere safe to go, and for how long will this safety last (Edwards & Halpern, 1991; Elman & Edwards, 1991)? Could she ensure her children's safety? How much disruption will all family members have to face in regard to schooling, work, ability to earn, prejudice and so on? Research (e.g. Kiely & Richardson, 1991) shows that women and children generally suffer dire financial and social consequence after divorce.

Recognizing the factors which give Mrs Y less choice in this situation, and working with the ways in which gender role beliefs in the culture have influenced the ways in which Mr and Mrs Y and their children behave, does not mean that the therapist is dragging her own political values into the therapy. It is the only way in which she can begin to contextualize the actions of the participants, so that there is no question of blaming either of the marital partners unilaterally: instead they are offered the opportunity to begin to increase their options for action within and outside of their relationship. By understanding how they have come to hold the beliefs which now contribute to their stereotyped and rigid interactions, they can begin to exercise some choices.

As Goldner and her colleagues have pointed out (1990) in order to work adequately with all relevant factors, in a manner that has the potential for freeing men and women to choose to relate non-abusively to others, therapists should employ four levels of description or explanation. She calls these *the psychodynamic level*, referring to the internal descriptions of self and other carried by individuals; *the social learning level*, which refers to the ways in which particular men and women have been socialized; *the socio-political level*, which refers to all external power differentials, including men's subjective sense of entitlement and privilege to rule women, and women's belief that they must serve men; and *the systemic level*, which refers to the transactional sequences around the immediate problem, and the processes related to the individual, couple, family, treatment and social contexts of clients. Here, as in other areas of therapeutic endeavour, the therapist needs to refrain from making either/or choices, and to search for a way of working clinically at a 'both/and' level.

THERAPIST POWER

Systemic therapy, influenced by second cybernetic ideas of co-construction and the impossibility of instructive interaction, and feminist therapy, influenced by attempts to move away from hierarchical, professionally-imposed styles of working, have both explored the ways in which therapists may shed power in the relationship with clients (Andersen, 1990, Brodsky & Hare-Mustin, 1980, Hoffman, 1990, 1991, Jones, 1990). Family therapists, working with teams and screens, have abandoned their earlier styles, in which the consultation team behind the screen was kept anonymous and used to make pronouncements of great power and éclat. Attempts have been made to purge the theory of its adversarial and militant metaphors (Selvini & Selvini, 1991). Greater attention has been paid to the degree of openness and democracy displayed by the therapist in regard to ways of working (cf Chapter 2), but also to demonstrating real respect for clients' own understanding of what might or might not fit for them, and for their creativity and common sense in deciding what constitutes solutions, and when therapy should end. Despite these advances, there are many aspects of therapist power (attributed and/or claimed) which remain unexamined in practice.

When a client approaches or is referred to a therapist, there is immediately a difference between them which may be translated into a power difference. The therapist is on home territory—and since the home territory is primarily that of being in a familiar professional situation, this idea would apply even to those therapists who make home visits—while the client is likely to be new to the idea and rules of therapy. The therapist has 'played this game' many times before, the client seldom or never. The client is by definition unhappy, confused or uncertain, and is coming to discuss private matters with a stranger. The therapist, regardless of what her personal problems may be, is not engaging in the relationship with the client in order to expose her own troubles. It is a one-sided intimacy, where the client will be expected to be self-revealing and the therapist not, or certainly not to the same degree or about the same topics. Any reader who has visited their doctor when feeling under the weather but unsure of the cause will know just how much a normally confident person's sense of helplessness can be activated by contact with a professional helper.

In addition to the contextual cues discussed above, there are other factors which will contribute to the therapist finding herself in a situation of unequal power with clients. Western culture tends to attribute a somewhat intimidating power ('X-ray eyes') to therapists; the fact that clients have been unable to resolve their difficulties without help will add to the strength of this attribution on the part of the client towards the therapist. Therefore, whether or not the therapist chooses to see herself as being in an unequal power-imbued relationship with the client, she is likely to be perceived as such. The therapist is less likely to abuse this power if she acknowledges its presence, than if she believes her own propaganda and considers that she has succeeded in shedding her power. In common with feminist therapists, systemic therapists can behave in ways throughout their work with clients which lean towards the re-empowering of clients, the demystification of therapist power, and the widening of client choices, also in respect of the client's attitude towards and judgement of the therapist, while nevertheless not shirking the professional responsibility to be skilled, experienced and competent.

A systemic therapist is in charge of the conduct of a session. With few exceptions she decides when it will start and end; no matter how much she behaves in responsive and reflexive ways in selecting her questions and topics with reference to client overtures, she nevertheless has more choice than the clients do about the direction of the therapeutic discussion. Indeed, this is her responsibility. It is therefore important to remain aware that every question asked, every focus chosen, every line of discussion explored, means the underscoring of those particular questions, foci, etc. as significant, and by implication the relegation of other unexplored topics to obscurity.

Recognition of these built-in inequities within the therapist–client relationship leads us to areas where therapists may abuse the power vested in them. Blatant abuses have been adequately described (Aghassy & Noot, 1990, Chessler, 1979, Masson, 1988, Showalter, 1985); the focus here will be on the more subtle ways in which therapists may use the power of their judgement and perception to blind them to client situations.

Example

A male therapist discusses a client couple with colleagues. The wife in the couple has said that she wishes to leave her husband, no longer loves him, and no longer desires him sexually. The husband cannot accept this, has become very depressed, and his wife has expressed her willingness, given their long relationship, to work with him in therapy on finding his feet again. The therapist, in discussion with his colleagues, refers to the fact that the woman is wearing a pink blouse, and looks attractive; he states that this shows that she wishes to make herself sexually attractive to her husband, and therefore cannot mean what she said about her attitude towards the marriage. She is therefore shamming for some reason, and the task of the therapist will be, in part, to call her bluff.

A deconstruction of the therapist's statement will reveal a number of assumptions underlying the judgement made about the female client. His statement can be boiled down to the following components: She looks attractive to the therapist, therefore she has attempted to make herself attractive, which shows that she wants to attract her husband sexually.

(a) The therapist has noticed what the female client is wearing, and whether she looks attractive or not. Has he noticed what the male client is wearing, and does he find him attractive? Psychiatric and clinical literature is of course full of examples in which women's mental and moral health is judged on their impact on the eye of the observer. Had the woman in this couple looked ugly or slovenly (to the therapist) this might, also, have been taken into account in his diagnosis, while the man's appearance remained equally unnoticed.

The therapist is allowing his own *unexamined* response to influence his judgement of the woman, and therefore to steer the direction in which he will lead therapy, and the way in which he will interpret the couple's difficulties. Since such unexamined responses are in part socially constructed, this example might be equally pertinent if the therapist were described as female. While the therapist's gender is likely to be relevant to the judgement of the woman's attractiveness, the power which infuses his declaration about the woman client rests on his assumptionthat his view is objective, and therefore represents a truth about the client, as well as on his role as an arbiter of mental health. The fact that such a judgement is made, on such grounds, about the woman and not about the man reflects the cultural stereotypes which organize the therapist and the clients. While they remain unexamined, such stereotypes will continue to influence therapy.

(b) Women are socialized to present themselves as attractively as they can manage. They grow up to experience themselves as held within, and given identity within the eye of the observer (Berger, 1972; De Beauvoir, 1953; Greer, 1970). Women do not easily experience themselves as having validity independent of their appearance, and thus the act of choosing clothes that will make her look good is likely to be second nature to the female client, and not bound up with a particular intentionality on a particular day towards her husband or, indeed, towards the therapist. However, her good taste in the choice of her blouse, and her 'presentation' are seen as active declarations in regard to the other, and as being primarily other-directed; i.e. there is no consideration of the possibility that she might be looking good because it makes her feel good, because her mother trained her always to dress properly when leaving the house, or because she put on the first things that came to hand. There are two profoundly sexist implications which underlie the therapist's assumptions, namely that a woman and her inmost feelings can be defined by how a man sees her, and that a man's attraction to her is her responsibility. This attitude is on the same continuum as the one that holds rape victims guilty for wearing shorts.

(c) The therapist assumes that his perception is normative, not subjective. That is, he does not consider that the degree to which he sees the female client as attractive may be a problem in therapy, particularly given the couple's situation, which might affect his even-handedness in his work with them. Instead, he attributes his own feeling—attraction—to the woman, and continues from there as if he is objective, that is outside the situation described, and offering an impartial assessment of what is 'really' going on between the couple.

(d) No really means yes, when said by a woman. The application of this belief to legal and social attitudes to rape does not need to be documented here. In therapy it means that a therapist showing the bias discussed here, will weight the contributions of the man and the woman client differently, and will use his therapist power to undermine the validity of the woman's discourse. Is it a coincidence that this will happen at a point where the woman is expressing a choice?

Example

A female therapist meets with a couple whose six-year-old daughter has been sexually abused by a man outside the family. The therapist is aware of the mother's guilt over her failure to protect her child, and spends a large part of the session exploring the degree to which the mother should or could take responsibility for what happened. The father is relatively silent throughout the session, or, to put it another way, the therapist addresses few remarks or questions to the father, other than commenting on how supportive he has been to his wife. Examining the assumptions underlying the therapist's behaviour again yields ideas and stereotypes derived from social and personal constructs likely to have a deleterious effect on whatever benefit the partners might derive from therapy.

(a) The therapist's behaviour is organized by an *unexamined* attitude which regards mothers as the primary parents; she therefore understands the mother's sense of guilt, chooses it as a focus for the session, and may even assist her in getting this into a reasonable perspective.

(b) However, because of her unexamined assumptions it does not occur to the therapist that the father may be feeling as distressed, guilty and involved as the mother. To the degree that she does not invite him to explore such feelings, she invalidates them in the context of therapy.

(c) In addition, the father is struggling with his own confused sense of being implicated in the abuser's actions, because of their shared gender, and would like an opportunity to evaluate his past and future relationship with his daughter in the light of this experience. The therapist does not pick up any of the cues which might make this possible, which has the effect of making the man even more uncertain about the validity of his ideas, since for him this would constitute exploring new ground. Does the therapist hold an (unexamined) view that the father, because he is a man, *does* share in the abuser's misdeeds?

(d) The therapist sees herself as a friendly, open and unauthoritative person, and if asked to examine her actions in therapy, would probably say that she is more organized by being a woman (i.e. someone who is good at facilitative relationships, but not very dominant) than by being a professional who holds authority (i.e. someone whose acts and utterances are imbued with expertise and power). Therefore she does not consider the impact of her silent communication to the man. From his perspective she carries considerable authority as an expert in human relations, and on the nature of the effects of sexual abuse. Thus her failure to validate his position has the effect of disqualifying his experience and any attempts he may have wanted to make to help himself and his daughter in the future.

THE CONTEXT OF POWER

The increased awareness, in Western societies, of the existence and incidence of the emotional, physical and sexual abuse of children has obliged family therapists working in these societies and cultures to expand their systemic theory so as to account for these actions as well as to find therapeutic ways of dealing with them. Observation shows that relationships of dominance and abuse occur in a variety of situations: in these societies it is primarily men who behave violently towards women, children and other men; adults (female and male) who abuse children and old people; whites who oppress blacks or other ethnic and religious minorities; heterosexuals who set the norms which marginalize homosexuals; the employed who legislate for the unemployed, and so forth (Boyd-Franklin, 1989; Collins, 1991; Kingston, 1982; Ussher, 1991). The common denominator in these relationships is the continuum between power and powerlessness. This does not, of course, mean that every adult, white, employed male abuses the power available to him; nevertheless, as Hare-Mustin points out, (1991b, p. 8) 'although individual men say they do not feel powerful, men as a class dominate women as a class, and benefit from that domination'. As a white who grew up in South Africa, I could paraphrase the above to say that while not every white person in an Apartheid society acts (or thinks and feels) in a racist manner, nevertheless every white in such a society receives the benefits and privileges that derive from their membership of the dominant group. As Kingston (1982) has pointed out those who are in positions of potential power, by virtue of their socially, historically and individually mediated situations, will be less likely to misuse power when they acknowledge its existence, in particular if their preferred self-image does not include concepts of powerfulness. As a client who had been sexually abused as a child said, when reflecting on a new relationship with a loving partner: 'I've realized for the first time how much power I have been given because of being loved so much. This is a new feeling for me; I must be careful not to abuse it.'

Patriarchal or androcratic cultures (Eisler, 1988) are based on patterns which are hierarchically structured and therefore construe difference as conveying implications of superiority or inferiority, and greater or lesser access to choice, information, wealth or authority. When therapists acknowledge this, they place themselves in a position to act ethically, that is, 'to act so as to *increase* the number of choices' (Von Foerster, 1990). Behaving ethically, within the belief structures of an observing-system stance, also means bearing in mind that one's own current stance is contingent and open to reassessment; that one's perceptions are always and inevitably subjective, historically and contextually influenced, selective, and (paradoxically) elective. In other words, although our views are open to many influences we also hold responsibility for them. Thus the views examined in this chapter, about the nature and relevance of power relationships in families and between clients and therapists, must also be understood as not representing immutable truths, but as reflecting a temporary position within a continually evolving process; indeed, the best that can probably be said for such a point of view is the fact that it remains open to change. This makes it possible for a therapist to hold certain values and perceptions 'and yet to accept their relativity in recursivity. . . systemic thinking . . . an ethical attitude which demands from a person to have the courage to permanently reflect about his or her own premises' (Krüll, 1987). Or, to put it another way, 'As advocates of systemic irreverence we suggest one way to survive in the field, and perhaps the world: to stay alive and flexible, to question any naive belief in "Truth"' (Cecchin et al., in press).

CHAPTER 8 Working with systems other than families: 1. Consultation

BACKGROUND

Because the systemic approaches use a theory of interactive systems, with the focus on communication and patterning over time, rather than a theory of individual or family health and pathology, it has been a logical step to extend the work of systems practitioners into consultation with systems other than families. In general the same principles are seen to apply, whether working with a family or, for example, a work group. Of course there are differences which need to be considered when moving from therapy with families to consultation to a 'stuck system' of therapist plus family, or to larger groups not united by ties of blood or intimacy. Over time these wider applications of the skills learned in the therapy room have received increasing attention from systemic therapists.

The idea that consultation may be useful connects with the basic tenets of systems thinking. Gregory Bateson (1978a, 1980) introduced family therapists to the idea that 'binocular vision' or 'double description' may lend new perspective to the perception of the observer. This concept has been applied in a variety of forms throughout the history of family therapy; a number of current applications will be discussed.

One of the definitions of the word consultation given by the *Chambers Concise Dictionary* is 'to consider jointly'. Many therapists (e.g. Wynne et al., 1986) would like to use the term consultation for a range of activities including therapy, because consultation implies a relationship where the client/consultee freely seeks the (usually) brief assistance of the consultant, and remains in charge of what will be accepted or rejected, while the consultant's task is to use professional skills to maintain a relative meta-position ('meta' in the sense of joining with, but not being wholly part of) in respect of the consultee's system, in order to facilitate change of perception or action on the part of the consultee; this fits with current trends in systemic therapy.

Like much contemporary family therapy, consultation tends to be brief, problem-focused, alert to strengths and resources, and collaborative. Terminology is always problematic. For example, the more usual definition of consultation is the act of seeking or giving advice—a position which most systemic therapists would repudiate. The terms 'therapy' and 'patient' have, to systemic therapists, unacceptable connotations of illness and cure; the term client, while preferred by many in its sense of one who employs a professional, has unfortunate associations of dependency (Chambers, 1988); long use in social work contexts has, for some practitioners, strengthened this meaning. Terms like 'customer', 'service user' or even 'user' have been proposed and discarded because of negative associations in their popular use. It is an interesting thought that the inability to find generally satisfactory, 'ideologically pure' terms to describe one's practice, and those members of the public on whom it depends, may well suggest a deeper malaise within the 'mental health' field than the discomfort displayed at the verbal level.

Discussion of consultation in this chapter will exclude therapy in the usual sense, i.e. as described in the previous chapters. Similarly, consultation between peers working together in a therapy team (in case discussion, in the therapy room, via one-way screen or closed-circuit video, or in reflecting teams), as discussed in Chapter 2, will not be considered here.

CLIENT-FOCUSED CONSULTATION

Because systems theory implies that different views may be obtained from different perspectives, therapists may ask for consultation when they and/or their clients feel that the therapist/client system has become 'stuck', i.e. that therapy is not leading to resolution of difficulties as the therapist and the clients expect it to. This consultation may be sought from peer colleagues or from acknowledged experts. The primary assumption is not that the consultant can help because she is more skilled than the consultee, but because she is able, by virtue of her consultant role, to hold a meta-position relative to the 'stuck' system. This meta-position is relative, not absolute; that is, the consultant, by virtue of engaging in consultation, becomes a part of the new system which is problem-determined in relation to the situation that brings about the request for consultation.

The acknowledgement that a relative meta-position can only be partial, but can be held to some degree, and with diminishing effect over time, is similar to the attempt to maintain distance by a team behind a one-way screen, by means of spatial differentiation, widely-spaced interviews, and so on (cf Chapter 2). The consultant's different perspective on the situation, when conveyed to the consultee (usually the primary therapist) is then likely to reintroduce double description into the thinking of the consultee or the consultee plus clients, and thus to free them up to continue their work.

Consultation to a primary therapist about work with clients may take the form of a discussion between this therapist, perhaps accompanied by colleagues or seniors, and one or two consultants. A systemic consultant is unlikely to offer views about the primary therapist's work with a case without taking into consideration the therapist's work context, so that the participation of involved colleagues may be crucial. The advantage of using more than one consultant is that they can differentiate their own roles within the consultation, thus building in another meta-layer of observation. In a model similar to that of the team approach to therapy, one consultant will interview the consultee(s) while the other holds more of an observing position; consultant and meta-consultant may then take time out for discussion, elaboration of hypotheses, and the planning of responses to the consultee.

Either in consequence of the sort of consultation discussed above, or as a first option, the consultant may meet with the primary therapist together with the client family. There are several reasons for doing this. Sometimes a straightforward request for such a consultation is made by a therapist, often one who is sophisticated in the use of such a structure. At other times the initial request may be for the consultant to accept referral of a family, where the original therapist describes themselves as having failed; this may be responded to with the suggestion of arranging a consultation meeting for all involved first, to assess the situation, and with the explicit goal of seeing whether the consultant's fresh perspective might help to resolve the impasse between therapist and clients. It is particularly important to be alert to unvoiced feelings of failure when families are referred on, by family therapists, to those seen as more expert. Taking such a referral, and doing successful work with the family, is likely to leave the original therapist feeling incompetent, whereas acknowledging that anyone and everyone is likely to feel stuck at times, and can benefit from consultation, may eventuate in a newly empowered therapist continuing their own work with their clients.

When meeting with a therapist and client family the emphasis of the interview is on the relationship between them, and on what has led them to feel stuck in their joint work; all participants may not, of course, agree that they are stuck, and this in itself is likely to provide interesting new information to the therapist/client system. The consultant will have access to her team for inter-session discussions, while the primary therapist is seen as a member of the consultee system; this implies, for example, that the therapist will remain with the family while the consultant meets with her team for the inter-session discussion (Van Trommel, 1984).

It is not useful for a consultant therapist to take over the therapist's function and conduct a therapy session with the clients in the presence of the therapist. The result of such actions is likely to leave the therapist feeling deskilled, and to put the clients in a difficult position, in that they may wish to take advantage of the skills of the new therapist/consultant, but doing so may make them feel disloyal to the primary therapist. Thus the consultant will begin by talking with the therapist and the clients about the history of their relationship, their different views as to how therapy is going and what impasses may be occurring. Since the primary therapist is usually the consultee rather than the family members, who may merely have complied with their therapist's request to come to a consultation interview, good manners dictate that the consultant should start with the therapist's view of the reasons for seeking consultation, and should, moreover, act in such a way throughout the consultation as to validate the therapist rather than increasing their sense of failure.

Example

Mark Thomas, a probation officer, referred a family he was working with in consequence of Peter, 15, having been placed on a supervision order for repeated delinquent acts. Mr Thomas said that he was obliged to continue his supervision of Peter, but felt he had failed in his attempts to work with the family, and wanted the work taken over by someone more 'expert'. He readily agreed to a consultation interview, as did Peter's family.

In the consultation meeting Mr Thomas described his own observation that he repeatedly sided with Peter against his father. This was related to his experience of Peter's father as very aggressive, which he confessed he felt intimidated by, and which made him see Peter as a victim. He considered this unhelpful both as regards any possible therapeutic work with the family, and as regards the requirement on him, as a probation officer, to keep a realistic eye on the possibility of Peter re-offending. He had no such difficulty about objectivity when working with Peter on his own. Exploration of this, and of the family members' views about the process and difficulties of the family therapy, led to a new and significantly different exchange of views between Mr Thomas and Peter's father. The latter described himself (with backing from his wife) as having survived a period of considerable depression following back injury and redundancy from his labouring job. Peter's trouble with the police had come as a last straw to this stressed family, and it seemed imperative to them that the father should show himself capable of filling the role of head of the household in relation to discipline, since he felt a failure in every other respect. Discussion of their joint sense of failure led to an exploration of the circularity of the pattern in which they were involved, so that the more Peter's father saw Mr Thomas as speaking for Peter (who tended to be quiet and inarticulate), the more he felt threatened in his authority and closeness in relation to his son; the more he responded to this by asserting his displeasure with Peter, the more Mr Thomas felt obliged to protect Peter. The opportunity to discuss this, together with other observations about pattern elicited during the interview, and commented on by the consultants, allowed both worker and family to feel validated, and enthusiastic about continuing their joint work.

Sometimes a decision by a professional colleague to refer a case to the consultant for therapy may be appropriate; it may, for example, be based on an informed decision that a different theoretical approach will be more appropriate at this stage of a client's development. A joint consultation interview with the original therapist and the clients may then form a bridge, avoid future problems of loyalty or rivalry, and may play a part in allowing the previous therapy relationship to be terminated appropriately.

Example

A colleague who works in a different psychotherapeutic model (individual cognitive therapy) wanted to refer a client because he felt that the client would at this stage benefit from an interactional model, but also asked for one or two joint sessions together with the client. He had worked over a period of some years with the individual client— a man who had no other social relationships—and felt that he had helped him with aspects of his difficulties. However, they had now agreed that they could not usefully go further, and that the therapist's way of working was unlikely to provide further resolution of the remaining difficulties. The therapist's major reason for wanting a joint consultation was that, in his view, he was having more difficulty letting go of the relationship than the client. In the course of two three-way meetings the patterns relating to this were explored and clarified, so that the initial therapist felt less guilty about ending work with the client; this exploration proved of great value to the consultant in later work with the client, since, not unexpectedly, the patterns that had allowed the first therapist to feel so enmeshed and helpless and responsible were in part a function of the kind of invitation to relationship that this client extended to would-be helpers.

Consultation in relation to work with a family may also, under certain circumstances, take place without clients or an external consultant; i.e. professionals involved with a particular family may jointly consult with one another. Such consultation will have the intention of clarifying inter-professional boundaries, differences or similarities of viewpoint or in the patterns of interaction established with clients.

Example

Mrs Peters requested family therapy for herself, her husband and her two adolescent children. She was dissatisfied with previous involvements with other professionals, and wanted 'an independent opinion' and 'a fresh start'. As is usual in beginning to work with clients who are, or have been, involved with other professionals, the therapist spent some time discussing the nature of the family's previous involvement with workers, including what had seemed to be more or less helpful. While such discussion can often help a therapist to gain understanding of the family's norms and preferences in regard to professional assistance, and can guard against the repetition of unhelpful patterns and suggestions, the therapist and team in this case found, after only a few sessions, that they had arrived at a point that seemed to replicate that arrived at with previous workers, so that Mrs Peters felt prompted once again to begin the search for an independent opinion. Since the relationship between therapist, team and family was a cooperative one, though unfruitful, an agreement was made to try something different.

Following a joint therapist, team and family meeting with a consultant, it was agreed that the therapist would convene a meeting of the relevant professionals who had, in the recent past, been involved with the family. While the family agreed to this, and cooperated in supplying a list, it was decided that they would not attend this meeting; its focus would be, explicitly, on the multi-professional patterns of involvement, many of which seemed to be doing duplicate work, some of which had become involved via Mrs Peters's search for independent opinions, and others via statutory and legal responsibilities. The meeting would be chaired by a professional who had had no involvement with the family.

Accordingly, the therapist wrote to those professionals whose details had been supplied by the family, explaining the purpose of the meeting, and asking that they send one representative only from each agency currently or very recently involved with the family or its individual members. They were also asked to extend the same invitation to other agencies that, to their knowledge, were similarly involved.

Fifteen people attended this meeting, each representing a different professional organization. Some of them had not known of the involvement of the others; some had not been mentioned by the family, either because the family had forgotten about them, or because the family did not know that they were involved! A salutary experience for all participants came from calculating the cost of the meeting in terms of the hourly wages of all those present, and in considering the similarity of patterns of interaction and impasse as they emerged from the various narratives. A proposal emerged from this meeting, namely that the family therapist would be given six months of 'clear space' to see whether one way of working, uncomplicated by alternative and different interventions from other professionals, might be helpful to the family. This meant that all the other professionals, including those representing the police and the courts, would 'hold off' for six months; requests from the family for 'fresh views' during this time would be referred back to the family therapist. If it proved impossible to hold off, e.g. if crises demanded immediate action, such action would be discussed with the family and the family therapist to see whether alternatives were available.

These decisions were discussed with the family, who agreed to attempt also to abide by the six-month moratorium. The therapist, with input from the family, sent a 'newsletter' after each family therapy session to all members of the professional network, in order to enable them to be reassured that they were not neglecting their professional responsibilities by taking no action. In the mean time the family therapy was enhanced by the therapist and her team's perception of the 'isomorphism at multiple systemic levels' (Imber-Black, 1991) which had been afforded by the meeting, so that ideas about family patterns and their replication in network relationships became usefully available to the work with the family.

It is important, when receiving a request for consultation, as well as when starting a consultation interview, to be clear about boundaries and responsibilities. The consultant is not clinically responsible for the case, and does not decide what use, if any, will be made of the consultation. The sorts of questions systemic therapists ask themselves when receiving therapy referrals take on an added dimension when consultation is requested, since the work is even more likely than in the case of therapy to involve multiple contexts and systems; lack of clarity, confusion around boundaries and roles, and lack of attention to the other systems (professional, community, sociopolitical, etc.) involved with the worker or the clients can undermine the effectiveness of the consultation.

Who is asking for the consultation? What is this person's relationship to the clients, and position in their agency? The person making the request, and coming to the consultation, may not be the person from whom the impetus derives. For example, a junior worker may be seeking consultation at the urging of a senior who is in doubt about her competence, or in defiance of a senior with whom she disagrees. If new ideas emerge in the course of the consultation, is the consultee in a position, in their agency hierarchy, to implement these? Why is consultation being sought now?—i.e. what events in the worker's agency, the clients' lives, or the interaction between these, may be creating a crisis or an impasse at this moment? Are there other agendas besides consultation? For example, a therapist who is feeling isolated—perhaps due to staff turnover and loss of close working colleagues—may seek consultation as a way of connecting with like-minded others, or to get support in maintaining a particular theoretical stance in an unsympathetic work environment. A consultation request may be an unacknowledged bid for training or professional development. Selvini (1984) points out that the person making the consultation request may be someone who finds themselves 'the loser' in agency interactions, so that the request may be a bid for alliance or covert coalition. Failure to clarify matters such as these will lead to confusion and dissatisfaction for all involved.

Example

May Smith asked for a consultation interview together with a family she was working with, with a view to possible subsequent referral. She had attended a training event at the consultant's institution, and—perhaps because of the false sense of familiarity induced by this—the consultant and her colleagues did not clarify the nature of the request, with the result that they found, after the consultation session, that they had contributed to a worsening of an already difficult situation.

Ms Smith was a trainee who was coming to the end of her placement in an agency where she had been assigned as a keyworker to a young woman (Barbara Brown) who had a long history of outpatient and inpatient treatment, dating from early adolescence. Ms Smith had befriended Ms Brown, and had got to know her parents in numerous meetings which were not quite designated as therapy nor, wholly, as friendly liaison. In her meetings with Ms Brown, Ms Smith had been talking to her about self-assertion, and had welcomed a few recent attempts on Ms Brown's part to assert her wishes. However, given Ms Brown's history and the nature of the wishes expressed, these attempts alarmed her family, the staff of the residential unit, and the psychiatrist in overall charge of her case, all of whom saw this new behaviour as indication of an imminent relapse. It emerged in the course of the consultation that all these professionals had advised against attendance at the consultation, considering a family therapy approach as likely to do more harm than good. The family had decided to attend because, as Ms Brown said, they were fond of Ms Smith and wanted to help her. However, they were anxious about the loyalty conflict this entailed with their daughter's main professional helpers, and had therefore kept their attendance at the consultation a secret.

This is an obvious example of what to avoid! It was clear that Ms Smith was at the bottom of the hierarchy in her place of work, both because of her student status and her imminent departure. Her hopes for Ms Brown, partly based on friendship and partly on newly encountered systemic ideas, put her in conflict with the more experienced professionals who had the authority to make decisions about Ms Brown's treatment. Her search for an alliance (or covert coalition) with a prestigious institution representing the style of working she thought appropriate for the Brown family, was meant to be her parting gift to the family; instead, it became a source of contention which forced the family into a conflict of loyalties. Although the consultant and her colleagues subsequently did what they could, via open communication with all members of the wider professional system (with the negotiated permission of the family), to retrieve the errors made by them, this was not wholly successful.

Thorough exploration of the context and meaning of requests can clarify what the relevant system is, and which bits of work need to be done first before others can be attended to. In complex cases the consultant's relative meta-position in relation to all members of the consultee system can become crucial.

Example

Mr Vaughan, a social worker, asked the consultant to see a foster mother (Mrs Price) and her two foster children with a view to helping him assess whether the children were well placed with her, and whether she should be encouraged to pursue her intention of adopting them. Exploration of the context and history of the request revealed a very tangled and problematic situation, with major disagreement amongst professionals and between professionals and Mrs Price. Because of this it was decided that seeing the children and offering yet another opinion was unlikely to be helpful at this stage. Instead, Mr Vaughan and Mrs Price were offered a joint consultation, as the two persons most directly involved in the care of the children, most overtly in conflict, and with most direct authority to negotiate and carry out decisions.

Initially both of them found the idea of joint consultation difficult, but agreed to try it. Mr Vaughan was reluctant to be placed on a level with Mrs Price, given their conflict and the erosion of his sense of authority and certainty; Mrs Price made it clear that she was willing to attend any and all meetings, on the advice of her solicitor, only in order to 'show willing', and without expecting to benefit. The consultant considered it appropriate to treat them as equal participants, since they were both being paid by the State to ensure the welfare of the children fostered with Mrs Price; she was respectful towards Mrs Price's scepticism and guardedness, and worked in such a way as to make it clear that seeing Mr Vaughan as a co-consultee did not diminish his status as a respected colleague.

Discussion with the two of them suggested that the hostility between them, and the threatened breakdown of plans for the children, could be seen as a function of the way their pattern of communication had become entangled with factors outside of, but relevant to, their joint concerns. Before Mr Vaughan's joining the service a number of decisions had been made about the children with which both he and Mrs Price, to different degrees, disagreed. It was clear that he did not feel able, as a professional, to speak freely about his disagreement with his new colleagues and seniors in Mrs Price's presence; she, on the other hand, expressed hers vocally and, despite a long and previously satisfactory relationship with the social service department (as foster mother to other children), was now seen as a troublemaker. Given Mr Vaughan's concern about past errors committed by his agency he had attempted to see the children, and also Mrs Price, frequently, since on the one hand he felt that they had been neglected by his predecessors, and on the other, given Mrs Price's antagonistic attitude, he could not be certain that she was the best person to have care of the children and needed to satisfy himself on this score. Since he did not feel at liberty to explain all of this, and since both Mrs Price and the children had become very suspicious and alarmed at any attention from social workers, fearing that they might be separated, he was met with hostility and silence. This increased his alarm about the welfare of the children, and made him more intent on seeing them, particularly without Mrs Price, so as to hear what their concerns might be, and for fear that her by now overt antagonism to the social services was influencing the children against speaking to him. His attempts to do so increased Mrs Price's sense of persecution.

Joint exploration of these and related matters led to the establishment of a workable, if not cordial, cooperation. Over the lengthy period leading to adoption of the children by Mrs Price she and the children, as well as Mr Vaughan and other professional workers involved in the situation, used the consultant and her colleagues from time to time as an 'independent' group to assist with the thinking through of new steps and difficulties.

A source of potential difficulty is the confusion that sometimes arises between consultation interviews and so-called demonstration interviews. The latter constitute a phenomenon that has become a feature of some family therapy teaching events, and consist of a visiting therapist, in the course of a workshop or conference, interviewing a family plus primary therapist while the workshop attenders simultaneously observe the interview via a one-way screen or closed-circuit television. While this sort of event was initially greeted enthusiastically by most, its drawbacks have become increasingly obvious, and have recently begun to be discussed in print (Cade, 1989/1990; Harari & Bloch, 1991).

The training context will put pressure on the consultant to attend primarily to the requirements of the audience—that is, to demonstrate the skills for which they have been hired by doing an entertaining interview focused more on the interests of the viewers than on the requirements of the consultee or the family. Most therapy (and this includes consultation) is only intermittently riveting to the onlooker; some of the most valuable work may be done in quiet, painstaking attention to detail and to relationship. This is why most trainers, if they use case material for teaching, will use edited videotape which, moreover, can be viewed and reviewed. With the best will in the world a consultant may not be able to avoid having primary therapeutic and consultation agendas contaminated by their involvement in a conference context.

It is unlikely that the best interests of the family and consultee will be served by such a demonstration. Indeed, the most honest way to introduce such a setting to clients would be to say (as some trainer/consultants do) that the clients are there primarily for the benefit of workshop or conference attenders, and may or may not themselves benefit incidentally. The consultant in such a setting is unlikely to be in a position to do a careful examination of the context and history of the consultation request, as discussed above (and also by, *inter alia* Imber-Black and numerous others (Wynne et al., 1986)); a 'one-shot' connection is unlikely to give rise to responsible follow-through on any further work that needs to be done, let alone the longer-term follow-up and feedback which will inform a consultant's future work. In addition the request for consultation may often be inappropriate. Consultees may have been 'selected' by those more senior in the hierarchy, or in organizing roles in conferences, and may then have to find a family to bring to the consultation. Such a family may be chosen not because there is an impasse in the therapist/client relationship, which is the appropriate reason for seeking consultation, but because they reflect relatively well on the consultee, who may be understandably unwilling to expose all their doubts and missteps to an audience of strangers.

CONSULTATION DIRECTED TO WORKING GROUPS

Many of the principles discussed in the previous section apply when consulting to groups of people with dilemmas related to their work settings, or working relationships with colleagues, rather than to client/therapist impasses. Requests for consultation may follow the reaching of an impasse or crisis (Bloch, 1986), but may likewise be triggered by positive changes or the possibility of new initiatives and directions. Systems therapists are working as consultants in an ever-widening range of settings such as schools, the courts, religious organizations, the full spectrum of health organizations, special task groups, community groups and businesses (cf Campbell et al., 1989; Dowling & Osborne, 1985; Gorell Barnes, 1991; Salamon et al., 1991; Steier & Smith, 1985; Wynne et al., 1986). Borwick (1986) warns that systems therapists should not expect to consult to businesses without a thorough understanding of how such organizations work, and in particular of how they differ from families. His warning that, although systems theory may have wide relevance, the thoughtless application of techniques from one context to another may have unforeseen and unwanted results, applies to more than consultation to businesses organizations. The Milan group have pointed out (Cecchin & Fruggeri, 1986) some of the perils of attempts to carry techniques from one setting to another. When their trainees, who worked in contexts very different from theirs, tried to apply techniques they had observed in Milan to their own settings, they found that, while it may be useful to think systemically, one's particular actions must be determined by the requirements, constraints and possibilities of the particular contexts in which they occur. When consulting to working groups it is important to bear in mind that, unlike families, their relationships—which are temporary and dissolvable—are organized primarily by common tasks, not by intimacy and emotion; thus the consultant's focus is not on emotional relationships but on role relationships (Borwick, 1986; Mason, 1991/1992). Deciding who should be involved in such a consultation, i.e. which members constitute the significant system, may be more complex than when working with families; it may, at times, be inadvisable to meet at all unless the relevant group can be convened (Cecchin & Fruggeri, 1986).

Consultations to working groups, particularly when problem-focused, are likely to be brief, i.e. to consist of one or a few meetings only, and may fulfil a variety of functions, including overt or less direct requests for education and support. It therefore becomes crucial, as in the categories discussed in the previous section, to be clear about the nature and source of the request, the responsibilities of the consultant and the consultee(s), and the boundaries to be observed. Similarly, knowledge of the context of the consultee organization, its place in its community, and the external influences impacting upon it, can make a considerable difference to the applicability or otherwise of the consultation offered.

As Imber-Black (1986) points out, organizations in the mental health field can be particularly beset by built-in incompatibilities, e.g. the injunction to be cost-effective, set against the injunction to be therapeutically effective. Those workers dealing with the assessment, disclosure and treatment of sexual abuse provide a case in point.

In such contexts external pressure derives, in part, from the intense media interest displayed when misjudgements occur, so that workers may feel that they have no leeway for failure, and that their choices are limited to omnipotence or ignominy. At the same time financial pressure means that many of them will carry excessively large case loads, which may prevent them from paying what they would regard as adequate attention to any one case. At every level of such an organization staff are likely to feel overburdened and under-resourced. The outcome of such tensions may be that workers resort to carrying out the letter of the law; while it may be sensible, in a situation of little support and constant scrutiny, for workers to 'cover their backs', the resultant sense of not doing what may be humanly and therapeutically the best for their clients will lead to depression and a sense of burn-out.

A consultant in such a situation may well decide that the most useful input would be to offer assistance in gaining a broad view of the situation—which will counteract each individual workers's sense of individual failure—and to offer educational input on the way in which 'helper systems' may come to mirror 'client systems'. In other words, organizations set up to combat and treat abuse may well develop into abusive systems, where the workers experience themselves as the victims of their managers, their clients, the government, the law and the media. The outcome of such consultation should lead to both workers and managers being able to consider the legitimacy of adequate staffing, training and support.

When the request for consultation comes from one part of a beleaguered system, and is likely to be seen by other parts of the system as a bid for coalition on the part of the primary consultee, it becomes imperative for the consultant(s) to proceed in such a way as to be seen as even-handed and open to a multiplicity of views. The consultant does not have an axe to grind as regards outcome, but is there to facilitate discussion, negotiation, and perhaps change amongst the members of the consultee system. As some of the participants in the following consultation said at follow-up: 'It taught us that there is a wealth of experience and advice available (within the system)—and that all we have to do is ask', and 'relationships were definitely improved; much greater respect is afforded each other. Since then there has been agreement to setting up a six-monthly "audit" and joint meeting to look at our working practices.' On the other hand the opinion of other participants in the same consultation was, that although the situation had changed for the better, they did not think that this was due to the consultation and felt that any improvements were due to the efforts of the group itself.

Example

A request for consultation came from Ms Johnson, who had recently taken up a post in a new area. Because of changes in the law, her position placed her hierarchically above other professionals who would traditionally have been seen as more autonomous, and as being above her in the professional hierarchy. Her function was to oversee good practice in relation to clients' rights, and she soon ran into major disagreement with the staff of a well-established residential agency. The disagreement took on major proportions, involving differences in theoretical orientation, tradition, and interpretations of the issues involved. Neither side felt able to alter their points of view, and although Ms Johnson had the right to enforce her views legally, she thought that this would bode ill for future working relations. She therefore asked for outside consultation, with the sceptical agreement of the other professionals involved in the dispute.

The consultation was arranged on 'neutral ground', and took the form of a circular interview of about four hours with the twenty-odd mental health professionals assembled, followed, after discussion between the consultants, by a sharing of observations and ideas by both consultants, which utilized suggestions for action which had already begun to emerge from the consultee group. The consultant and her colleague/consultant made it clear from the beginning that they understood the impact of their having been invited on the initiative of Ms Johnson, and attempted to communicate, by the nature of their questioning, that they were equally interested in the validity of the views of all concerned, were alert to resources and creativity on the part of the participants, and that eventual decisions would rest with the consultee system, not with the consultants. Since actions count louder than words, they were also careful to give the same message at all communication levels throughout their time with the consultee group, e.g. they avoided sitting down with only Ms Johnson at lunch-time.

As stated earlier, consultation requests can often contain many layers, e.g. the request may be for help with resolving an impasse, for educational input and information, or for modelling of interviewing and consultation processes and techniques.

Example

A group of therapists working together in a state-run clinic asked for a consultation to discuss future developments in their service provision, in the light of pressure from financial managers, increased demands on their time from service-users, and changes in their own theoretical orientation in the direction of a systemic approach. Part of their recognized function was to provide consultation to other professionals working outside of their agency in 'the field'.

In response to this request the consultants proceeded, in the first part of the consultation, as in the example described above: that is, a long circular interview elicited the views, attitudes, differences, similarities and so on within the large group of colleagues, followed by a discussion meeting between the co-consultants, who then fed back to the consultee group. Following this, and after discussion of responses by the consultees to the consultants' opinions, the focus of the meeting then moved to a more overtly educational one. The consultants and consultees went back over the consultation, which had been videotaped, and discussed points of theory and technique, with particular attention to how these could be applied in the consultees' work with their own consultees. The 'unpacking' of the components of the consultation served not only a training function, but also helped to shift the complementary consultant/consultee relationship to a more symmetrical one of colleagues who all worked as consultants to different systems.

A multiple focus, while potentially problematic, can also help to engage all the participants in a large system which is the recipient of consultation. Borwick (1986) in his consultation to business groups, will at certain points in the process break the group up into smaller task-focused groups, whose deliberations are then fed back to the consultants and other participants. The Stockholm team of Ylva Almquist-Fritz, Eva Rosenberg and Lars Theander (Mason, 1991/1992) use ideas, derived from the reflecting team approach of Tom Andersen and his group (1990), in their consultations to business organizations. Thus they will interview sub-systems of the organization, while their own team and other sub-groups of the organization observe; this is followed by each of these groups having the opportunity to voice their reflections on the interview and on each others' comments. As they point out, this reflective process offers an efficient use of time and an active involvement to all.

The nature of certain consultation requests may make it impossible for a consultant to claim full 'neutrality' towards people and ideas. Groups may request consultation in relation to their attempts to move towards anti-racist or anti-sexist practice, or because of a particular ideology which informs the work of an agency (e.g. Women's Refuges) and may therefore choose a consultant specifically because of their interest or expertise in such an area. At the same time, it is unlikely that all members of such a group will share the group ethos to the same degree, so that a consultant's ability to be open to polyphonic discourse will be crucial.

Example

A group of workers in a residential unit for young people requested consultation around the issue of their own attitudes towards gender and sexism, which they saw as problematic within staff relationships and in relations between staff and young people in the unit. The consultants were approached specifically because they were known to have an interest in this area, and had published on the topic.

At the start of the consultation process, having introduced the way of working (i.e. a circular interview conducted by the consultant while her male colleague observed the interview from outside the group) both consultants declared their bias in regard to the focus. They discussed their interest in the topic of gender-sensitive practice, talked briefly of the history of the development of this interest in their work setting, and of the fact that their own positions on a 'gender-sensitive continuum' were different, reflecting, *inter alia*, their different professional histories and gender. They also declared their commitment to respecting all points of view. Thus, while they did not make a futile attempt to pretend that they had no personal views, they committed themselves to a position of respect for difference among individuals and attitudes, and emphasized that members of the consultee group, individually, would be responsible for what the group did with the outcome of consultation.

This stance was utilized throughout the consultation by the demonstration of even-handed interest in the eliciting of the wide range of views present in the group, and in the positive framing of views which dissented from the majority position. The following extracts from the discussion will illustrate this process.

Male worker 1: 'I've got to be honest—my own feeling is, we have a lot of personal experience like our own family upbringing. It's inevitable, though we won't push it on to the kids, that it will come out somewhere. I don't know about this gender business . . . I'm going to be very interested to see what the hell does come out of this morning.'
Consultant: 'Does this mean you're sceptical?'
M.W.1: 'I am, I really am. Having said that, I shall be very interested though . . .'
Cons: 'What's your worst guess?'

The discussion continued with an exploration of his worst guess—that nothing would come of the consultation. The group went on to discuss the fact that, in the view of the majority, the other major sceptics had absented themselves from the room.

Interestingly these absent sceptics were identified as being, on the one hand, those high in the hierarchy who were seen as hostile to changes which would imply greater gender sensitivity and gender equality in the work group, as well as, on the other hand, a small group of workers strongly identified with a feminist position, who had said that they did not believe change would come from the consultation, and were unwilling to participate in a farce. This is a significant view, since workers are often alive to the possibility that management may arrange consultation as a sop, to calm down dissent, but without the intention or the hope that it will effect change. The consultants had expected all members of the group to be there, since careful preparation had included attention to the hierarchy of the organization, and the location and authority of the consultation request, and since a major commitment had been made by the organization, e.g. closing the unit down for the day, so as to enable all workers to attend. Nevertheless, finding that there were last-minute absences, they decided to proceed, while incorporating absent members in the discussion via repeated speculation on their probable views, and on the assumption that, if the consultation did constitute a significant perturbation in this work system, the members present might be able to carry the consequences of consultation to their absent colleagues.

The discussion of different group members' attitudes towards the consultation continued, and a second sceptic identified himself.

M.W.2: 'If you're talking statistically I suppose there is a difference between how men and women will react in a given situation, but amongst the people in here it's very difficult to say that all the men react sort of macho, and all the women nag. . . . The conflict is a conflict of styles, not a gender issue.'
Cons: 'You are not in agreement about the reasons for today's meeting?'
M.W.2: 'No. To be honest with you I thought I'd come here, chat away for a few hours, and leave no different.'

This was met by considerable hostile laughter from other group members, which prompted the consultant to say:

Cons: 'We all here know enough about group work to know that it is useful to have people in the group who voice the sceptical position. Otherwise one can get swept into a group enthusiasm that is not necessarily anchored.'

This statement may be seen as reframing the sceptical position as helpful to the group, and as restraining the group from attempting to change too rapidly; these are ideas which are familiar in systemic therapy, as well as useful at a commonsensical level. The group hoping for a more gender-sensitive approach to their working relationships had in the past kept quiet, since each person considered her or himself to be alone, and the general ethos of the unit (not to mention the wider social context) had made them assume they were in a minority. As views were canvassed through the group, an exhilaration built up from the discovery that these attitudes seemed to express the views and intentions of the majority; it is but a short step from there to an assumption that there is no problem, and a quick relapse into the status quo ante.

At a later stage in the interview, when the group was exploring areas that participants wanted to change, the issue of the sexual double standard came up.

Female worker 1: 'One of the things I'm quite angry about is—maybe it's not even recognized by some of the men—but if you've got a female child, and she's deemed as promiscuous, she's labelled as promiscuous, you can have an equally promiscuous boy and that's not even picked up. That's something that I notice when I'm reading files—that's never dealt with.'
M.W.2: 'That example was brought up before, but especially for myself, that wasn't really an issue.'

Later the discussion about workers' willingness to tackle their own prejudices became heated.

M.W.3: 'How can we ask anything of the children if we're not prepared to think about what *we're* doing?'
Cons: 'Hang on to the fact that there are differences of opinion in this room. It's not about convincing each other in this short space of time, it's about getting some idea of what the issues are.'
M.W.3: 'The issue is about the use of the male gender—white and male is the common denominator, and female/black is a deviation from that.'
M.W.2: 'I can't say I'm not sexist or racist. I never considered myself to be sexist or racist, but as the boundaries of those terms are being pushed out you come to the conclusion that you must be . . . but if nothing else, today has taught me something, and that's the point about boys being promiscuous.'
Cons: 'Be careful! [To M.W.1] You'll be abandoned and left as the only one in the sceptic's position!' The laughter this time had much more of a shared and amused quality.

After discussion between the consultants they presented their views of group patterns to the group, with an emphasis on the questions that had occurred to them, e.g. 'How come, if the wish to move towards a more gender-sensitive practice was held by a majority of the group [which had emerged during the interview], had it been so difficult to speak out initially on this topic?' 'How might this phenomenon affect their ideas for future action?' In addition, the consultants told some anecdotes from their own experiences, again highlighting differences between them. The intention was to continue to legitimate a continuum of difference amongst workers, in an atmosphere of humorousness about past conflict. At the request of the consultee group the consultants then moved on to give information about experiential exercises they had found useful in their work, and which the consultees could use as and when it seemed appropriate to them.

While many consultations will be brief and time-limited, certain types of requests will entail ongoing, open-ended consultation. A therapist might meet regularly with a consultant for the discussion of the therapist's ongoing cases. The focus of the consultation, however, will be more on the consultee's professional development, and will contain a training element. Such consultation might coincide with, or be interspersed within, more formal training structures.

Ongoing consultation may also be sought to enable workers to stand back and think about their own working context. Such consultation is most likely to be useful if there is a shared theoretical base for the analysis of pattern and structure, so that this can form the background to considering how such factors influence daily functioning within a working group. This makes it crucial for the consultant to understand the meta-context of the consultees' organization. Time can usefully be spent on mapping the network of the organization internally and externally, and for exploring the role of management hierarchies, and local or national policies and financing decisions on day-to-day work. While the consultation is not in the first place problem-focused—that is, it has not necessarily been organized in response to a problem or a new development—problems that crop up in the course of the consultation will require to be understood within the wider context. In addition to such an understanding, respect for the existing management and other structures is also of importance; it is easy for long-term consultants to be tempted to take over management responsibilities, especially if they are internal to the wider organization, or combine different roles within it. Thus it can be useful, from time to time, for consultants and consultees, together and separately, to consider the impact of the consultant/consultee relationship on other roles and relationships within the organization.

Example

Two female managers of a social services unit arranged to have regular consultation with a woman consultant. They shared a theoretical orientation, and an interest in gender and role attributions; the focus of the consultation was explicitly defined as (a) helping them think about their position as two women managing a mixed-gender team, and in turn being managed by a predominantly male management team; (b) thinking about existing and potential new policies; (c) dealing with any management or organizational problems as they came up; and (d) providing a space for nurturance and 'time-out' for themselves.

These goals were accepted by their managers and by the team they managed. They and the consultant, however, took care to be alert to indications from either of these two groups that they might be feeling excluded, and responded to such intimations by arranging open discussion meetings with members of the management team, or workshops with the service team. The consultations happened about six times per year over a period of several years; the infrequent contact, and the consultant's position outside the organization to which the consultees belonged, ensured sufficient difference in perspective to allow consultation to be useful. On follow-up they summarized some of the effects of consultation as follows: 'It enabled us to consider how to place ourselves strategically within an organization undergoing constant changes. It enabled us to ensure the survival of our service (and ourselves!) with a degree of humour, and allowed us to maintain an appropriate distance from the minutiae of work.'

In conclusion, while a systemic consultant will draw heavily on the theory and techniques of family therapy, there are irreducible differences between the nature of the consultation agreement, whether with a primary therapist and client family, or with a work-focused group. These differences must be respected and understood in order to maximize the usefulness of ideas offered by the consultant. Since this implementation of systems thinking is more recent than therapeutic applications, its practice can be enriched by increased discussion, follow-up and research on the approaches to, and the effects of consultation to systems other than families.

CHAPTER 9 Working with systems other than families: 2. Training

BACKGROUND

Family therapy is a relative newcomer to the field of psycho-therapy; accordingly it is only in recent years that training has begun to be formalized. This goes hand in hand with the development of family therapy into a profession, rather than a collection of skills which mental health professionals could simply add to their range. The family therapy pioneers trained themselves through practice and mutual influence. Such informal training continues to be a significant influence in the development of family therapists, who see workshops, conferences, reading and work in teams as an intrinsic part of their professional development.

There is, nowadays, increasing agreement on what a family therapist should know in order to be recognized as competent by her peers. Formal training is accordingly being seen as a requirement for family therapy practice in many countries, e.g. the United States, and, more recently, in Europe (including the United Kingdom). Thus professionals qualified in Psy-chology, Psychiatry, Social Work and allied fields are now undergoing specialized training in family therapy courses, usually linked to academic institutions such as universities, and such qualification is now more often being required by employers for posts designated as involving not just work with families—which social workers, for example, have long done—but as bringing a particular orientation to work with families, couples, individuals, consultation and so on. The pressure for the professionalization and accreditation of family therapists has, in Europe, received impetus from the creation of the European Community, with its implication for free movement of workers from one part of the Community to another, and therefore a requirement that qualifications should be transferable.

In general training starts with introductory courses which might be available not only to those beginning a training in family therapy, but to many others, such as academics, who wish to acquire a general understanding of the approach. Introductory or foundation level courses will then allow the trainee, after passing selection requirements (such as a designated length of time after professional qualification— usually two or three years—a specified number of annual hours of work with families, and whatever personal qualities the particular institution seeks in its trainees) to go on to intermediate or more advanced training, which will eventually lead to a qualification as a practitioner in family therapy. For the most part this training is part-time, so that the trainee's course-based learning becomes integrated with their changing practice in their own agency. In order to intensify this process the Milan group, for instance, suggest that trainees should take a year out from the course before the final year (Pirotta & Cecchin, 1988).

Family therapy training uses many teaching techniques, some of which are common to many other training areas. What is most particularly associated with it is the use of role play and live supervision. In general in this chapter a distinction will be made between training (which includes all aspects of the learning process for trainee family therapists), and supervision, which will refer specifically to the live observation and guiding of the trainee's work with clients, by means of a one-way screen (cf also Chapters 1 and 2 for a fuller discussion of the rationale behind the use of the one-way screen and the team). The use of live supervision is inextricably linked with the evolving theory and practice of family therapy, and will be discussed in detail below (cf also, for example, Anderson & Rambo, 1988; Liddle et al., 1988; Roberts, 1983).

The term 'trainer' will be used in general in this chapter; the term 'supervisor' will be used when specifically referring to live-supervised training.

ISOMORPHISM BETWEEN THERAPY AND TRAINING

There is general agreement among all schools of family therapy training (e.g. Liddle & Saba, 1983; Liddle, 1991) that training and therapy are similar in structure (they are 'isomorphic') and that similar theoretical considerations apply to each. Thus ideas about how adults learn will be connected with theories about how people change, and the trainer's style of functioning with trainees will give information about how she works with clients, and vice versa.

Trainees who apply for a two- or three-year course, leading to a qualification in family therapy, may be seen as implicitly making a number of requests and statements. These may include some or all of the following: a desire to enhance their existing skills; a desire to change orientation and to learn the approach taught at the training institution; permission for a moratorium, that is, time out of their usual context, to think about where they stand and how they view their practice; a wish for professional enhancement, to be gained by a further professional qualification; a change of professional direction, e.g. from mainstream psychiatry, or from a field such as teaching, towards a more psychotherapeutic identity. All these, and others, will form part of the complexity that makes a trainee eager to learn as well as protective of the skills and theories they bring to training; that is, while they will be keen to change they will also be reluctant to give up ideas and practices which have stood them in good stead in the past, or which they still cherish, even though they may no longer be useful, or may not easily fit into the model being taught on the course.

Thus the trainer will want to understand how the trainee functions, and to respect their resources as well as the times when they find it difficult to take new functions on board. It is more useful to ask a trainee to begin to work with families in such a way as to show the trainer what it is they usually do, and then to discuss the consequences of this way of working, than to attempt to force the trainee to work differently by pointing out 'errors' (cf Pirotta & Cecchin, 1988). If the trainer believes, as a therapist, that there are many 'realities' which are equally valid, though not necessarily equally desirable, then their conduct as a trainer should also reflect this. At the same time there is an assumption that learning new skills, and being in a trainee role, creates anxiety and a sense of loss of certainty, so that the trainer will, in the early part of training, take responsibility for many functions— including the safety of the learning context—which later will be shifted to the trainee. This shifting structure will be discussed in more detail below.

A further assumption that flows from the isomorphism between theories of training and therapy is the belief, held by 'second-order' trainers, that structure-determinism means that trainees will take what makes sense to them from the training, and will transform it to fit with their own style and beliefs. A 'first-order' trainer, for example, may intervene frequently and directly in a trainee's work, e.g. via multiple messages to the therapist during a session, containing very detailed instructions about what to say and do; even more directly, an ear-bug may be used, so that a trainee will be instructed, from moment to moment by (as trainees sometimes call it) 'his master's voice' in the minutiae of interaction. When the trainer assumes that 'instructive interaction' is impossible or unpredictable, she is more likely to focus supervisory energy on discussion outside of the main body of the session, that is, in the pre-session hypothesizing period, during the inter-session discussion, and after the session, during discussion and video supervision slots. Messages to the trainee therapist during the session will be kept to a minimum, delivered as succinct suggestions via an intercom telephone, or during an inter-session discussion. An inter-session discussion happens when the trainee is called out of the room for consultation, or decides to leave the room, to have a fuller discussion with the supervisor and the trainee team about feeling stuck, the desire to change direction or hypotheses, etc. Thus the aim will be to invite the trainee to consider alternative hypotheses and styles of interaction, via consideration of the patterns of relationship of which the trainee and the training context form an intrinsic part. This also reflects the view (Cecchin & Fruggeri, 1986) that there can be a significant difference between teaching technique versus teaching a way of thinking. Technique is not always translatable from one context to another, and can dry up in crisis, or become stereotyped and non-responsive to client difference; having a coherent theory base, however, will enhance the likelihood of being able to think flexibly—and invent new techniques—when required. It must also be borne in mind that the majority of family therapy trainees, at the live supervision stage of training, are fully qualified mental health professionals with some, or even considerable, experience in family therapy.

The increasing professionalization of family therapy, with its concomitants of accreditation of courses and examination of trainees, brings a particular tension to systemic trainers. The field of systems-based therapy, like Dr Pangloss (Voltaire, Tr. 1947) has operated on the assumption that human beings do the best they can given the constraints of their situation; thus the task of the therapist, and of the trainer, is to search for strengths and resources, and to value and respect people as they are and might be, rather than to find fault with them for how they are. This attitude can be difficult to reconcile with the Pass-Fail ethos of examinations.

TRAINING STRUCTURES

General Patterns

There are as many training structures as there are training courses, but certain general patterns can be discerned. Most courses which aim to 'produce' advanced systemic family therapy practitioners use a structure which moves a trainee from observer to apprentice therapist to independent practitioner/consultant. Thus most courses will start with the trainee observing the work of the trainers, live and on videotape. A valuable aspect of live observation is the opportunity for trainees to observe the consultant/therapist relationship in action, and to be reminded of the fact that therapy does not always proceed as smoothly as it can seem to do on edited videotape. Seeing a trainer/therapist and their colleagues struggle to formulate their hypotheses, to engage with families and to search for change can be a lesson in the necessity of error-activated learning,[1] which will stand trainees in good stead when their own turn comes. The way in which the Milan trainers divide trainees into T-teams and O-teams (Therapy-teams and Observation teams) (cf Boscolo & Cecchin, 1982; Pirotta & Cecchin, 1988; Roberts et al., 1989) which initially observe the work of the trainers, but later join in as consultant team and meta-observation team, is a template for the shifting structure of apprenticeship. In addition it functions as a valuable learning tool, since the less directly involved position of the Observation team, which observes the trainee, her team and supervisor working with the family, facilitates the adoption of a meta-perspective, and the realization that the system under observation includes the therapy team as well as the client family.

As shown in the research done by Short (1986) a typical training structure is likely to begin with control fairly tightly in the trainer's hands, and to evolve to the point where the trainer is no longer involved in the work except as an observer or consultant. The trainer is likely to take major responsibility in the early phases of a training course for certain aspects of the management of the therapy/training situation.

Clinical responsibility

If training occurs in the trainer's agency, she is likely to be required by agency regulations to hold clinical responsibility throughout. Whether

---

[1] As Bateson points out (1978a) human beings are capable of making choices which, though not leading to the desired results, can provide information which would contribute to the making of future choices, i.e. to the development of skill. Gaining the expected result from an action (zero-learning) teaches us nothing new; gaining an unexpected or undesired result leads us to punctuate events differently, so as to attempt to reach a different understanding or outcome, and thus, if repeated, can teach us to learn about our punctuation of events (learning about learning). It follows then that making errors is potentially more useful than never making any, just as struggling at the limits of our understanding or our theory is potentially more useful than basking in the confidence of perfect certainty.

or not this is the case, in the early stages of live supervised training she may experience tension between the trainee's learning needs, and the therapeutic welfare of the clients. Discussion of this with the trainees, as well as spelling out what emergency measures may be taken, is likely to lead to relief on both sides, and paradoxically makes it less likely that the trainee or trainer will ever feel anxious enough to require major intervention in the session by the trainer.

Hierarchy

As in the above example, being clear about issues of hierarchy avoids confusion, and helps to pave the way towards a shifting of power (empowerment) as the course progresses. A pretence of democracy and equality, when this does not fully describe the relationships, can lead to more abuse of power, not less. For example, a trainee (G), about half-way through the live-supervised component of the training, had a difficult decision to make about who, in a complexly organized family, to invite to a next session. The supervisor suggested that the rest of the group (three fellow-trainees and the supervisor) should mull this over for the rest of the day, while getting on with other training activities, and should then each give G one suggestion about whom to invite at the end of the day, so that she could think it over overnight and make a decision by the next morning. This was duly done; when the supervisor expressed her opinion, which was different from those of the rest of the group, G said, 'Well obviously I'll do that—I know which side my bread's buttered'. As a pointed joke it was a useful comment on the phase of training in which the group found itself; they had, over the previous month or so, begun overtly to shift from a predominantly supervisor-led style of working to one where more active participation was being invited from the trainee group. Nevertheless the supervisor also chose to comment on this remark, saying that, since she was the supervisor, and since examinations loomed large in the trainee's minds at that point, it was of course inevitable that her voice would be experienced as carrying more weight; nevertheless, whilst acknowledging this, she thought it would be useful if G could find a way of mulling over all the suggestions equally before making her decision. It may be that such a request has a paradoxical element: if the trainee's bread is buttered on the side of pleasing the supervisor, will she more do this by adopting the supervisor's suggestion about whom to invite, or the supervisor's suggestion to value all contributions equally? In the event, G returned the following day with a solution of her own, which combined aspects of all the suggestions made to her.

Information overload

In the early stages of live supervision the trainer is likely to act as a filter between the group and the trainee therapist. Thus, for example, when the trainee therapist comes out of the therapy room for an inter-session consultation, the supervisor will be the only spokesperson; this procedure will then shift at later stages, and with respect to the trainee's indications of readiness. Similarly if messages are to be communicated to the trainee therapist by intercom telephone during a session, this will, in the beginning, be done by the supervisor. The purpose of such a filtering structure is to shield the trainee from overload. Even though advanced trainees are, by definition, skilled and experienced professional workers, the effects of being in a trainee role should not be underestimated. On the other hand, some trainers prefer from the beginning of live supervision to use reflecting team techniques (cf Chapter 2), in the presence of the family or during the inter-session consultation to the trainee. The latter involves the trainee in listening to the views expressed by her fellow-trainees and supervisor, making her own synthesis, and returning to the session with the clients to use this as she wishes. While this approach has the advantage of being highly coherent with a co-constructive philosophy, it has been suggested (David Campbell & Ros Draper, personal communication) that implementing this approach in the early stages of live supervision can leave trainees feeling confused and unsupported.

Theory Training

Whether or not a family therapy training course has been preceded by introductory level training, the first part of the course, preceding live supervised therapy practice, will be where most attention is paid to formal study of theory. This may proceed via didactic input from trainers, in the form of lectures on theory, perhaps illustrated with examples from their own work. In the early stages of training many courses find it necessary to give trainees an overview of all the mainstream 'schools' of family therapy, and accreditation bodies may insist on this. Such theoretical training may be offered by course trainers, who will also later supervise the trainees, or visiting teachers may be brought in to enable trainees to experience variety.

In most forms of professional training there is, or has at some time been, a debate about the fox versus hedgehog schools of training. That is, should trainees (and trainers), like the fox, know something about many things, or should they, like the hedgehog, know a lot about one thing? Accreditation bodies are likely to opt for the fox model, since they themselves are in the position of having to reconcile many competing approaches; trainees who are sufficiently well informed to choose a particular training institute or teacher may prefer the hedgehog method.

A considerable proportion of the theory training may be done via reading seminars, where trainees have responsibility for presenting and discussing selected papers; papers may initially be selected by the trainers, thus conforming to a basic curriculum, and then further reading may happen at the behest of trainees themselves. The trainer's role in such reading seminars is to stimulate critical discussion, since the tendency either to reject new views out of hand, or on the other hand to accept anything because it has been published recently, will probably always be endemic in groups, particularly groups of normally independent-minded adults who are in the process of enjoying the second adolescence bestowed by training, look forward with apprehension to being examined, and suspect that, in their trainers' minds, there may be a correct answer after all.

As with the hedgehog/fox debate, there are two predominant schools of thought about the content of theory training and reading seminars. The one school holds that theory development should be covered, so that it is possible for each new generation of trainees to place the ideas they work with in an historical context. This point of view is coherent with the historical and contextualizing approach of Milan-systemic therapy. Knowing the derivation of an idea, being aware of 'good' ideas which have gone out of fashion, or come back into fashion, may help trainees to hold a sceptical view, to deconstruct whatever the current dominant texts are, and to test theories for their usefulness in practice. The second school of thought prefers to present trainees with 'state of the art' literature. This has the advantage of allowing more time to

come to terms with what may be new concepts and applications, so that trainees in this approach will be less likely
than those following a historical path, to have only a superficial
acquaintance with current trends in theory. On the other
hand such a focus on that which is hot off the presses may,
like other 'post-modern' activities, run the risk, in its a-
historicism, of leaving trainees with a shallow grasp on the
'ecology' of the ideas they work with, and make them less
able to critique new developments.

The teaching of theory on the course can be amplified by
work done outside the course by trainees in the form of
written assignments, on aspects of theory and its application
to cases, as well as homework tasks which require trainees
to apply the hothouse thinking of a course to other contexts,
including their own professional setting. Such assignments
can be straightforward—e.g. a critique of a particular aspect
of theory, the mapping out of an approach to a particular
referral, etc.—or can use tasks on questions apparently
unrelated to family therapy, thus encouraging trainees to
expand their flexibility in lateral thinking. For example, a
group of trainees (towards the end of 1989) derived much fun
and not inconsiderable learning from a homework task asking
them to answer the question 'Can one person unilaterally
bring about change in the system of which they are part?' by
using Michael Gorbachev and events in the then Soviet Union
as an example.

Training Exercises

Experiential learning has always been seen as important in
family therapy training, and most trainers will have had the
opportunity to see trainees work with simulated families
(role play) before they meet clients. However, many other
experiential forms of learning, besides role play, can be used
(cf for example Campbell et al., 1988). While most contemporary
family therapy trainers do not expect trainees to have
undergone their own individual or family therapy before or
during training (which was the expectation in some centres

in the past) there is nevertheless a recognition that the person of the trainee and therapist is relevant to the quality and type of therapy that will be done, and to the learning patterns that will be experienced as most helpful. Thus aspects of training courses will be structured in such a way as to encourage trainees to examine the influence on their work of their own families of origin, values, and personal patterns of interaction and perception (cf *Genogram* section below).

In the systemic approaches there is an assumption that it is the act of observation which produces punctuation, information, and action. Thus it is useful for much of this observation to be done in contexts (like role-play or video-observation) where the action can be slowed down, repeated, turned on its head, and generally subjected to meta-observation. Experiential learning is not only about the acquisition of skills, though it is invaluable for that; it is also a forum where trainees can experiment and observe themselves experimenting. In addition, like humour, play produces a marvellous context for learning.

Play

Example

Philip Brown came to a supervision seminar with two specific requests, which he presented to the group and the supervisor in a focused way by means of videotaped extracts from a previous therapy session. In his work with an embattled couple, who had screamed aggressively at each other throughout most of the first session, he felt that he had handled two areas less well than he would have liked, and he asked for help with them. (1) He wanted to be able to persist with his line of questioning and not get sidetracked; (2) he wanted to interrupt their habitual pattern of escalating counter-accusations, since these clearly were non-productive in the session, but he wanted to do so without engaging in a symmetrical matching of styles. Philip was a therapist capable of clear, focused thinking, as evidenced by his presentation of his dilemma; he was particularly interested in questions of changing gender roles, and in ways of enabling men to feel masculine without obeying the stereotyped injunctions to be violent and domineering, as his client had done. His usual quiet and facilitative style, which had proved useful in the past, was too low-keyed to register with his current clients, who simply swept him aside while continuing with their usual battle. This had the effect of making him speak more hesitantly and softly, in his efforts not to join the battle on the only terms that, during the session, had seemed available to him, namely matching escalating aggression with aggression.

After some discussion with the trainee group (four including Philip) and the supervisor, the latter suggested a role play game. Two of Philip's colleagues played a couple (loosely based on the clients, but without any attempt to give an accurate portrait). They had overt permission to use any means, fair or foul, to prevent Philip from persisting with his line of questioning. The idea was that, having had the opportunity to play with the worst catastrophes he could imagine, the reality of the therapy situation would seem less threatening, and having faced his ferocious colleagues (and supervisor!) he could, via time out for discussion, repetition of sequences, and the achievement of an observing stance in relation to himself, practice more effective ways of connecting with such clients. The third trainee team member acted as observer, with a particular focus on what worked well for Philip, and what the processes were that led him to act in a disempowered manner.

The 'couple' threw themselves into their roles with gusto, and it was soon observed that, as long as Philip retained an edge of enthusiasm or enjoyment in the proceedings, he was able to appear authoritative and calm. However, as soon as he became caught up in the tension of the process he seemed to feel disqualified by the couple—and angry?—and his speech became hesitant and apologetic, filled in particular with phrases such as 'could I just . . .'. Having discussed this, the supervisor then sat next to Philip while the 'interview' continued, with the pretence that the pencil in her hand was an electric-shock machine (such as she and Philip fantasized were used in old-fashioned behaviourist experiments), and that she would shock Philip by poking him in the ribs each time he said 'just' or 'only'. This turned the game into high farce, but after three prods Philip, who was highly entertained by the procedure, abandoned his hesitant speech. The group then, via more discussion and practice of techniques such as breathing, voice production and posture, continued to explore Philip's learning targets.

The use of humour, play and silliness in this example make a serious point. Philip had been not been consciously aware of the way in which his language shifted towards a more ineffective speech style at certain points. He had become aware of this when watching himself on video, but it had happened again during role play. It was important for him to find a way of punctuating his awareness of hesitant speech patterns so that he could avoid using them in a situation where they were counterproductive, yet doing so during play made it easier to do this and to change than a serious or willed effort might have done. As Bateson points out (1978a) humour and play can be seen as 'trans-contextual' phenomena which can enhance the likelihood for learning to take place. It is also likely that making the same observation in two different contexts (his review of videotape, and the game) increased the likelihood that this learning would be transferred to the context of the next therapy session. Acting in this way—e.g. from the supervisor's part, parodying an extreme type of instructive dominance, and from his colleagues part, behaving worse than any client was ever likely to do, both being done in a context where Philip had given permission for these actions, and was part of the planning for them, has a multiplicity of effects, some of which can only be guessed at. The consequence of this particular teaching game was that Philip's style was significantly different in the next session; he acted with quiet but firm and warm authority, remaining loyal to his own ideas about non-oppressive action as well as fulfilling his task as a therapist to whom the couple looked for help in breaking the vicious circle of their interactive pattern.

Other advantages of such 'non-serious' playing can be illustrated by another occasion, when a group of trainees were doing a similar exercise, designed to help the interviewer stay on track while interviewing another trainee, with the rest of the group encouraged to use any means to distract the interviewer. One trainee, who had until then seen herself and been seen by the others as somewhat of an outsider to the group, and who usually presented as formal and reserved, astonished everyone by the magnificence of her histrionic skills. This meant that all, including the supervisor, saw her in a new light, so that it became possible to encourage her to take more risks in exploring her range of behaviours in therapy.

Role play

Most family therapy trainers will use the repeated experience of working with simulated families to teach skills. Such role-played families can be invented, or can represent attempts to play families actually being seen in therapy. The latter situation is most useful where therapists finds themselves unable to behave even-handedly to all family members; playing the person to whom the therapist feels least sympathetic can offer an opportunity to develop empathy and shift perspective. The advantage of role play for skills learning is that the action can be interspersed with discussion, suggestions for alternatives, extended hypothesizing, requests by the trainee therapist for help, and so on. Ways of doing things can be tried out without the trainees having to commit themselves to working in that way; this may have a function similar to experimental tasks or hypothetical questioning in therapy. Particular skills such as circular interviewing can be practised under safe conditions; the use of observers can bring awareness of the value of different perspectives; and trainees, if they have not worked with an observing team and a one-way screen before, can become used to the exposure which so characterizes family therapy practice. When role playing, the 'therapist' can be replaced at regular intervals by another trainee ('tagging'), with the supervisor making sure that trainees end their spell as therapist on an upbeat, rather than stopping them when they are stuck.

Role play can also be a major opportunity for trainees to experience the way in which observation and interaction function to bring forth certain patterns; when working with actual client families in therapy it can be easier to overlook this and assume that the interactive pattern observed is 'really there', is fixed, and that the therapist has not contributed to it. An example of a game played with many variations by systemic trainers (cf for example Pirotta & Cecchin, 1988) is the following: someone who volunteers to be an interviewer is taken out of the room, and given the instruction that, when summoned, they will, as a therapist, join a family in a therapy room. Out of the hearing of the interviewer, the group of people who have volunteered to role play are told that they will be a family. They are asked not to discuss the allocation of roles or relationships; instead, each one is asked, silently, to think about who they would like to be in this family, and what sort of person they would be; they are also asked, in their minds, to allocate roles in a similar way to the others. Family and interviewer are then brought together. Once the interview has proceeded for some time the role play is stopped, the 'family' and the 'interviewer' are told of the instructions given to the others, and their observations are then discussed. Starting with an almost blank canvas means that the influences of the participants, the contexts, and assumptions by the participants can be drawn out more clearly, and can prove very thought-provoking—e.g. did the interviewer's assumption of being a therapist (which the family did not receive in their instructions) produce a system with a problem amenable to therapy? How did this happen? What were the first words said, and how did they influence the next words said? What influence did the workshop context and relationships amongst participants have on the way roles were allocated and accepted? How was someone 'persuaded' to become a problem-carrier, or a spouse, or a child? How did individuals' initial (silent) decisions change under the influence of group process? These are just a few examples of issues that will be highlighted by participants' own observations.

Genograms

While, as said above, personal or training therapy is not a requirement for trainee family therapists, there is nevertheless an increasing acknowledgement that the personal history and life of the trainee will be influential in their work with clients. Trainers recognize the importance of keeping a boundary between supervision, which may at times deal with personal elements, and therapy, which is not the business of the supervisor or the rest of the trainee group. Getting trainees to use their own genograms (family trees) in one way or another during training can be useful, both because of the content of such training exercises, and as a signal that the person of the therapist/trainee is relevant to therapeutic work done.

One way of doing genogram work is to ask trainees, in the supervision groups in which they will work with clients, to present their genograms, one by one, to the rest of the group and the supervisor. They have overt permission to omit personal material they do not wish to discuss within the context of the course. One of the group, with consultation from the others, then interviews the genogram presenter, with two aims: (1) to practice circular interviewing skills, and (2) to find out how their colleague's family history contributes to their functioning as a family therapist, and their choice of family therapy as a preferred therapeutic mode. The task of the consultants is to help the interviewer adhere to these two aims. This exercise is not only useful for the trainees themselves, perhaps making new connections between work and private patterns, but means that certain data are available to the supervision group—what life stage a trainee is at, whether they have children or not, what cross-cultural experience their families may embody, etc.—which can help the group's understanding of a trainee therapist's particular strengths or areas of inexperience or difficulty.

Sequential discussion

This is a hypothesizing technique which has many useful applications (Campbell et al., 1988, Pirotta & Cecchin, 1988). For example, when a trainee presents work from their agency for consultation, the rest of the group may be asked to hypothesize sequentially, while the trainee presenter listens without comment. Thus group member A will make a statement (which is a hunch based on available information, generic hypotheses and so on) of no more than two sentences. The next person will add their own statement, making sure that it is linked explicitly or implicitly to the previous statement. Linking can be in the form of agreement, disagreement or amplification. This process goes around the circle several times. What usually happens is that a consensus begins to emerge around hypotheses that are fuller and more inclusive than those presented initially. The sequential discussion can be directed at hypotheses related to the clients' functioning, the therapist's difficulties with the case, or any other focus. At a certain point the procedure will be brought to a halt, and the presenter asked to comment on the ideas they have heard. This technique can also be used for pre- and post-session hypothesizing.

The advantages of sequential discussion are that it gives everyone in the group an equal voice, it ensures that participants respond thoughtfully to the contributions of others rather than simply thinking about their own idea, and it provides a vivid experience of the way that the whole becomes more than the sum of its parts. It is coherent with the idea of non-instructive interaction, in that it makes explicit the assumption that the listener will hear and digest what is being said in their own way, and will exercise choice about what to take on board and what to discard or to put aside for thinking about later. This experience, among other uses, helps trainees also to remember that clients go through similar processes in therapy, and that it may not be necessary to dot every i and cross every t for clients, who will use their own judgement to decide what fits for them.

Interviewing exercises

As Campbell and his colleagues (1988) point out, exercises should not be used by rote, but should rather emerge from the specific context and situation. Many opportunities will arise, in the training structures preceding live supervision, and during the non-client-related parts of supervised training, that will give rise to exercises that allow trainees to practice interviewing skills. Trainees can be asked, at the beginning of the live supervision part of the training course, to interview each other in front of the group about their own learning style. While this functions as a skills exercise, it also gives the supervisor and the rest of the group the opportunity to learn from the trainee what sorts of contexts and experiences enhance or block their learning. Some people have to experience things in practice before they can make sense of the theory that underlies it; others have to understand something cognitively before they can try it out, and so on. This exercise can be repeated at various stages, to signal shifts in the training modality, for example with a focus on what a particular trainee, at this point, wants/needs to learn. In similar vein, trainees can be asked to interview a supervisor about their supervisory style.

More formal exercises can be used to focus on particular skills, especially in the pre-supervision stage of training. Groups of three trainees can work together as follows: person A agrees to be interviewed and presents a small problem from their own life (e.g. I always squeeze the toothpaste tube in the middle, and this drives my spouse, parents, children, cat, superego wild); B interviews A about this, with particular attention to how this constitutes a problem for whom, what the attitudes of others are or might be about it, what has been tried to solve it, what meanings are attached to the behaviour for the different participants, what the likely consequences of change or no change will be. Person C observes this process, and has the task of keeping the interviewer B on track, assisting with new lines of questioning and thinking when required, and so on. After a set time (e.g. 10 minutes) the interview stops, and B and C discuss their hypotheses about A's situation while A listens without commenting; after five or ten minutes this discussion stops and A gives feedback on responses to the interview and the discussion between B and C.

Anti-discriminatory Practice

As discussed in Chapter 7, family therapists have in recent years begun to try to incorporate anti-discriminatory concepts into their work, with a concomitant attention to these themes in the training of future family therapists. Accreditation guidelines issued by family therapy associations (e.g. AAMFT in the USA, and AFT in the UK) explicitly require training programmes seeking accreditation to demonstrate that adequate attention is being paid on their courses to questions of discrimination on the grounds of gender, race, disability, age, and so on (cf for example Storm, 1991). Many training programmes have integrated such views in their teaching, including the acknowledgement that the problem of how to deal with power, hierarchy, inequity and the abuse of such differences in access to choice has not yet been solved; this has meant that trainers themselves have had to look to their own practice and attitudes, seek out further training for themselves, and examine the practices of their agencies and their training courses. However, research by Coleman and her colleagues (1990) into the attention paid to questions of gender in family therapy training in a large number of training schools (mainly in the United States but also in some other countries) found that the subject of gender was largely absent in most family therapy training, and when dealt with was often done so only superficially. It was particularly striking that questions of gender in supervision seemed not to be addressed frequently.

There are numerous issues that could be expected to be part of the normal functioning of training groups, for example, the routine inclusion of gender, cultural and ethnic context (including the possibility of the experience of discrimination) in pre-session hypothesizing; expecting trainees to be able to deal with inter-familial violence and sexual abuse when it occurs in families they are seeing; monitoring the numerical representation of women and men, and ethnic minorities, in trainee and trainer groups, and responding positively to imbalances; and paying attention to the effect of gender in training relationships (Caust et al., 1981, Avis, 1989). As regards the latter point, it is possible that there may be significant differences in how male or female trainees learn from female or male trainers; observation suggests that there are differences in cultural and socially acquired learning styles and the ways in which hierarchical relationships are construed, so that research on these and related topics will enable trainers to perform their tasks more efficiently and ethically, and to match trainee and training requirements more satisfactorily.

Despite the findings of Coleman and her colleagues (1990), it is nevertheless notable that the question of how to enable trainers and trainees to become culturally aware and gender sensitive is receiving increasing attention in the literature and in the curricula of family therapy training courses. There have been debates about the relative merits of expecting family therapists to acquire detailed knowledge of cultural groups other than their own, versus the view that over-emphasis on ethnic identity and difference can obscure similarities between people, distract attention from the unique problems that bring families to therapy, avoid focusing on other contextual issues, such as poverty and unemployment, and militate against the development of an open-minded, integrated and sensitive approach to work with all clients (Falicov, 1988, McGoldrick et al., 1991).

Supervision

As discussed in the introduction to this chapter, most supervisors use a model in which trainees move from close supervision to increasing autonomy. It is useful at the beginning of supervision to make overt the implicit contract— that one person agrees to be trained, and the other to train— so that actions, training structures and potential difficulties that flow from this can be dealt with.

The major focus of supervised training is on trainees' work with clients. The theoretical and skills foundation will have been laid in earlier phases of the training; in the supervision phase theory and skills need to be integrated by the trainee, and tested out in practice, so that a coherent stance towards their therapeutic work will begin to develop for trainees. Several components of supervision will be discussed separately.

Video review and video supervision

Trainees review videotapes of their work with clients on the course together with their colleagues from the supervision team. The purpose of this, besides the usual clinical purpose of doing more thinking about the clients with whom they are working, is to observe themselves as therapists, in the light of comments from the supervisor and their fellow-trainees, and of their own critique of their work. Doing this within the trainee team once again makes use of the richness and complexity of viewpoints brought by a group, which enhances the opportunity to take a meta-observing stance towards one's own functioning.

On the basis of this video review the trainee will select sections of videotape to bring to a video supervision slot for discussion. The supervisor may also request to see a particular section of tape, in order to use it as a teaching point. The likelihood is that aspects selected will reflect less than satisfactory work by the trainee therapist, points of 'stuckness', illustrations of interaction that seem puzzling, and so on, rather than the examples of skilled and satisfactory work that a trainee may want to show when functioning, for example, as a teacher or when presenting work to an examination panel. The assumption is that looking at and discussing such examples will allow the whole trainee group to learn, and that error-activated learning is useful. A point mentioned earlier in this chapter needs to be emphasized again here. Trainees who see families under live supervision are not novices. They are likely to be qualified mental health professionals, with some years of experience in their own professional discipline and in family therapy behind them. 'Less than satisfactory work', 'stuckness', and so on, can be experienced by any therapist at any time. The fact that trainees experience this, and that such experiences are used to enhance their learning, does not mean that families are, unethically, being subjected to incompetent therapists in the interests of training.

Example

Liz Sherman saw an young man (Harvey Miller, 23), who had a psychiatric history of breakdown and inability to cope with tertiary education or work, together with his mother (58), who had been widowed 7 years previously. On two occasions in the first session a particular sequence of actions occurred: Liz asked a question about Mr Miller's death (the second time in response to a message from the supervisor), Mrs Miller showed some distress (e.g. pressing a handkerchief to her eyes), Harvey apologized to his mother, and the conversation shifted so that, after a few minutes, he and Liz were engaged in an intense discussion of his inability to work, study or make relationships outside the family, while Mrs Miller sat back in her chair with a small kindly-looking smile.

In the video supervision Liz said that she had found it difficult to comply with the supervisor's message asking her to return to the topic of Mr Miller's death, experiencing it as cruel. She was also bothered, during the session and on reviewing the tape, by what she saw as an adversarial tone in her discussion with Harvey about his psychological and social problems. She had not noticed, in the session, that she was leaving Mrs Miller out of large parts of the discussion. Instead of treating these occurrences as the 'errors' of an trainee therapist, they were discussed as phenomena which could help to stimulate the supervision group's curiosity so as to make better sense of the clients' situation, and of how best to respond to them. This attitude towards these occurrences is based on an assumption that any therapist, whether a trainee or a qualified and highly experienced practitioner, can be influenced by events and feelings within themselves and between themselves and the clients. Such influence can then allow a therapist's attention to focus on one aspect of the complex family tapestry, while losing sight of others. Regarding the therapist as part of the observing system means that the therapist's participation in the whole system's patterns of feeling and interaction becomes a source of valuable information for all concerned.

The team wondered, for example, whether Harvey's behaviour in the session could be seen as a representation, in miniature, of a larger life pattern. Schematically this would look as follows: father dies, mother is upset, Harvey has a problem and engages a mental health professional, mother is not upset any more. Such a hypothesis would lead Liz in the next session to explore the family's beliefs about adulthood and leaving home, the meaning of widowhood, whether mother and son viewed each other as fragile and unable to cope with each other's distress or autonomy.

Turning to Liz's discomfort about her (unusual) adversarial interaction with Harvey, the team's feedback was that she had sounded like an impatient careers counsellor (a job she had done in the past). Liz reported that she had experienced Harvey as sounding self-pitying (i.e. his distress had not felt 'genuine' to her), and she had felt irritated by this. Was it possible that, once she had 'joined' the family system sufficiently to start playing by their rules (i.e. in cooperating with them to avoid the taboo areas of death and grief, and to focus on Harvey as 'the problem'), she felt invalidated as a systemic therapist, and fell back on a previous style of functioning, while feeling irritated, not only with Harvey, but with herself? Her sense of Harvey as self-pitying was also explored, and various hypothetical meanings assigned to this, e.g.: What might it be about her values, or his behaviour, or the situation, that diminished her sense of compassion and made her judgemental? What was it about the way he was communicating that signalled that he need not be taken seriously?

The team also speculated about the difference between Liz's experience, in the therapy room, of an intensity of dangerousness and fragility around the idea of talking directly about a death which had occurred 7 years previously, and the observers' sense that Mrs Miller had not seemed severely upset. It is known that the therapist's experience of affect can differ markedly from the behind-the-screen team's more cognitive meta-perspective, and that both of these are valuable and can combine to give a fuller systemic view. Discussion of both these perspectives thus allowed both to be taken seriously. In addition the training context was explored. This session took place early in the supervision group's life: to what extent were Liz and her trainee team-mates influenced by performance anxiety, the desire to impress the supervisor by competing for the validity of their different perspectives, and a fear that the supervisor or the model might not prove sensitive to the fears of clients and trainees?

The above example, with its brief reference to some of the themes that might be explored in video supervision, serves to illustrate the usefulness of re-viewing the interactive patterns of the clients, the clients plus therapist, and the clients plus therapist plus team plus supervisor. Liz worked flexibly and inventively with Harvey and Mrs Miller in the next session, explored the hypotheses generated by the team's discussion, and generated further new ideas for exploration. Equally importantly, this example served as a significant marker for the whole supervision group, who were excited by the process of the exploration, and now felt more confident that there would be coherence between the style of supervision and a theoretical model which takes the stance that feeling stuck, and becoming curious about one's own observed processes, can be useful, as it may enhance the possibility of achieving change.

Consultation to agency cases

Trainees are encouraged during the supervision part of the course, as well as during earlier phases, to bring cases they are working with in their home agencies, and non-clinical organizational problems, to the supervision group. This is explicitly framed as not being supervision of the case—e.g., as Pirotta and Cecchin (1988) point out in discussing the work of the Milan teachers, no follow-up enquiry will be made about the development of the work after it has been presented—but as consultation and an opportunity for the whole group to learn. The focus is explicitly on what will work in the trainee's agency; this is important, as it helps to bridge the gap between what can be seen as the idealized and unreal context of the training institution and the 'harsh realities' of the trainee's working situation, hierarchical position, agency constraints and so on, and can encourage trainees to think systemically about and in all their contexts. Trainees can be encouraged to make maps of their professional networks, so that any case or organizational issue discussed will be presented against the background of the relevant context.

The observing team behind the screen

There is general agreement amongst trainers that four trainees makes an ideal size of supervision group: small enough to give each trainee adequate space for development, and large enough to make for diversity and balance. Larger groups are used, sometimes perhaps more because of financial and contextual constraints than for ideological reasons. In the early stages of supervision the group behind the screen will be given specific tasks to do while their colleague is interviewing a family: thus one will be drawing a genogram as information about the family constellation is elicited; one will keep 'process' notes, that is a tracking of themes discussed with annotations of the times, as indicated on the videotape, when these occur, so that the trainee, when reviewing the tape, can more easily get access to a particular part of the session; a third will be making notes about particular language styles, metaphors and expressions used by clients, so as to assist the trainee in adapting their language use more to that of the family members. In addition one of these will be making verbatim notes of the supervisor's comments, again with time annotations. If such notes were not taken, each trainee, when it was their turn to be the therapist, might be worrying about what was being said about their performance; conversely it would block the supervisor from making teaching points behind the screen for fear of enhancing trainee anxiety. Knowing that what she says is written down to be relayed to the trainee therapist after the session means that the supervisor can make full use of the training opportunities presented behind the screen.

At a later stage of live supervised training each trainee will be asked to instruct their colleagues on what sorts of notes they find useful and what not, so that note-taking starts being tailor-made to individual requirements. This also coincides in time with other shifts in activity behind the screen.

Initially the observing team members are likely to be more passive, more concerned with their specific observation and note-taking tasks, and comments to the therapist will be relayed via the supervisor. At a later stage they will be encouraged to become more active.

The trainee therapist

At the beginning of live supervision the supervisor may ask the trainee to work with clients in the way they would normally do. This request has several uses. It allows the supervisor to see what the trainee's style and skills are (while making allowances for nervousness because of the training context); it acknowledges that the trainee is already a skilled professional; and it then allows the supervisor and trainee together, as they examine the consequences of the trainee's usual way of working, to draw up an agenda for what the trainee may want to learn from supervision. The trainee also knows that, barring major crises or specific factual demands, the supervisor will not intervene (via intercom telephone or a knock on the door) for the first part of the session—actual times may vary from supervisor to supervisor, but in general lies somewhere between fifteen minutes and half an hour. This allows trainee therapist and clients to establish their own rhythm, and to get sufficiently connected in any session to allow the supervisor and observing team to get a sense of the patterns of interaction they are observing.

There is usually explicit agreement that the trainee will come out of the room when asked to do so, and may also choose at any time to leave the family and join the group behind the screen for consultation. When asked to pursue a particular line of enquiry they will do so; if they feel unable to do so, because they disagree strongly or do not understand the request, they will come out for discussion.

Initially the supervisor will be the person who communicates with the trainee when delivering in-session messages and during the consultation period before the end of the session. The purpose of this is to shield the trainee therapist from overload, and to give the trainee group time to gel and to develop a cooperative style and group ethos. As time moves on these patterns will all shift. Thus consultations will increasingly become group events, perhaps initially via sequential discussion, and only later as a 'free-for-all' or 'orgy of lineal hypothesizing' (Pirotta & Cecchin, 1988, p. 51). This greater freedom in the group is likely to promote more creativity, but at too early a time can become chaotic and disconcerting for a therapist who is holding together a variety of concerns: therapeutic responsibility for the clients, the newness of being under observation in a training context, and the negotiation of roles and relationships with group members and with the supervisor. Having tried a variety of styles of discussion and feedback, the trainee therapist will be encouraged to inform the group which style of consultation suits her best.

At this stage the group behind the screen need to have moved from a major concentration on note-taking (cf previous section) and to be moving towards more active participation in discussion behind the screen, together with the supervisor, and eventually to taking over the supervisory role. Preparation for this, via role-play, will lead to trainees, by the end of the supervision course, taking full responsibility for consulting to each other, with the supervisor now supervising the process of the team's co-working.

The supervisor

Supervisors and trainers, like family therapists, were originally self-trained. As the field of family therapy has developed, the training of supervisors has also become more formalized. It stands to reason that those who train family therapists should themselves be skilled and experienced, and able demonstrably to do what they require their trainees to do.

In addition, however, trainers using live supervision perhaps require certain specific skills and capacities which are not essential to other forms of training. It can be possible to learn much from someone who behaves in charismatic, self-absorbed, inconsistent, competitive, intrusive or bizarre ways, as everyone who has at some time been inspired by an eccentric teacher will testify. However, the conditions of live supervision call, as a minimal requirement, for certain specific qualities in the supervisor: patience, the ability to hold at least two contexts (therapy and training) simultaneously in balance, and an authentic trust in the capacity of people (trainees and clients) to interact, when supported in a safe context, in ways which enhance the resourcefulness of all participants.

Conclusion

A final isomorphism between theories about teaching and about therapy lies in the idea of co-evolution. In training, as in therapy, *all* participants expect to undergo some level of change, to be affected by the process, to exert mutual influence, and to co-construct new meanings, not only with clients, but with each other. The Welsh language excellently demonstrates the systemic attitude towards teaching and learning: the word 'dysgu' (pronounced 'dusgy', like 'rugby') means to teach *and* to learn. When one wishes to be more specific it is therefore necessary to say 'I "dysgu" as a teacher' or 'I "dysgu" as a learner'. This serves constantly to remind the speaker of the mutuality of the teaching/learning continuum; it would be useful if family therapy trainers and trainees, teachers and learners, could find a similar word to keep the interconnected nature of their mutual endeavours constantly in focus.

POSTSCRIPT Developments in the systemic therapies

Writers in the field of the systemic therapies regard current changes in the thought and practice in our field as being of the nature of a 'new epistemology' or a 'paradigm shift' (Hoffman, 1988, MacKinnon & Miller, 1987, among many others). Epistemology, 'the theory of knowledge' (Chambers, 1988), or how we know about our knowing, is at a higher logical level than theory, and theory (that is, the explanations we construct) flows from epistemology. Thus a changed epistemology suggests that we have changed our way of understanding the world, our place in it, and our view of the limits and patterns of our apprehension of it, in a radical manner. Paradigm means 'a conceptual framework within which scientific theories are constructed' (Chambers, 1988). Thus a paradigm shift would imply non-trivial changes in the way we view reality, which would then have major implications for the theories and actions which flow from such a view.

Do current systemic theories of therapy constitute a new epistemology or paradigm shift, or do they simply reflect variations *within* an unchanged world-view? This question is not merely academic, but has serious implications at pragmatic and ethical levels. I shall attempt, in this Postscript, to explore different sides of the argument, leaving the answer(s) to the reader.

LOOKING ON THE BRIGHT SIDE

By taking on board ideas from many different disciplines, as discussed particularly in Chapters 1 and 7, systemic therapists have moved a long way away from the early mechanistic and normative applications of General System Theory. Concepts derived from second cybernetic formulations about observing systems (Von Foerster, 1981) have allowed systemic therapists to take more responsibility for their own views and perceptions, and for the way in which their presence and participation in therapy influences descriptions of the clients' reality. Constructivism (e.g. Von Glasersfeld, 1987, 1988, Watzlawick, 1984) and the ideas derived from the biologically-based theories of Maturana and Varela (1972, 1988) have undermined therapists' certainty about the objectivity of their judgements of others or the possibility of unilaterally changing others, and have paved the way for a style of therapy that is more democratic, and more ready to accept that there can be many opinions and solutions, and that these can be accorded equal validity.

Social constructionist ideas (e.g. Gergen, 1985; Gergen & Davis, 1985) and application of the critiques of Foucault (1972, 1979, 1980) have invited therapists to become more aware of the way in which values, perceptions and assumptions about reality are profoundly influenced by social contexts, and thus political (in the sense of 'partisan', or not neutral). These ideas, together with feminist critiques (e.g. Goldner, 1985, 1991b, 1992a; Gorell Barnes, 1990; Hare-Mustin, 1986, 1991a; Jones, 1990, 1991; McCarthy, 1990; MacKinnon & Miller, 1987) from within the family-therapy field, have led therapists to question how certain theories, values systems or descriptions become dominant, and how those attempting to describe such processes are inevitably also influenced by, because part of, those processes.

Family therapists have begun to look at problems of power and inequity within the cultures in which family therapy is practised, and have also begun to acknowledge the power attributed to therapists within social systems, and the implications this has for the ethics of therapy. Thus Atkinson and Heath (1990a) can say:

> Second-order family therapists will continually recognize and acknowledge that their views are not objective or 'true' in any determinable way, but rather that they are constructed from the limited (but important) viewpoint of the therapist, and that clients should feel free to disagree. (p. 152)

I would add that 'second-order' therapists also need to acknowledge that the therapist's voice is likely to carry more weight in therapeutic settings, so that it may be no easy matter for the client to disagree.

In summary then, the consequence of theoretical and (perhaps) epistemological change is a therapeutic approach that does not deal in concepts of dysfunction or pathology, that respects clients' uniqueness, that values the variety and 'multiversal' nature of human beings and their patterns, that demystifies its own expertise without abandoning professional responsibility, that shows systemic curiosity and irreverence towards any dogma (including its own), that acknowledges the influence of social context (including discourses of power and inequity) on the lives of therapists and clients, and that attempts to act ethically by increasing the choices of all those involved in therapy.

BUT. . .

Different ways of interpreting the meaning of the new influences in the family therapy field may lead to different applications, or to the attribution of different meanings to applications. Constructivist positions can lead to amoral and non-responsible positions, i.e. it is possible for a therapist to say that since instructive interaction is impossible (Maturana & Varela, 1988), and since the *client's* structure-determinism will specify what a client will make of therapy, this then relieves the therapist of all need to take responsibility for the consequences of therapy. The respectful 'being-with' stance of some therapists (Andersen, 1990) can be exaggerated by others into an assumption that the therapist no longer needs skills, and that it is enough simply to be there. Reflecting team techniques (Andersen, 1990), which are intended to respect the clients' ability to take from the team's diversity of views that which fits, and to construct new meaning systems in response, can be used as yet another technique for manipulating and managing client responses.

In a 'post-modern' world (Doherty, 1991) the stance that regards all perceptions as equally valid, and that does not recognize any external or given standard for judgement, can become a stance of 'no value'. If we say that different perceptions or stances are equally valid, but differ in the desirability of their consequences, this raises the question of who is to judge the desirability of the consequences. If our criteria for the acceptability of a certain action is whether it 'fits', or works, or enables us to survive (Von Glasersfeld, 1988), then how do we judge the ethics of our actions? Krüll tackles this difficult topic by subjecting her own feminist values about the rights or wrongs of patriarchy to a systemic lens, in order to 'present the feminist construction of the world as one about which we as feminists are convinced without claiming it to be the only true perspective' (Krüll, 1987, p. 140).

Without attention to the influence of social constructs on the meaning systems of *all* participants in therapy, the 'neutrality' or 'curiosity' of systemic therapists can participate in the maintenance of the status quo, and the consequent silencing and oppression of some members of client systems. A 'power-blind' stance is most easily and most often maintained by those who find themselves part of dominant groups. If a therapist and some members of the client group share membership of socially dominant groups, and share the world-views that go with such membership (e.g. male, white, heterosexual) it is quite likely that a therapist's discounting of questions of power in relationships and society will contribute to the subjugation of other perspectives and voices in the client group.

The cybernetic model has been regarded as too mechanistic and thus responsible for the mechanical metaphors, e.g. of power and control, which have bedevilled the arguments of systemic therapists. Attempts have been made to resolve this problem by constructing linguistic models of human interaction (Anderson & Goolishian, 1988, 1990). The view that 'change is the evolution of new meaning through the narratives and stories created in the therapeutic conversation' (Anderson & Goolishian, 1990, p. 161) can be distorted to a view that dismisses the lived experience of client's lives as mere 'stories' (Parry, 1991) which can be rescripted at will. Thus 'when you stop describing therapy (or life, presumably) in terms of power, power isn't a problem any more' (Atkinson & Heath, 1990b, p. 166).

If we are to act ethically, in Von Foerster's phrase (1990) so as to increase choice for *all* system members, then we need to ask whether our construction of the world is likely to enhance or hinder this process. 'Drawing distinctions is, thus, not only an epistemological act, it is a political act' (MacKinnon & Miller, 1987, p. 151). There is nothing intrinsic to a constructivist, 'second-cybernetic', 'observing-system' perspective to determine whether the actions that flow from it will be radical or conservative. The attention recently focused on social constructionist positions suggest that many systemic therapists have found constructivism, taken to its logical conclusion, to be a dead-end, and are hoping that the inclusion of the social context of relationships, roles and meaning systems will enable therapists to remain open-minded and curious while not discounting the extra-individual and extra-familial influences which shape the realities within which we and our clients live.

THE CONTEXT OF THERAPY

Why has family therapy developed in the latter half of the twentieth century? This question can also be embedded in a wider one which asks why therapy, i.e. the professionalization of help-giving, has emerged, for the most part, during the twentieth century. In the Western world, regardless of whether going to a therapist is seen as a source of social embarrassment or social prestige, it has become an accepted part of our assumptions about what is available to those people who find themselves troubled by non-material distress. The questions raised here will be addressed by, firstly, considering the meaning and place of therapy (i.e. all the professional psychotherapies) in general, and then by looking at the situation of family therapy in particular.

Why Therapy?

One explanation may be that professional therapists are necessary because, in the post-industrial West, family and social life has changed so profoundly that individuals no longer have access to the traditional social structures and networks from where they would previously have obtained help, advice, or a listening ear. Greater mobility and urbanization, the fragmentation and diversity of modern family life (Gergen, 1991), mean that professionals now have to function as 'paid intimates'. Lasch (1977) suggests that the take-over by professionals of many functions previously belonging to the family (e.g. training and care-taking) have in fact had the effect of weakening the family.

Another explanation would suggest that therapy is an indication that the cultures in which it flourishes have attained a higher level of functioning. Suffering and abuse are not accepted fatalistically in these societies; instead there is an assumption that everyone is entitled to a better, happier life. One could say, with Maslow (1968) that once human beings are assured of the satisfaction of their basic needs for shelter, sustenance and species survival, they then begin to search for self-actualization, and that therapy offers a context for such a search.

Rieff (1966) would offer an alternative to this view, by positing that, in the materialistically fortunate cultures of the 'First World', an assumption has arisen which sees happiness or immediate relief of stress as everyone's prerogative, so that in the absence of a constant sense of self-fulfilment people seek therapy to restore that to which they feel entitled. A

Foucaultian analysis, on the other hand, might see therapy as the way in which society both creates and manages those whom it marginalizes, so that therapists are constructed by, and in service of, the social order, regardless of the degree of 'enlightenment' of their theories and practices (Foucault, 1967; Goffman, 1961). Masson (1988) sees all therapy as intrinsically abusive of clients, and holds the view that help in trouble can only be obtained from interactions between hierarchical equals, which, in his view, therapists and clients can never be in relation to each other.

Are We Part of the Problem or Part of the Solution?

In thinking about the place of family therapy within the growth of the 'mental health industry', it is interesting to reflect that family therapy came to the fore at a time when the family, as a social structure, was seen to be changing its organization and function on the one hand, or to be threatened with disintegration or obsolescence on the other. A glance at professional literature, popular magazines or films, etc. of, say, the nineteen-fifties will show just how much assumptions about family life have changed in a relatively short period. Increases in divorce and remarriage, and the acceptance of non-patriarchal, non-heterosexual or non-child-bearing structures within society's definition of 'the family' offer greater choice and flexibility. At the same time changes in methods of production, and women's education, mean that social and economic survival may not be as linked to family life as has been the case in the past, or as may still be the case in non-Western cultures.

What does it mean, then, to observe that this period of great change in family life is also the period during which family therapy has become established? In addition, 'the popularity of the new epistemology and Milan approach is linked in time to the growing dominance of conservative politics in Western countries' (MacKinnon & Miller, 1987, p. 153). Are these connections significant or insignificant? It is possible to speculate about more and less desirable meanings to this coincidence.

Apparent advances in knowledge can, in retrospect, be found to have served the interests of the status quo, and to have had the effect of subjugating the desires and interests of those it apparently served. For example, Friedan (1963), describing her study of the (non)-careers of women graduates following World War Two, describes her surprise as she slowly started to realize that there were connections between the ways in which highly-educated women were living as frustrated housewives, and the larger social patterns which were served by this return to 'early marriage and the large families that are causing the population explosion; the recent movement to natural childbirth and breastfeeding; suburban conformity, and the new neuroses' (Friedan, 1963, p. 28), etc. Following the trauma of the death of many young men during World War Two, and the return of others who needed their jobs back, psychological theories arose (e.g. Bowlby, 1951) which emphasized the necessity for women to spend all their time in the home and in the intensive rearing of children. There is no suggestion here that a therapist like Bowlby deliberately thought up a theory to achieve these ends. Of more interest, and relevance, is the idea that social and psychological theories are brought forth, or receive acceptance, because they fit the prevailing patterns within the dominant discourse of society. In a time when more babies are needed, when soldiers and civilians feel traumatized by the experience of loss, brutality, and death, a theory emerges which emphasizes the naturalness of women's caring 'instincts', and simultaneously removes women from the job market, while urging them to create a haven for those whose natural function it is to face the 'real' world outside the home.

If we were to look back in ten, or twenty, years time, would we see our systemic theories as fitting in such a way into the maintenance of a particular social order, a social order which is invested in the prevention of change, rather than the open exploration of flexibilities? Foucault (1972, 1980) argues that what is spoken, who may speak, and whether or how speech is heard, are issues of power, and that such power relations are socially organized. Our definitions of reality (even if these maintain that there is no reality!) emerge from our cultural context and are socially constructed, despite our experience of them as being individually chosen and autonomous.

A more optimistic and flattering view of the emergence of systemic approaches is offered by a construction which sees the systems approaches as part of a changing world order, which is less destructive than the one that has been dominant over the last few thousand years. Capra (1982) postulates a view of cultures as rising and falling, like waves, and sees, amidst the destruction accompanying the death of the old culture, signs of a rising culture which includes 'the emerging systems view of life, mind, consciousness, and evolution . . . and an ecological and feminist perspective which is spiritual in its ultimate nature and will lead to profound changes in our social and political structures' (Capra, 1982, p. xix). He sees this as accompanied by a profound shift in cultural values, and his detailed descriptions of the characteristics of this new wave fit, in many respects, with the new values embraced by systemic therapists taking an 'observing-system' perspective. Taking this view, systemic approaches could then be seen as both part of a new social construction, and as subversive of the old one.

Eisler, too, sees the possibility of participating in the establishment of 'a new world order: one where our essential interconnection with one another and our planetary habitat is recognized and institutionally supported (Eisler, 1991, p. 1). She offers (Eisler, 1988) a classification of social and cultural structures into two categories:a *dominator* model, where difference gives rise to ranking and dominance of some over others, and a *partnership* model, where difference does not act as the signal for inferiority or superiority. As Hoffman (1990) has discussed, new directions in the systemic therapies can be seen as approaching the values embodied within a partnership model.

The theories of systems researchers (Abraham & Shaw, 1984; Prigogine, 1976, 1980; Prigogine & Stengers, 1984) suggest that whether systems change in response to external or internal perturbation or not will be affected by the state in which the system is at the point when difference, or a potential perturbation, occurs. In a system in a state of stability considerable perturbation can occur and be, so to speak, absorbed by the system, so that no lasting change will be effected. On the other hand, when a system is 'far from equilibrium' even small fluctuations in its organization can act as 'attractors' or 'innovators' which will then have the effect of leading to potentially major transformation. The nature and direction of such change will be unpredictable. It is perhaps not too far-fetched, given the social, political and ecological upheavals of recent times, to claim that the world is presently in a state far from equilibrium, and that the presence of ideas about ecological or system wholeness, interconnectedness, partnership, co-construction, the giving up of the desire to control others, and so on, may act as catalysts for change. Since we know that actions may have consequences, and since we cannot predict all the consequences of our actions, 'the problem of how to transmit our ecological reasoning to those whom we wish to influence in what seems to us to be an ecologically 'good' direction is itself an ecological problem. We are not outside the ecology for which we plan—we are always and inevitably a part of it' (Bateson, 1978a, p. 480).

REFERENCES

Abraham, Ralph, and Shaw, Christopher (1984) *Dynamics: The Geometry of Behaviour*. Santa Cruz, California, Aerial Press.

Ackerman, Nathan W. (1958) *The Psychodynamics of Family Life*. New York, Basic Books.

Ackerman, Nathan W. (1966) *Treating the Troubled Family*. New York, Basic Books.

Aghassy, G., and Noot, M. (1990) *Seksuele Kontakten binnen Psychotherapeutische Hulpverleningsrelasies.*'s-Gravenhage, VUGA. (First names not given)

Andersen, Tom (1987) Reflecting teams: dialogue and meta-dialogue in clinical work. *Family Process* **26**:4, 415–428.

Andersen, Tom (ed.) (1990) *The Reflecting Team: Dialogues and Dialogues about the Dialogues*. Broadstairs, Kent, Borgmann.

Anderson, Harlene; Goolishian, Harold A.; and Windermand, Lee (1986) Problem-determined systems: toward transformation in family therapy. *Journal of Strategic and Systemic Therapies* **5**:4, 1–14.

Anderson, Harlene, and Goolishian, Harold A. (1988) Human systems as linguistic systems: preliminary and evolving ideas about the implications for clinical theory. *Family Process* **27**:4, 371–393.

Anderson, Harlene, and Goolishian, Harold A. (1990) Beyond cybernetics: comments on Atkinson and Heath's 'Further thoughts on second-order family therapy'. *Family Process* **29**, 157–163.

Anderson, Harlene, and Rambo, Anne (1988) An experiment in systemic family therapy training: a trainer and trainee perspective. *Journal of Strategic and Systemic Therapies* **7**:1, 54–70.

Atkinson, Brent J., and Heath, Anthony W. (1990a) Further thoughts on second-order family therapy—this time it's personal. *Family Process* **29**, 145–155.

Atkinson, Brent J., and Heath, Anthony W. (1990b) The limits of explanation and evaluation. *Family Process* **29**, June, 164–167.

Atwood, Margaret (1990) *Cat's Eye*. London, Virago Press.

Avis, Judith Myers (1989) Integrating gender into the family therapy curriculum. *Journal of Feminist Family Therapy* **1**:2, 3–24.

Bateson, Gregory (1958) *Naven*. London, Wildwood House (2nd Edition, 1980).

Bateson, Gregory (1978a) (reprint) *Steps to an Ecology of Mind: Collected Essays in Anthropology, Psychiatry, Evolution and Epistemology*. London, Paladin/Granada Publishing.

Bateson, Gregory (1978b) The double bind—misunderstood? *Psychiatric News* 13.

Bateson, Gregory (1980) *Mind and Nature: A Necessary Unity*. Glasgow, Fontana/Collins.

Bateson, Gregory; Jackson, Don D.; Haley, Jay; and Weakland John H. (1956) Toward a theory of schizophrenia. *Behavioral Science*, 251–264.

Bell, John E. (1967) Family group therapy—a new treatment method for children. *Family Process* **6**, 254–263.

Berger, John (1972) *Ways of Seeing*. London, British Broadcasting Corporation and Penguin Books.

Birch, Jim (1991) Re-inventing the already punctured wheel: reflections on a seminar with Humberto Maturana. *Journal of Family Therapy* **13**:4, 349–373.

Bloch, Donald A. (ed.) (1973) *Techniques of Family Psychotherapy*. New York, Grune & Stratton.

Bloch, Donald A. (1981) Foreword. In: Hoffman, Lynn, *Foundations of Family Therapy: A Conceptual Framework for Systems Change*. New York, Basic Books.

Bloch, Donald A. (1986) The family therapist as consultant to health care organizations. In: Wynne, Lyman C., McDaniel, Susan H., and Weber, Timothy T. (eds), *Systems Consultation: A New Perspective for Family Therapy*. New York, The Guilford Press.

Borwick, Irving (1986) The family therapist as business consultant. In: Wynne, Lyman C., McDaniel, Susan H., and Weber, Timothy T. (eds), *Systems Consultation: A New Perspective for Family Therapy*. New York, The Guilford Press.

Boscolo, Luigi, and Cecchin, Gianfranco (1982) Training in systemic therapy at the Milan centre. In: Whiffen, Rosemary, and Byng-Hall, John, *Family Therapy Supervision: Recent Developments in Practice*. London, Academic Press.

Boscolo, Luigi; Cecchin, Gianfranco; Hoffman, Lynn; and Penn, Peggy (1987) *Milan Systemic Family Therapy: Conversations in Theory and Practice*. New York, Basic Books.

Boszormenyi-Nagy, Ivan, and Framo, James (eds) (1965) *Intensive Family Therapy: Theoretical and Practical Aspects*. New York, Harper & Row.

Bowen, Murray (1966) The use of family theory in clinical practice. *Comprehensive Psychiatry* 7, 345–374.

Bowen, Murray (1978) *Family Therapy in Clinical Practice*. NewYork, Jason Aronson.

Bowlby, John (1949) The study and reduction of group tension in the family. *Human Relations* 2, 123–128.

Bowlby, John (1951) *Maternal Care and Mental Health*. Geneva, WHO.

Boyd-Franklin, Nancy (1989) *Black Families in Therapy: A Multisystems Approach*. New York, The Guilford Press.

Braverman, Lois (1986) Social casework and strategic therapy. *Social Casework* 67: 234–239.

Brodsky, Annette M., and Hare-Mustin, Rachel (1980) *Women and Psychotherapy: An Assessment of Research and Practice*. New York, The Guilford Press.

Bührman, M. Vera (1984) *Living in Two Worlds*. Cape Town, Human & Rousseau.

Cade, Brian W. (1982) Humour and Creativity. *Journal of Family Therapy* 4:1.

Cade, Brian W. (1989/90) Demonstration interviews: some questions and comments. *Dulwich Centre Newsletter* Summer, 21–26.

Cade, Brian W.; Speed, Bebe; and Seligman, Philippa (1986) Working in teams: the pros and cons. In: Kaslow, Florence W., *Supervision and Training: Models, Dilemmas, and Challenges*. New York, The Haworth Press.

Campbell, David, and Draper, Rosalind (eds) (1985) *Applications of Systemic Family Therapy: The Milan Approach*. London, Grune & Stratton.

Campbell, David; Draper, Ros; and Huffington, Clare (1988)

Teaching Systemic Thinking. London, DC Associates.

Campbell, David; Draper, Ros; and Huffington, Clare (1989) *A Systemic Approach to Consultation.* London, DC Associates.

Capra, Fritjof (1975) *The Tao of Physics.* London, Fontana/Collins.

Capra, Fritjof (1982) *The Turning Point.* London, Fontana Paperbacks.

Carr, Alan (1991) Milan systemic family therapy: a review of ten empirical investigations. *Journal of Family Therapy* **13**:3, 237–263.

Carter, Elizabeth A., and McGoldrick, Monica (1981) *The Family Life Cycle.* London, Gardner Press.

Caust, Barbara L.; Libow, Judith A.; Raskin, Pamela A. (1981) Challenges and promises of training women as family systems therapists. *Family Process* **20**:4, 439–447.

Cecchin, Gianfranco (1987) Hypothesizing, Circularity, and neutrality revisited: an invitation to curiosity. *Family Process* **26**:4, 405–413.

Cecchin, Gianfranco, and Fruggeri, Laura (1986) Consultation with mental health systems in Italy. In: Wynne, Lyman C., McDaniel, Susan H., and Weber, Timothy T. (eds), *Systems Consultation: A New Perspective for Family Therapy.* New York, The Guilford Press.

Cecchin, Gianfranco; Lane, Gerry; and Ray, Wendel A. (in press) From strategizing to non-intervention: toward irreverence in systemic practice. *Journal of Marital and Family Therapy.*

Chambers Concise Dictionary (1988) Cambridge, Chambers.

Chessler, Phyllis (1979) *Women and Madness.* Harmondsworth, Penguin Books.

Coleman, Sandra B.; Avis, Judith M.; and Turin, Mindy (1990) A study of the role of gender in family therapy training. *Family Process* **29**, 365–374.

Collins, Patricia H. (1991) *Black Feminist Thought: Knowledge, Consciousness and the Politics of Empowerment.* Perspectives on Gender, Vol. 2. Boston, Unwin Hyman.

Cooper, Jannette (1990) Not Just Words. Dissertation, University of Wales Diploma in Family Therapy.

Cronen, Vernon E.; Johnson, Kenneth M.; and Lannamann, John W. (1982) Paradoxes, Double Binds, and Reflexive

Loops: An Alternative Theoretical Perspective. *Family Process* **20**, 91–112.

Cronen, Vernon E., and Pearce, W. Barnett (1985) Toward an explanation of how the Milan method works: an invitation to a systemic epistemology and the evolution of family systems. In: Campbell, David, and Draper, Rosalind (eds) *Applications of Systemic Family Therapy: The Milan Approach.* London, Grune & Stratton.

De Beauvoir, Simone (1953) *The Second Sex.* London, Jonathan Cape.

Dell, Paul F. (1985) Understanding Bateson and Maturana: toward a biological foundation for the social sciences. *Journal of Marital and Family Therapy* **11**:1, 1–20.

Derrida, Jacques (1976) *Of Grammatology* (Tr.). Baltimore, The Johns Hopkins University Press.

De Shazer, Steve, and Molnar, Alex (1984) Changing teams/ changing families. *Family Process* **23**:4, 481–486.

Doherty, William J. (1986) Quanta, quarks and families: implications of quantum physics for family research. *Family Process* **25**, June, 249–263.

Doherty, William J. (1991) Family therapy goes postmodern. *The Family Therapy Networker* September/October, 37–42.

Dowling, Emilia, and Osborne, Elsie (eds) (1985) *The Family and the School.* London, Routledge & Kegan Paul.

Edwards, Rosalind (1991) Lone parent families, poverty and employment. *Highlight* No. 102, National Children's Bureau, London.

Edwards, Susan S.M., and Halpern, Ann (1991) Protection for the victim of domestic violence: time for radical revision? *Journal of Social Welfare and Family Law* No. 2, 94–109.

Eichenbaum, Luise, and Orbach, Susie (1983) *What do Women Want?* London, Fontana/Collins.

Eisler, Riane (1988) *The Chalice and the Blade: Our History, Our Future.* San Francisco, Harper & Row.

Eisler, Riane (1991) Foundations for a new world order. Paper presented to Heidelberg Conference, April.

Elman, R. Amy, and Eduards, Maud L. (1991) Unprotected by the Swedish welfare state: a survey of battered women and the assistance they received. *Women's Studies International Forum* **14**:5, 413–421.

Erickson, Milton, and Rossi, Ernest L. (1976) *Hypnotic Realities*. New York, Irvington.

Falicov, Celia Jaes (1988) Learning to think culturally. In: Liddle, Howard A., Breunlin, Douglas C. and Schwartz, Richard S. (eds) *Handbook of Family Therapy Training and Supervision*. New York, The Guilford Press.

Foucault, Michel (1967) *Madness and Civilization: A History of Insanity in the Age of Reason*. London, Tavistock.

Foucault, Michel (1972) *The Archeology of Knowledge*. London, Routledge.

Foucault, Michel (1979) *Discipline and Punish: Birth of the Prison*. New York, Vintage Books.

Foucault, Michel (1980) *Power/Knowledge: Selected Interviews and Other Writings* (Ed. Colin Gordon). New York, Harvester Wheatsheaf.

Friedan, Betty (1963) *The Feminine Mystique*. Harmondsworth, England, Penguin Books.

Frude, Neil (1991) *Understanding Family Problems*. Chichester, John Wiley & Sons.

Fruggeri, Laura, and McNamee, Sheila (1991) Burnout as social process: a research study. In: Fruggeri, Laura; Telfner, Umberta; Castellucci, Anna; Marzari, Maurizio; and Matteini, Massimo, *New Systemic Ideas from the Italian Mental Health Movement*. London, Karnac Books.

Gaćić, Branko (1992) Belgrade systemic approach to the treatment of alcoholism: principles and interventions. *Journal of Family Therapy* 14:2, 103–122.

Gergen, Kenneth J. (1985) The social constructionist movement in modern psychology. *American Psychologist* 40:3, 266–275.

Gergen, Kenneth J. (1991) The saturated family. *The Family Therapy Networker* Sept/Oct, 27–35.

Gergen, Kenneth J., and Davis, Keith E. (eds) (1985) *The Social Construction of the Person*. New York, Springer-Verlag.

Goffman, Erving (1961) *Asylums*. New York, Anchor.

Golann, Stuart (1988) On second order family therapy. *Family Process* 27, 51–65.

Goldner, Virginia (1985) Warning: family therapy may be hazardous to your health. *The Family Therapy Networker* 9:6, 19–23.

Goldner, Virginia (1991a) Feminism and systemic practice:

two critical traditions in transition. *Journal of Family Therapy* **13**:1, 95–104.

Goldner, Virginia (1991b) Sex, power and gender: a feminist systemic analysis of the politics of passion. In: Goodrich, Thelma J. (ed.), *Women and Power: Perspectives for Family Therapy*. NewYork, W.W. Norton & Co.

Goldner, Virginia (1992a) Making room for both/and. *The Family Therapy Networker* March/April, 55–61.

Goldner, Virginia (1992b) Toward a systemic theory of gender. Paper presented to workshop in Ireland, May.

Goldner, Virginia; Penn, Peggy; Sheinberg, Marcia; and Walker, Gillian (1990) Love and violence: gender paradoxes in volatile attachments. *Family Process* **29**:4, 343–364.

Goodrich, Thelma J. (ed.) (1991) *Women and Power: Perspectives for Family Therapy*. New York, W.W. Norton & Co.

Gorell Barnes, Gill (1990) The 'little woman' and the world of work. In: Perelberg, Rosine J., and Miller, Ann C. (eds) *Gender and Power in Families*. London, Tavistock/Routledge.

Gorell Barnes, Gill (1991) Consultation to a disaster unit: exploring contradictions in the system. *Context: A News Magazine of Family Therapy* **9**, 14–19.

Green, Robert-Jay, and Herget, Mary (1991) Outcomes of systemic/strategic team consultation: III. The importance of therapist warmth and active structuring. *Family Process* **30**, 321–336.

Greer, Germaine (1970) *The Female Eunuch*. London, Paladin.

Gurman, Alan S., and Kniskern, David P. (eds) (1991) *Handbook of Family Therapy*, Vol. II. New York, Brunner/Mazel.

Hafner, R. Julian (1989) Health differences between married men and women: the contribution of sex-role stereotyping. *Australia and New Zealand Journal of Family Therapy* **10**:1 13–19.

Haley, Jay (1961a) Control in brief psychotherapy. *Archives of General Psychiatry* **4**, 139–153.

Haley, Jay (1961b) Control in the psychotherapy of schizo-phrenics. *Archives of General Psychiatry* **5**, 340–353.

Haley, Jay (1964) *Strategies of Psychotherapy*. New York, Grune & Stratton.

Haley, Jay (1969) *The Power Tactics of Jesus Christ and Other Essays*. New York, Grossman.

Haley, Jay (1976) *Problem Solving Therapy*. San Francisco, Jossey Bass.

Haley, Jay, and Hoffman, Lynn (1968) *Techniques of Family Therapy*. New York, Basic Books.

Harari, Edwin, and Bloch, Sidney (1991) Potential perils of the demonstration-consultation interview in family therapy: a case study of contextual confusion. *Family Process* **30**, 363–371.

Hare-Mustin, Rachel T. (1986) The problem of gender in family therapy theory. *Family Process* **26**, 15–27.

Hare-Mustin, Rachel T. (1991a) Sex, lies and headaches: the problem is power. In: Goodrich, Thelma J. (ed.), *Women and Power: Perspectives for Family Therapy*. New York, W.W. Norton & Co.

Hare-Mustin, Rachel (1991b) Clinical implications of the changing role of women. Paper presented at the International Colloquium on Women in Family Therapy, Copenhagen, May.

Hoffman, Lynn (1981) *Foundations of Family Therapy: A Conceptual Framework for Systems Change*. New York, Basic Books.

Hoffman, Lynn (1985) Beyond power and control: toward a 'second order' family systems therapy. *Family Systems Medicine* **3**:4, 381–396.

Hoffman, Lynn (1988) A constructivist position for family therapy. *The Irish Journal of Psychology* **9**:1, 110–129.

Hoffman, Lynn (1990) Constructing realities: an art of lenses. *Family Process* **29**:1, 1–12.

Hoffman, Lynn (1991) A reflexive stance for family therapy. *Journal of Strategic and Systemic Therapies* **10**:3/4, 4–17.

Howell, Hilary (1992) Into the lion's den: an exploration of therapist's power within systemic family therapy. Dissertation, University of Wales Diploma in Family Therapy.

Imber-Black, Evan (1986) The systemic consultant and human-service-provider systems. In: Wynne, Lyman C., McDaniel, Susan H., and Weber, Timothy T. (eds) *Systems Consultation: A New Perspective for Family Therapy*. New York, The Guilford Press.

Imber-Black, Evan (1991) A family-larger-system perspective. In: Gurman, Alan S. and Kniskern, David P. (eds) *Handbook of Family Therapy, Vol. II.* New York, Brunner/Mazel.

Jackson, Don D. (1968) *The Mirages of Marriage.* New York, Basic Books.

Jenkins, Hugh, and Asen, Karl (1992) Family therapy without the family: a framework for systemic practice. *Journal of Family Therapy* **14**:1, 1–14.

Jones, Elsa (1987) Brief systemic work in psychiatric settings where a family member has been diagnosed as schizophrenic. *Journal of Family Therapy* **9**:1, 3–25.

Jones, Elsa (1988) The Milan method–quo vadis? *Journal of Family Therapy* **10**, 325–338.

Jones, Elsa (1990) Feminism and family therapy: can mixed marriages work? In: Perelberg, Rosine J. and Miller, Ann C. (eds) *Gender and Power in Families.* London, Routledge.

Jones, Elsa (1991) *Working with Adult Survivors of Child Sexual Abuse.* London, Karnac Books.

Jukes, Adam (1990) Making women safe. *Social Work Today* June, 14–15.

Kassis, Jeffrey P., and Matthews, William J. (1987) When families and helpers do not want the mirror: a brief report of one team's experience. *Journal of Strategic and Systemic Therapies* **6**:4, 33–43.

Kaye, John (1990) Toward meaningful research in psychotherapy. *Dulwich Centre Newsletter* No. 2, 27–38.

Kearney, Philip A. (1991) Redressing the colonial imperative in new combinations. Paper presented to the 3rd World Congress on Family Therapy, Jyvaskyla, Finland.

Kelly, George (1955) *The Psychology of Personal Constructs.* New York, Norton.

Keeney, Bradford P. (1988) Autonomy in dialogue. *The Irish Journal of Psychology* **9**:1, 101–109.

Kenny, Vincent (1988) Constructions of self-organizing systems.*The Irish Journal of Psychology* **9**:1, 1–24.

Kiely, Gabriel, and Richardson, Valerie (1991) *Family Policy: European Perspectives.* Dublin, Family Studies Centre.

Killick, Stella (1986) An investigation into clients' and therapists' account of a Milan-style family therapy session with particular reference to intervention. M.Sc Dissertation, University of Warwick.

Kingston, Philip (1982) Power and influence in the environment of family therapy. *Journal of Family Therapy* **4**, 211–227.

Kingston, Philip, and Smith, Donna (1983) Preparation for live consultation and live supervision when working without a one-way screen. *Journal of Family Therapy* **5**, 219–233.

Koestler, Arthur (1964) *The Act of Creation*. New York, The Macmillan Company (Picador, 3rd printing, 1978).

Korzybski, Alfred (1941) *Science and Sanity*. New York, Science Press.

Krüll, Marianne (1987) Systemic thinking and ethics. Political implications of the systemic perspective. In: Hargens, Jürgen (ed.), *Systemic Therapy: A European Perspective*, 1990, Broadstairs, Kent. Originally in: *Zeitschrift für systemische Therapie* **5**:4, 250–255, 1987.

Laing, Ronald D., and Esterson, Aaron (1964) *Sanity, Madness and the Family*, Vol. I, *Families of Schizophrenics*. London, Tavistock Publications.

Lasch, Christopher (1977) *Haven in a Heartless World: The Family Besieged*. New York, Basic Books.

Lask, Bryan, and Speed, Bebe (1992) Correspondence. *Journal of Family Therapy* **14**:3, 345–347.

Liddle, Howard A., and Saba, George W. (1983) On context replication: the isomorphic relationship of training and therapy. *Journal of Strategic and Systemic Therapies* **2**, 3–11.

Liddle, Howard A.; Breunlin, Douglas C.; and Schwartz, Richard C. (eds) (1988) *Handbook of Family Therapy Training and Supervision*. New York, The Guilford Press.

Liddle, Howard A. (1991) Training and supervision in family therapy: a comprehensive and critical analysis. In Gurman, Alan S. and Kniskern, David P. (eds) *Handbook of Family Therapy*, Vol. II. New York, Brunner/Mazel.

Luepnitz, Deborah Anna (1992) Nothing in common but their first names: the case of Foucault and White. *Journal of Family Therapy* **14**:3, 281–284.

MacKinnon, Laurie Katherine, and Miller, Dusty (1987) The new epistemology and the Milan approach: feminist and sociopolitical considerations. *Journal of Marital and Family Therapy* **13**:2, 139–155.

McCarthy, Imelda Colgan (1990) Paradigms lost: re-membering her stories and other invalid subjects. *Contemporary Family Therapy* **12**:5, 427–437.

McGoldrick, Monica; Preto, Nydia Garcia; Hines, Paulette Moore; and Lee, Evelyn (1991) Ethnicity and family therapy. In: Gurman, Alan S. and Kniskern, David P. (eds) *Handbook of Family Therapy* Vol II. New York, Brunner/Mazel.

McGoldrick, Monica; Anderson, Carol M.; and Walsh, Froma (1989) *Women in Families: A Framework for Family Therapy.* New York, W.W. Norton & Co.

McNamee, Sheila (1987) Accepting research as social intervention: implications of a systemic epistemology. *Communication Quarterly* **36**:1.

Madanes, Cloé (1981) *Strategic Family Therapy.* San Francisco, Jossey Bass.

Madanes, Cloé (1984) *Behind the One-way Mirror: Advances in the Practice of Strategic Therapy.* San Francisco, Jossey Bass.

Maslow, Abraham (1968) *Toward a Psychology of Being.* New York, Van Nostrand-Reinhold.

Mason, Barry (1991/1992) Reflecting teams: Ylva Almquist-Fritz, Eva Rosenberg, & Lars Theander in conversation with Barry Mason. *Context: A News Magazine of Family Therapy* No. 10, 24–26.

Masson, Jeffrey (1988) *Against Therapy.* London, Fontana/Collins.

Maturana, Humberto R. (1988) Reality: the search for objectivity or the quest for a compelling argument. *The Irish Journal of Psychology* **9**:1, 25–82.

Maturana, Humberto R., and Varela, Francisco J. (1972) *Autopoiesis and Cognition: The Realization of the Living.* Dordrecht, Holland, D. Reidel Publishing Co.

Maturana, Humberto R., and Varela, Francisco J. (1988) *The Tree of Knowledge: The Biological Roots of Human Understanding.* Boston, Shambala.

Mendez, Carmen Luz; Coddou, Fernando; and Maturana, Humberto (1988) The bringing forth of pathology. *The Irish Journal of Psychology* **9**:1, 144–172.

Minuchin, Salvador (1974) *Families and Family Therapy.* London, Tavistock Publications.

Minuchin, Salvador (1991) The seductions of constructivism. *The Family Therapy Networker* Sept/Oct, 47–50.

Minuchin, Salvador; Montalvo, Braulio; Guerney, Bernard, G.; Rosman, Bernice, L.; and Schumer, Florence (1967) *Families*

of the Slums: An Exploration of their Structure and Treatment.
New York, Basic Books.

Minuchin, Salvador; Rosman, Bernice L; and Baker, Lester
(1978) *Psychosomatic Families: Anorexia Nervosa in Context.*
Cambridge, Massachusetts, Harvard University Press.

Montalvo, Braulio (1973) Aspects of live supervision. *Family
Process* **12**, 343–359.

Myers, Norman (ed.) (1985) *The Gaia Atlas of Planet Management: For Today's Caretakers of Tomorrow's World.* London,
Pan Books.

Norris, Christopher (1987) *Derrida.* London, Fontana Press.

Papadopoulos, Renos K., and Saayman, Graham S. (1989)
Towards a Jungian approach to family therapy. *Harvest:
Journal for Jungian Studies* **35**, 95–120.

Papp, Peggy (1980) The Greek chorus and other techniques
of family therapy. *Family Process* **19**:1, 45–57.

Parry, Alan (1991) A universe of stories. *Family Process* **30**,
37–54.

Penn, Peggy (1982) Circular questioning. *Family Process* **21**,
267–280.

Penn, Peggy (1985) Feed-forward: Future questions, future
maps. *Family Process* **24**:3, 299–310.

Pirotta, Sergio (1984) Milan revisited: a comparison of the two
Milan schools. *Journal of Strategic and Systemic Therapies* **3**,
3–15.

Pirotta, Sergio, and Cecchin, Gianfranco (1988) The Milan
training program. In: Liddle, Howard A.; Breunlin, Douglas
C.; and Schwartz, Richard C. (eds) *Handbook of Family
Therapy Training and Supervision.* New York, The Guilford
Press.

Popper, Karl (1972) *The Logic of Scientific Discovery.* London,
Hutchinson.

Prigogine, Ilya (1976) Order through fluctuation: Self-organiz-
ation and social systems. In: Jantsch, E., and Waddington,
C.H. (eds) *Evolution and Consciousness: Human Systems in
Transition.* Reading, MA, Addison-Wesley.

Prigogine, Ilya (1980) *From Being to Becoming.* San Francisco,
Freeman.

Prigogine, Ilya, and Stengers, Isabel (1984) *Order out of Chaos:
Man's New Dialogue with Nature.* New York, Bantam.

Rieff, Philip (1966) *The Triumph of the Therapeutic*. Middlesex, England, Penguin Books.

Rilke, Rainer Maria (1929) Briefe an einen jungen Dichter. Inselverlag, No. 406. In: *The Concise Oxford Dictionary of Quotations* (2nd edn) (1981).

Roberts, Janine (1983) Two models of live supervision: collaborative team and supervisor guided. *Journal of Strategic and Systemic Therapies* 2:2, 68–83.

Roberts, Janine; Matthews, William J.; Bodin, Noor-Anisa; Cohen, Doris; Lewandowski, Linda; Novo, John; Pumilia, Joe; and Willis, Carlotta (1989) Training with O (Observing) and T (Treatment) teams in live supervision: reflections in the looking glass. *Journal of Marital and Family Therapy* **15**:4, 397–410

Roper-Hall, Alison (1991) Evolution of a model for evaluation applicable in everyday practice for the evaluation of a systemic therapy service. Dissertation, Diploma in Systemic Therapy, University of Birmingham.

Salamon, Ernst; Andersson, Mia; and Grevelius, Klas (1991) *The AGS Commission Model*. Stockholm, Sweden, The AGS Institute.

Satir, Virginia (1964) *Conjoint Family Therapy: A Guide to Theory and Technique*. Palo Alto, CA, Science and Behavior Books.

Scheflen, Albert E. (1961) *A Psychotherapy of Schizophrenia: Direct Analysis*. Springfield, Illinois, Charles C. Thomas, Publisher.

Scheflen, Albert E. (1978) Susan smiled: on explanation in family therapy. *Family Process* **17**, March, 59–68.

Selvini Palazzoli, Mara (1974) *Self-starvation: From the Intrapsychic to the Transpersonal Approach to Anorexia Nervosa*. London, Human Context Books (Tr.).

Selvini Palazzoli, Mara (1984) Behind the scenes of the organization: some guidelines for the expert in human relations. *Journal of Family Therapy* **6**, 229–307.

Selvini Palazzoli, Mara (1986) Towards a general model of psychotic family games. *Journal of Marital and Family Therapy* **12**, 339–349.

Selvini Palazzoli, Mara; Boscolo, Luigi; Cecchin, Gianfranco; and Prata, Giuliana (1977) Family rituals: a powerful tool in family therapy. *Family Process* **16**, 445–453.

Selvini Palazzoli, Mara; Boscolo, Luigi; Cecchin, Gianfranco; and Prata, Giuliana (1978) *Paradox and Counterparadox: A New Model in the Therapy of the Family in Schizophrenic Transaction.* New York, Jason Aronson (Tr.).

Selvini Palazzoli, Mara; Boscolo, Luigi; Cecchin, Gianfranco; and Prata, Giuliana (1980a) The problem of the referring person. *Journal of Marital and Family Therapy* **6**, 3–9.

Selvini Palazzoli, Mara; Boscolo, Luigi; Cecchin, Gianfranco; and Prata, Giuliana (1980b) Hypothesizing-circularity-neutrality: three guidelines for the conductor of the session. *Family Process* **19**, 3–12.

Selvini Palazzoli, Mara; Boscolo, Luigi; Cecchin, Gianfranco; and Prata, Giuliana (1980c) A ritualized prescription in family therapy: odd days and even days. *Journal of Marital and Family Therapy* **6**, 3–9.

Selvini Palazzoli, Mara; Cirillo, Stefano; Selvini, Matteo; and Sorrentino, Anna-Maria (1989) *Family Games: General Models of Psychotic Processes in the Family.* London, Karnac.

Selvini, Matteo, and Selvini Palazzoli, Mara (1991) Team consultation: an indispensable tool for the progress of knowledge. *Journal of Family Therapy* **13**:1, 31–52.

Short, Patricia J. (1986) Aspects of live supervision in training for systemic family therapy. M.Sc dissertation, University of Birmingham.

Showalter, Elaine (1985) *The Female Malady: Women, Madness, and English Culture, 1830–1980.* London, Virago Press.

Shweder, Richard A., and Miller, Joan G. (1985) The social construction of the person: how is it possible? In: Gergen, Kenneth J., and Davis, Keith E., *The Social Construction of the Person.* New York, Springer-Verlag.

Simon, Richard (1987) Goodbye paradox, hello invariant prescription. *The Family Therapy Networker* Sept/Oct, 17–25.

Skynner, Robin (1969) A group-analytic approach to conjoint family therapy. *Journal of Child Psychology and Psychiatry* **16**, 81.

Skynner, Robin (1976) *One Flesh, Separate Persons: Principles of Family and Marital Psychotherapy.* London, Constable.

Sluzki, Carlos E., and Ransom, Donald C. (eds) (1976) *Double Bind.* New York, Grune & Stratton.

Sluzki, Carlos E. (1985) A minimal map of cybernetics. *The Family Therapy Networker* May/June.

Smith, Donna, and Kingston, Philip (1980) Live supervision without a one-way screen. *Journal of Family Therapy* 2, 379–387.

Speck, Ross, and Attneave, Carolyn. (1974) *Family Networks.* New York, Vintage Books.

Speed, Bebe (1985) Evaluating the Milan approach. In: Campbell, David, and Draper, Rosalind (eds) *Applications of Systemic Family Therapy: The Milan Approach.* London, Grune & Stratton.

Speed, Bebe (1991a) Reality exists o.k.? An argument against constructivism and social constructionism. *Journal of Family Therapy* 13, 395–409.

Speed, Bebe (1991b) One head is better than two (or more): the advantages of the lone therapist. Paper to Conference, Heidelberg, April.

Spender, Dale (1980) *Man Made Language.* London, Routledge & Kegan Paul.

Steier, Frederick (ed.) (1991) *Research and Reflexivity.* London, Sage Publications.

Steier, Frederick, and Smith, Kenwyn K. (1985) Organization and second order cybernetics. *Journal of Strategic and Systemic Therapies* 4:4, 53–65.

Steinglass, Peter (1991) An editorial: finding a place for the individual in family therapy. *Family Process* 30:3, 267–269.

Stierlin, Helm (1977) *Psychoanalysis and Family Therapy.* New York, Aronson.

Storm, Cheryl L. (1991) Placing gender in the heart of MFT Masters programs: teaching a gender sensitive systemic view. *Journal of Marital and Family Therapy* 17:1, 45–52.

Tomm, Karl (1984a) One perspective on the Milan systemic approach. Part I. Overview of Development, Theory and Practice. *Journal of Marital and Family Therapy* 10, 113–125.

Tomm, Karl (1984b) One perspective on the Milan systemic approach. Part II. Description of session format, interviewing style and interventions. *Journal of Marital and Family Therapy* 10, 253–271.

Tomm, Karl (1987a) Interventive interviewing: Part I. Strategizing as a fourth guideline for the therapist. *Family Process* 26, 3–13.

Tomm, Karl (1987b) Interventive interviewing: Part II. Reflexive questioning as a means to enable self-healing. *Family Process* **26**,167–183.

Tomm, Karl (1988) Interventive interviewing: Part III. Intending to ask lineal, circular, strategic and reflexive questions. *Family Process* **27**, 1–15.

Ussher, Jane M. (1991) Family and couples therapy with gay and lesbian clients: acknowledging the forgotten minority. *Journal of Family Therapy* **13**:2, 131–148.

Van Trommel, Max J. (1984) A consultation method addressing the therapist-family system. *Family Process* **23**:4, 469–480.

Varela, Francisco J. (1989) Reflections on the circulation of concepts between a biology of cognition and systemic family therapy. *Family Process* **28**, 15–24.

Voltaire (1947) *Candide, or Optimism* (Tr. John Butt, 1947). London, Penguin Books.

Von Bertalanffy, Ludwig (1968) *General System Theory: Foundations, Development, Applications*. Harmondsworth, Penguin Books.

Von Foerster, Heinz (1981) *Observing Systems*. Seaside, CA, Intersystems.

Von Foerster, Heinz (1990) Ethics and Second-order Cybernetics. Paper delivered at the International Conference on Systems and Family Therapy: Ethics, Epistemology, New Methods. Paris.

Von Glasersfeld, Ernst (1984) An introduction to radical constructivism. In: Watzlawick, Paul (ed.), *The Invented Reality*. New York, W.W. Norton & Co..

Von Glasersfeld, Ernst (1987) *The Construction of Knowledge: Contributions to Conceptual Semantics*. Salinas, CA, Intersystems.

Von Glasersfeld, Ernst (1988) The reluctance to change a way of thinking. *The Irish Journal of Psychology* **9**:1, 83–90.

Von Neumann, John, and Morgenstern, O. (1944) *Theory of games and Economic Behaviour*, Princeton, Princeton University Press, cited in Bateson, Gregory, *Steps to an Ecology of Mind* (1978). London, Paladin/Granada.

Walters, Marianne; Carter, Betty; Papp, Peggy; and Silverstein, Olga (1988) *The Invisible Web: Gender Patterns in Family Relationships*. New York, Guilford.

Watzlawick, Paul (ed.) (1984) *The Invented Reality.* New York, W.W. Norton & Co.

Watzlawick, Paul; Beavin, Janet H.; and Jackson, Don D. (1967) *Pragmatics of Human Communication: A Study of Interactional Patterns, Pathologies, and Paradoxes.* New York, W.W. Norton & Co.

Watzlawick, Paul; Weakland, John; and Fisch, Richard (1974) *Change: Principles of Problem Formation and Problem Resolution.* New York, W.W. Norton & Co.

Weakland, John; Fisch, Richard; and Bodin, Arthur (1974) Brief therapy: focussed problem resolution. *Family Process* **13**:2, 141–168.

Whitaker, Carl A. (1969) A reevaluation of psychiatric help when divorce impends. *American Journal of Psychiatry* **126**, 57–64.

Whitaker, Carl A. (1975) Psychotherapy of the Absurd. *Family Process* **14**, 1–16.

Whitehead, Alfred N., and Russell, Bertrand (1910) *Principia Mathematica.* Cambridge, Cambridge University Press.

Wiener, Norbert (1948) *Cybernetics: or Control and Communication in the Animal and the Machine.* Cambridge, MIT Press.

Wood, Andrew (1990) The consumer's view of the team and the one-way screen: a preliminary investigation. *Dulwich Centre Newsletter* **2**, 21–23.

Wynne, Lyman (1961) Intrafamilial splits and alignments in exploratory family therapy. In: Ackerman, Nathan et al. (eds) *Exploring the Base for Family Therapy.* New York, Family Service Association of America.

Wynne, Lyman (ed.) (1988) *The State of the Art in Family Therapy Research.* New York, Family Process Press.

Wynne, Lyman C.; McDaniel, Susan H.; and Weber, Timothy T. (eds) (1986) *Systems Consultation: A New Perspective for Family Therapy.* New York, The Guilford Press.

Young, Jeff (1989/90) A critical look at the one-way screen. *Dulwich Centre Newsletter* Summer, 5–11.

AUTHOR INDEX

SUBJECT INDEX